GCSE Literature Boost: A Christmas Carol

T0314577

GCSE Literature Boost: A Christmas Carol uses academic criticism and theory to relight your literary passion for this classic text and put a newfound excitement in your pedagogy. Beginning with a whistlestop tour of literary theory and criticism from 400BC to the late 20th century, Hughes explains how you can introduce your GCSE English students to themes most often reserved for undergraduate courses improving their understanding of the text and broadening their knowledge of the subject as a whole.

Written in easily digestible chunks, each chapter considers a main theme or section of Charles Dickens' *A Christmas Carol* through different critical lenses summarising the relevant academic theories, and shows how you can transfer this knowledge to the classroom through practical teaching ideas. Features include:

- Case studies showing how English teachers have used academic theory in practical ways.

- Ideas for teaching linked to GCSE assessment objectives at the end of each chapter.

- Six key points at the end of each chapter that highlight the key takeaways from that chapter.

- Real examples of student work that can be used as models and exemplars.

This is essential reading for all secondary English teachers looking to create a climate of high expectations and improve their students' knowledge and understanding of the big ideas in literature.

Haili Hughes is an academic at the University of Sunderland, Director of Education at IRIS Connect and was an English teacher for sixteen years. She has written five education books, speaks all over the world and advises the Department for Education.

GCSE Literature Boost: A Christmas Carol

Using Critical Theory at GCSE

Haili Hughes

Routledge
Taylor & Francis Group

LONDON AND NEW YORK

Designed cover image: © Sarah Hoyle

First published 2024
by Routledge
4 Park Square, Milton Park, Abingdon, Oxon OX14 4RN

and by Routledge
605 Third Avenue, New York, NY 10158

Routledge is an imprint of the Taylor & Francis Group, an informa business

© 2024 Haili Hughes

British Library Cataloguing-in-Publication Data
A catalogue record for this book is available from the British Library

Library of Congress Cataloging-in-Publication Data
Names: Hughes, Haili, author.
Title: GCSE literature boost : A Christmas carol : using critical theory at GCSE / Haili Hughes.
Description: Abingdon, Oxon ; New York, NY : Routledge, 2024. |
Series: GCSE literature boost | Includes bibliographical references and index.
Identifiers: LCCN 2023051752 (print) | LCCN 2023051753 (ebook) |
ISBN 9781032591964 (hardback) | ISBN 9781032591957 (paperback) |
ISBN 9781003453468 (ebook)
Subjects: LCSH: English literature--Study and teaching (Secondary) |
Dickens, Charles, 1812-1870. Christmas carol.
Classification: LCC PR33 .H84 2024 (print) | LCC PR33 (ebook) |
DDC 823/.8--dc23
LC record available at https://lccn.loc.gov/2023051752
LC ebook record available at https://lccn.loc.gov/2023051753

ISBN: 978-1-032-59196-4 (hbk)
ISBN: 978-1-032-59195-7 (pbk)
ISBN: 978-1-003-45346-8 (ebk)

DOI: 10.4324/9781003453468

Typeset in Melior
by SPi Technologies India Pvt Ltd (Straive)

To all my classes, who have taught me as much in their literature interpretations as any theorist.

Contents

Foreword

Literature is human thought made manifest in an imperfect communication system. A writer might express themselves precisely as they mean to, but two different readers might not interpret the clusters of black symbols on the page in the same way. Writing systems around the world are generally successful when performing functional tasks – 'the sun will set today at 5:30pm' leaves very little room for interpretation. But there is no such clarity when Sylvia Plath writes in her poem, 'A Winter Ship' about the sun going down and the tips of the waves glittering like a knife.[1]

Plath chose these words in this order. She might have known exactly what she wanted to say – these lines might, to Plath, have been a perfect translation of her mind to the page. She might, however, have only had a vague sense of what she wanted to say. She might, actually, have been writing to work out for herself what she really thought: the act of writing is generative, after all. It is possible – likely, even – that Plath's intention was deliberately to create ambiguity and layers of meaning – that is what metaphor does.

Clearly, the 'meaning' of a text is complex from the moment words are committed to paper. But regardless of the author's own certainty or solidity of thought, there is a space which exists between a writer's intention for meaning, and the way a reader constructs it for themselves. Reading is an act of translation – symbols into words, words into phrases, clauses, sentences, paragraphs, texts, to meaning. The symbols on the page must be transformed into something meaningful by the reader, and that process is almost always done at a distance from the original writer. A space begins to open up between a writer's intention, and a reader's understanding. That space is broad and deep. It expands and shifts with the reader's experiences. It expands as time rolls on and the language of the writer becomes increasingly foreign to modern ears and tongues. It expands with every societal shift and semantic evolution.

This space between writer and reader is a chasm where readers create their own worlds of meaning, and texts themselves outlive their originators. The text, once extant only in the mind of a writer, can, in written form, become anything. A text can be re-imagined, blended, updated. Texts can meet new texts and begin to multiply. Our chasm might be better described as a creative melting pot, where ideas abound, and concepts are interrogated, shaped, synthesised and responded to. Texts are not alone in this place of transformation – they are just one form of art, and might exist in conversation with other means of human expression. Our Plath poem might meet a Freida Kahlo painting, a piece of contemporary dance or crop up in political rhetoric. The possibilities are limitless. Meaning is fluid.

The world of literary criticism has a famous analogy for this space between the writer's intention and the meaning constructed by the reader. Kenneth Burke describes it as an eternal conversation over a dinner table where participants arrive to join in, or stop and depart, in a never-ending stream:

> You listen for a while until you decide that you have caught the tenor of the argument; then you put in your oar. Someone answers; you answer him; another comes to your defence; another aligns himself against you, to either the embarrassment or gratification of your opponent, depending upon the quality of your ally's assistance. However, the discussion is interminable. The hour grows late, you must depart. And you do depart, with the discussion still vigorously in progress.[2]

But what does this mean for the study of literature at secondary school? University academics might imagine themselves in conversation with philosophers and writers of the past, contributing through their published theses to the melting pot of literary theory, but is this relevant to teenagers in their classrooms trying to fathom Dickens?

I think it is. Whether they know it or not, our students construct meaning every time they read anything. They engage in the eternal conversation every time they express an opinion about a text, even if it's just to say that they think Scrooge 'shouldn't have dumped Belle.'

The difficulty we have in secondary schools is making something so complicated feel genuinely useable in our context without detracting from the other pressures on our curriculum time. How can the chasm, or melting pot, or eternal dinner party be made relevant to an audience of teenagers?

Haili Hughes has taken on all of this complexity and made it work. Her years of experience in the classroom have made this book an absolute treasure trove of resources, strategies and provocations for teachers, so that their students can see their reading as part of something bigger. Reading literature is an interrogation of the way people think, remember, behave and create. Studying theory allows us to read and interpret in the knowledge that other readers and interpreters have been here, and are here, as well.

With a book like this, we can turn our classrooms into stages where our students' reading matters: where their voices are heard, and where they can contribute to the great eternal debate.

Jennifer Webb

Notes

1 Sylvia Plath, 'A Winter Ship' (1960), https://www.theatlantic.com/magazine/archive/1960/07/a-winter-ship/658146/.
2 Kenneth Burke, *The Philosophy of Literary Form* (University of California Press, 1974), 110–111.

Introduction

'I too am not a bit tamed, I too am untranslatable,
   I sound my barbaric yawp over the roofs of the world.'[1]

I first heard this quote from Walt Whitman's 'Song of Myself' while watching the film *Dead Poet's Society*. I was a bit late to the party, having always avoided films about teaching, seeing them as a bit like a bus man's holiday. I know that there are some who find the film problematic,[2] mostly due to its depiction of suicide but also the depiction of teaching literature, which is sometimes seen as misleading[3] and idealistic.[4] Yet I loved it, as the enthusiastic, passionate students featured in the film reminded me of an incredible year 9 class I had. I had already taught them for a year and had just found out that I was going to take them all the way through GCSE. The approach that Robin Williams' John Keating took with his pupils, where he encouraged them to have opinions about the great debates in society involved the use of this Whitman quote and I thought it apt.

This section begins with an image of a spotted hawk swooping by him for the kill, making a loud and clear sound, which startles the poet and shames him into realising that humans sometimes waste their time with 'idle talk, mocking and accusing others, while the hawk soars above us, making the ultimate mockery and accusation by squawking a nonverbal complaint about how humans waste their time instead of living untamed.'[5] The poet feels he should be more untamed, and that's what John Keating wants for his pupils and also what I wanted. I have never been the kind of teacher who's taught to the test; I want more for them. I want them to become active participants in society, not bystanders, to feel comfortable about articulating their opinions and to feel passionately about them.

Yet to build this confidence, this passion, our students need knowledge, to have been exposed to the wider debates and discussions in society. Though as Mark Finnis[6] asserts, not all of our students come to us with an equal exposure, or cultural capital.[7] Finnis uses an interesting analogy of a jar, where some students have a jar full of change when they arrive at school, representing their exposure to debates and wider knowledge and also their experiences. Yet for some of our

DOI: 10.4324/9781003453468-1

students, this jar may be emptier, with the teacher being the main contributor, and this is where using academic theory comes in.

English is a highly discursive, interpretive subject, where texts have a seemingly limitless potential for layered interpretations. This is mirrored in even the way many literature lessons are structured, with a communal reading of a text followed by discussions of meaning between students, with the teacher as a guide and facilitator. Indeed, I have often heard English teachers say that there are no wrong answers in English, and of course there are, but when it comes to interpretation of literature, all readers are equal and have as much right to contribute their ideas to discussions and debates as anyone else.[8] It is this discussion, this listening to other ideas, which helps us to construct our own knowledge in English,[9] and these ideas can also belong to critics, academics and researchers.

It has been my experience, over sixteen years in the classroom and now working with trainee English teachers, that interaction between students and teachers by discursive means helps to work through possible interpretations and crystalise their own perspective. Neil Mercer describes this process well: 'People ask questions; people share relevant information; ideas may be challenged; reasons are given for challenges; contributions build on what has gone before; everyone is encouraged to contribute; ideas and opinions treated with respect.'[10] Sometimes, students may need a teacher to help them with an initial idea, but that source can also come from a discussion outside of the classroom, like a scholarly source, such as an academic journal or a theoretical lens, or even with the critical reading of texts in context.

Of course, the GCSE marking criteria assesses context in Assessment Objective 3, but doesn't specifically make reference to using academic theory – the closest we might get to this is the top-level descriptor:

> a candidate's response is likely to be a critical, exploratory, well-structured argument. It takes a conceptualised approach to the full task supported by a range of judicious references. There will be a fine-grained and insightful analysis of language…convincing exploration of one or more ideas/perspectives/contextual factors/interpretations.[11]

But the essence of English surely does not only lie in what is assessed formally? Some teachers have honed in on the word 'conceptualised' and used academic theory to help students formulate these big ideas and concepts, but using academic theory could also help students be more perceptive and insightfully link their interpretations to the tradition of thought in their subject, of what's come before. A 'larger vision' if you like, which sometimes disrupts our own assumptions. These big ideas and concepts sometimes come from an emphasis on the contextual knowledge of a text, and while this is an essential part of literary study, using critical theory or theoretical lenses can also be an enjoyable way of doing this. As Bob Eaglestone says, part of teaching English is also teaching 'ways of thinking,'[12] and texts and academic theories can be a stimulus for these ways of thinking and wrestling with meanings.[13]

It was through this reading and my thoughts on *Dead Poet's Society* that I decided to integrate academic theory into my own teaching of English Literature and treat them more like undergraduates. I didn't encounter any academic theory or critical approaches to texts until I started my degree, and it really opened up the way I thought about texts. I had studied *Macbeth* as a GCSE text and then re-studied it during my first year at university through a psycho-analytical lens, and my head nearly exploded. Suddenly, the references to childlessness and the internal struggle of Macbeth, when analysed through the work of Jung and Freud made sense. It provided a richness, a golden thread for me to pin a thesis on and illuminate my own thoughts. Not only this, but I also felt part of something bigger, like I was situating myself within a long and varied history of debate in the discipline and contributing my voice.

So back to my wonderful class. I started to use academic journals and critical articles with them, alongside their literature study, not just as a discussion prompt and springboard for their own ideas, but also to model the kind of academic thinking I wanted them to emulate. Of course, this also included what academic writing in English looks and sounds like, such as the more sophisticated phrasing and tentative language we might see in high level analysis. Alongside some other strategies with this class, the introduction of using theory made a huge difference, with the students achieving twelve Grade 9s out of a class of 30 – almost 35% above the national average.[14]

How did I do it? It wasn't just as easy as plonking a stack of academic journals in front of them and saying have a read of these. Of course, there was lots of scaffolding involved, and it's much better to start early and introduce complex material or ideas more gradually. I started with this class in year 9 but after this, as a school, we began to use critical theory as early as year 7, by looking at things like the male gaze when analysing characters or using characters as vehicles for the author's message, to help students realise there are layers of interpretation and wider considerations in any literature text and also pave the way for analysing Macbeth through a feminist lens. Laying the groundwork this early also helps when students bump back into these concepts later on and re-visit ideas, so that the student gains deeper knowledge of the topic. This has the benefits of reinforcing concepts and ideas over time, so that students use prior knowledge to inform their future learning.

This is the approach Jerome Bruner proposed in his spiral curriculum.[15] The spiral approach to curriculum has three key principles: the content has to be cyclical, so that students return to the same concept or topic repeatedly throughout their schooling. Perhaps more importantly, the depth of the topic needs to be increased, so that students are able to explore the topic in more depth and with more complexity, not just to whole scale repeat what they have learned. Finally, student's prior learning needs to be unlocked and utilised when they return to the topic or concept, so that they are not starting anew – they already have the foundations they can build upon to link their new learning to.

This is important. My view is, if we just try to shoehorn this kind of critical thinking and engagement with academic texts in at the last minute, in year 11, it becomes a bolt-on. I've marked for AQA for years and often seen this reflected in student's work, where there is a random line inserted into their response about what Sigmund Freud thought, which hasn't been embedded into the response or moved on their analysis. Really, it's better to have the ideas that students get from academic criticism informing their thesis, something to polish the golden thread which links their argument together. This is my interpretation of 'conceptualised.' Alongside a focus on 'Big Questions' rather than routinised formulaic learning objectives.

Although there are some teachers who hate the idea of using critical theory with GCSE students and even younger pupils, I am not the only one who has embraced it. A simple trawl through *TES* or Litdrive will demonstrate that there are plenty of English teachers, up and down the country, who are enjoying using it in a variety of ways and are generously sharing their resources. Alongside these resources, teachers are providing incredible experiences for their students, such as delivering series of university style lectures on genre, theoretical lenses or big ideas in texts. English teacher Sana Master described this exact approach in a *TES* article[16] where she explained:

> Because we've laid the groundwork, when the students read about Lady Macbeth's tragic end, it leads to a discussion of the necessity for catharsis for the audience and deep responsibility the author has to satisfy his audience, be it contemporaneous with Shakespeare or modern. The sheer flooding of knowledge that they are provided with appears to open new vistas and suddenly the paradigm shift in class is palpable.

I've seen this approach used brilliantly, in a number of schools, including Laura Webb's Churchdown School Lit Fest, where students were treated to lectures from academics and writers on high-level concepts.[17] This book can be seen as a print version of these kind of sessions. There are hundreds of brilliant teachers doing innovative things in this area, and I have been lucky enough to have some of them contribute a case study to this book – feel inspired by them and give their strategies a try, I certainly will be.

This book, with its ten essays of 'big ideas,' can be great for students but also a wonderful way for individual teachers and English departments to strengthen their subject knowledge of *A Christmas Carol*, and of course, knowledge in English can be a highly contested thing. In England, subject knowledge has sometimes focused on content knowledge, such as the texts and authors in the national curriculum and GCSE specs[18] and teacher training may have focused on skilling up future teachers in these areas, to define what a teacher should know. However, knowledge framed around these content lists has faced criticism as being a knowledge shaped by metricity[19] and tick lists. For experienced teachers especially, this can feel a bit boring and reductive. I personally loved becoming a student again and re-visiting some of the theories I'd learned in my undergraduate English Literature study.

Of course, subject knowledge is important, one of the biggest influences on the likelihood of a student continuing with a subject is the quality of teaching that they experience. This is especially important in the current climate, where A-Level English entries have dropped by 20% since 2018 and 35% since 2013, according to Ofqual.[20] That's why it's so important that we as teachers are experts in our subject and that we continue to develop our expertise throughout our careers. As Berliner stated in his seminal work, 'The nature of expertise in teaching,' the development of expertise is not linear and experts are more flexible, with an ability to consciously process more complex information as they engage in their activities.[21]

This is why subject specific CPD is so important. The 'Subjects Matter' report[22] drew on a wide range of evidence across the UK about subject-specific continuing professional development in schools and how an approach to career-long professional learning would be of benefit to all subjects. The report categorises this knowledge into three areas:

● substantive knowledge of the content, comprising the facts, explanations and ideas of a subject or discipline;

● disciplinary knowledge relating to how practitioners think and behave and how they established the substantive knowledge;

● pedagogic content knowledge of how to develop students' substantive and disciplinary knowledge.

And as research indicates that high-performing education systems tend to have high investment in CPD,[23] then teachers being given the chance to develop in all these areas is vital.

Not only this, but subject knowledge can also increase teacher's confidence[24] as they feel more effective, increasing their feelings of self-efficacy. If more subject specific CPD goes even a tiny way to helping schools with the current recruitment and retention issues they face, then it's worth a try. More confident teachers, teaching more engaged students, will hopefully support the development of skills and improve life chances for our young people.

The book has two parts. The first runs through some critical lenses, how an English curriculum might be built to encompass some of them, and a handy table of how the lenses might link to *A Christmas Carol*, as well as some case studies from English teachers. The second part comprises ten essays, exploring some of the big ideas in the novella, informed by academic papers. I envisage this book also being used as a resource for departments to supplement their subject specific CPD and to be a springboard for conversations between teachers. They may vehemently disagree with some of the arguments put forward from academics in its pages, or have their own interpretations for the themes and ideas contained within which

I don't even mention. Isn't that the beauty of English? I have loved writing it and reading so many journals, it's really invigorated my passions for a text I've taught, every year, for sixteen years, and I hope it reinvigorates your teaching too.

Haili Hughes

Notes

1 Walt Whitman, *Leaves of Grass*, (Minneapolis: First Avenue Editions, 2015), 56.
2 'Dead Poets Society Is a Great Film But It's Also Highly Problematic,' *Affinity Magazine*, November 2, 2019, http://culture.affinitymagazine.us/dead-poets-society-is-a-great-film-but-its-also-highly-problematic/.
3 'Dead Poets Society Is a Terrible Defense of the Humanities,' *The Atlantic*, February 19, 2014, https://www.theatlantic.com/education/archive/2014/02/-em-dead-poets-society-em-is-a-terrible-defense-of-the-humanities/283853/.
4 'Revisiting Dead Poet's Society,' *Far Out Magazine*, June 2, 2021, https://faroutmagazine.co.uk/poetry-and-politics-revisiting-dead-poets-society-32-years-later/.
5 Ed Folsom, 'Translating Whitman's "Barbaric Yawp": Introduction,' *Comparative Yearbook* 4, (June 2013): 255–263.
6 Mark Finnis, *Independent Thinking on Restorative Practice: Building relationships, improving behaviour and creating stronger communities*, (Carmarthen: Independent Thinking Press, 2021).
7 Pierre Bourdieu, 'Les rites d'institution,' *Actes de la recherche en sciences sociales* 43, (April 1982): 58–63.
8 Paul Deane, 'Building and Justifying Interpretations of Texts: A key practice in the English Language Arts,' *ETS Research Report Series* 1, (September 2020): 1–53.
9 Victoria Faith Elliott, *Knowledge in English: Canon, curriculum and cultural literacy*, (London: Taylor & Francis Group, 2020).
10 Neil Mercer, 'The Seeds of Time: Why classroom dialogue needs a temporal analysis,' *Journal of the Learning Sciences*, 17, (January 2008): 33–59.
11 'GCSE English Literature Mark Scheme,' *AQA*, June 2018, https://filestore.aqa.org.uk/sample-papers-and-mark-schemes/2018/june/AQA-87021-W-MS-JUN18.PDF.
12 Robert Eaglestone, *Doing English: A guide for literature students*, (London: Routledge, 2017): 70.
13 Victoria Faith Elliott, *Knowledge in English*.
14 'Treating My GCSE Class Like Undergraduates Boosted Results,' *TES*, October 11, 2019, https://www.tes.com/magazine/archived/treating-my-gcse-class-undergraduates-boosted-results.
15 Jerome Bruner, *The Process of Education*, (Cambridge: Harvard University Press, 1960).
16 'Why You Need to Teach Critical Theory,' *TES*, July 24, 2020, https://www.tes.com/magazine/archive/gcse-english-why-you-need-teach-critical-theory.
17 'Churchdown Literature Festival,' Churchdown School, May 2022, https://churchdownlitfest.co.uk/.
18 John Gordon, 'More Than Canons: Teacher knowledge and the literary domain of the secondary English curriculum,' *Educational Research* 54, (November 2012): 375–390.
19 Martha Nussbaum, *Love's Knowledge: Essays on philosophy and literature*, (Oxford: Oxford University Press, 1990).
20 'Changes to GCSE Blamed for Crisis Drop in A-Level English Exam Entries,' *FE Week*, July 8 2022, https://feweek.co.uk/changes-to-gcse-blamed-for-crisis-drop-in-a-level-english-exam-entries/.

21 David C. Berliner, 'Describing the Behaviour and Documenting the Accomplishments of Expert Teachers,' *Bulletin of Science, Technology & Society* 24, (June 2004): 200-212.

22 'Subjects Matter,' Institute of Physics, December 2020, https://www.iop.org/sites/default/files/2020-12/Subjects-Matter-IOP-December-2020.pdf.

23 'Towards a National System of Subject-Specific CPD,' Chartered College of Teaching, September 21, 2021, https://my.chartered.college/impact_article/towards-a-national-system-of-subject-specific-cpd/.

24 Vanessa Kind, 'A Conflict in your Head: An exploration of trainee science teachers' subject matter knowledge development and its impact on teacher self-confidence,' *International Journal of Science Education* 31, (July 2009): 1529–1562.

References

AQA, "GCSE English Literature Mark Scheme." AQA. (June 2018). https://filestore.aqa.org.uk/sample-papers-and-mark-schemes/2018/june/AQA-87021-W-MS-JUN18.PDF

D. C. Berliner, 'Describing the Behaviour and Documenting the Accomplishments of Expert Teachers,' *Bulletin of Science, Technology & Society* 24, (June 2004): 200–202. DOI: 10.1177/0270467604265535

S. D. Bose, "Revisiting Dead Poet's Society." *Far Out Magazine*. (June 2, 2021). https://faroutmagazine.co.uk/poetry-and-politics-revisiting-dead-poets-society-32-years-later/

P. Bourdieu, "Les rites d'institution." *Actes de la recherche en sciences sociales* 43, (April 1982): 58–63.

Jerome Bruner, *The Process of Education*, (Cambridge: Harvard University Press, 1960).

Churchdown School. "Churchdown Literature Festival." Churchdown School. https://churchdownlitfest.co.uk/

Lauren Cho. 'Dead Poets Society Is a Great Film but It's Also Highly Problematic.' *Affinity Magazine*, (November 2, 2019). http://culture.affinitymagazine.us/dead-poets-society-is-a-great-film-but-its-also-highly-problematic/

P. Deane, 'Building and Justifying Interpretations of Texts: A Key Practice in the English Language Arts.' *ETS Research Report Series* 1, (September 2020): 1–53. DOI: https://doi.org/10.1002/ets2.12304

K. Dettmar, 'Dead Poets Society is a terrible defense of the humanities,' *The Atlantic* (February 19, 2014). https://www.theatlantic.com/education/archive/2014/02/-em-dead-poets-society-em-is-a-terrible-defense-of-the-humanities/283853/

Robert Eaglestone, *Doing English: A Guide for Literature Students*, (London: Routledge, 2017). DOI: https://doi.org/10.4324/9781315175690

Victoria Faith Elliott, *Knowledge in English: Canon, curriculum and cultural literacy*, (London: Taylor & Francis Group, 2020). DOI: 10.4324/9780429331275

Mark Finnis, *Independent Thinking on Restorative Practice: Building relationships, improving behaviour and creating stronger communities*, (Carmarthen: Independent Thinking Press, 2021).

E. Folsom, 'Translating Whitman's "Barbaric Yawp": Introduction.' *Comparative Yearbook* 4, (June 2013): 255–263. ISBN: 9781781353387.

J. Gordon, "More than canons: teacher knowledge and the literary domain of the secondary English curriculum." *Educational Research* 54, (November 2012): 375–390. DOI: https://doi.org/10.1080/00131881.2012.734723

H. Hughes, "Treating my GCSE Class like Undergraduates boosted results." TES (October 11 2019), https://www.tes.com/magazine/archived/treating-my-gcse-class-undergraduates-boosted-results

Institute of Physics, 'Subjects Matter,' Institute of Physics, (December 2020), https://www.iop.org/sites/default/files/2020-12/Subjects-Matter-IOP-December-2020.pdf

V. Kind, 'A Conflict in Your Head: An exploration of trainee science teachers' subject matter knowledge development and its impact on teacher self-confidence,' *International Journal of Science Education* 31, (July 2009): 1529–1562. DOI: http://dx.doi.org/10.1080/09500690802226062

Sana Master, "Why You Need to Teach Critical Theory," TES (July 24 2020), https://www.tes.com/magazine/archive/gcse-english-why-you-need-teach-critical-theory

N. Mercer, 'The Seeds of Time: Why classroom dialogue needs a temporal analysis,' *Journal of the Learning Sciences* 17, (January 2008): 33–59. DOI: https://doi.org/10.1080/10508400701793182

J. Noble, "Changes to GCSE blamed for crisis drop in A-Level English exam entries." *FE Week.* (July 8 2022), https://feweek.co.uk/changes-to-gcse-blamed-for-crisis-drop-in-a-level-english-exam-entries/

Martha Nussbaum, *Love's Knowledge: Essays on philosophy and literature.* (Oxford: Oxford University Press, 1990). ISBN: 9780195074857

C. Tracy and L. Childs, 'Towards a National System of Subject-specific CPD,' The Chartered College of Teaching (September 21 2021), https://my.chartered.college/impact_article/towards-a-national-system-of-subject-specific-cpd/

Walt Whitman, *Leaves of Grass.* (Minneapolis: First Avenue Editions, 2015). DOI: https://doi.org/10.2307/j.ctt1djmfw7

A whistlestop tour of some theoretical lenses

This section aims to give a brief overview of some of the literary schools of thought and theoretical lenses, but it is by no means a comprehensive list or an in-depth study. For more on these, I would recommend *Literary Criticism and Theory: From Plato to Postcolonialism* by Pelagia Goulimari.

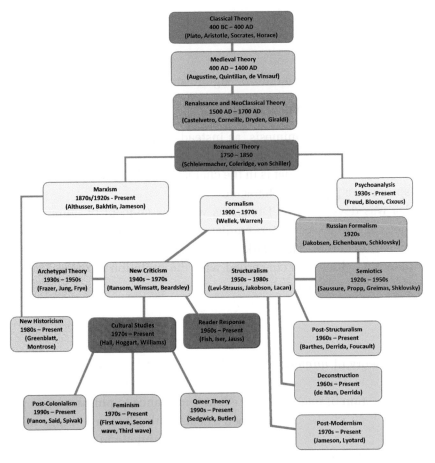

Figure 1.1 A model of schools of literary thought from 400BC to the 1990s.

DOI: 10.4324/9781003453468-2

Classical Theory

Religious texts are the focus of literary criticism during this time period, and this theory is based on the idea that literature is a representation of life and is based on mimesis, a Greek word which stands for imitation. Mimesis positioned the physical world as a model for beauty, truth and the good, and early theorists tried to determine whether a literary work imitated life and if so, in what way? In Classical Theory, the reader locates the textual meaning in the reality of nature represented by it, by seeking out the antecedent of the literary works and the many dimensions of reality or nature. These might include:

- life signified by metaphor
- figurative language
- plot and structure
- mythological connections
- literary archetypes
- religious imagery
- rhetorical devices
- psychological, political and cultural significance
- sociological and philosophical realities.

Diegesis is the opposite of mimesis, as instead of showing or using some of the methods above, diegesis is the telling of the story by a narrator. The narrator or author indirectly describes what is in the characters' minds and emotions, is omniscient or speaks as a particular character.

This idea was developed by Dionysius with his concept of imitation, a technique of rhetoric which sees writers emulating, adapting, reworking, and enriching a text by an earlier author. This marked a departure away from some of the earlier ideas of mimesis, which was concerned with the imitation of nature, rather than the imitation of other earlier writers.

Key ideas

Plato: In his theory of *mimesis*, Plato said that all art is mimetic by nature; art is an imitation of life. He believed that 'idea' is the ultimate reality. Art imitates idea and so it is imitation of reality. He gave first importance to philosophy as philosophy deals with the ideas, whereas poetry deals with illusion – things which are removed from reality. Plato rejected poetry as it is mimetic in nature on the moral and philosophical grounds.

Aristotle: According to Aristotle, metre/verse alone is not the distinguishing feature of poetry or imaginative literature in general. Instead, he classified various forms of art with the help of object, medium and manner of their imitation of life, so writing could be characterised and classified into genres by the types of characters, the form and the techniques they employed. This led to Aristotle's work on tragedy, where he defined the genre, set out his six formative elements of tragedy (plot, character, thought, diction, spectacle, song) and outlined the key characteristics of a tragic hero.

Socrates: Socrates believed that understanding the philosophical ideas in literature was a collaborative effort and disavowed all knowledge. When analysing characters, he believed that understanding people's motivations was complex and that people were not just in possession of one virtue. Instead, the virtues constitute a unity, which are inter-entailing in such a way that one cannot have any single virtue without having all the others.

Horace: Horace was concerned with the purpose of poetry and other literature and whether it was *dulce et utile* – sweet and useful. Horace argued that literature serves both a didactic purpose and also provides pleasure, which was in contrast to Plato, who believed that the two purposes are incompatible. Horace saw poetry as a useful teaching tool because it is pleasurable, which makes it popular and accessible. He saw nature as the primary source for poetry, but argued that poets should imitate other authors as well as imitating nature, so needed to know the literary traditions which came before and respect their traditions.

Medieval Theory

The Middle Ages preserved the rhetorical tradition of classical times, adapting it to its own needs. There was a quite prescriptive side of medieval literary theory, which saw manuals being created, which gave instructions for composition to prospective authors. There was also a rich tradition of textual commentary of the classics, the Bible and other theological writings. Medieval criticism tends not to direct its attention to the way works should be, but to the way they are. The ultimate basis for medieval knowledge is faith in the authority of the Scripture, and with threats from Pagan learning, they had to grapple with different interpretations of the Bible. Many critics of this period were priests, monks or theologians, and so their criticism and theories had strong connections to the Church and the Bible.

From the point of view of literary criticism, this time can be divided into three periods: the Dark Ages, from the 6th to the 8th century, very few documents from this period survive; the High Middle Ages, up to the 12th century, there was little variety in debate and little knowledge of the classics during this period, and the dominant tradition in philosophical thought was Platonic, with a lack of faith in human agency and a reliance on authority and revelation; and the 12th century

Renaissance in Western Europe, when critics attempted to use Aristotelian thought to apply to Christian dogma. This began to also herald a movement towards humanism.

Key ideas

Augustine: Much of his thought is distinctly religious, and he believed that knowledge of truths will make a person happy, as a wise man is a happy man. Unlike sceptics like Socrates, Augustine believed that knowledge is possible, but he didn't dismiss the senses as wholly deceptive. Although he did believe that the true objects of knowledge are that the truths we can know with greatest certainty are the truths that are universal, necessary, and eternal and that these are the highest form of knowledge, while sensory knowledge is the lowest. This means that these eternal truths have to be found within the mind independently of sensory experience.

Quintilian: He wrote a twelve-volume textbook on rhetoric, which described the theory and practice of rhetoric and also the education and development of the orator. He suggested that the perfect orator needs to be a good man before he can become a good speaker. He also claimed that in order for a speech to be honourable, it needs to stay genuine to the intended message, known as the 'good man theory.' He also gave his own definition for the art of rhetoric, as a good man who is skilled at speaking and that history, a knowledge of justice and philosophy can increase a speaker's eloquence and style. His moral stance on oratory still has influences today.

De Vinsauf: He wrote a treatise on poetry, which was widely influential and provided guidance in the rules and practice of poetry, along with the study and imitation of great poets. Many trainee poets used this book as a manual on how to write poetry. De Vinsauf saw poetry as a branch of rhetoric, and formed five rhetorical offices (invention, arrangement, style, memory and delivery). He likened the creation of a poem's subject matter to the building of a house, where a builder must design a house and know what it will look like before he begins to build. Therefore, a poet must know what the poem will be about and contain before he writes. This is a quite rational view of poetry, whereby the act of composition occurs entirely in the mind prior to writing. This idea of a writer consciously crafting his poems also related to the words and techniques used, and that we should use words not just for their superficial qualities of sound and appearance, but with due consideration of their meaning in a given context.

Renaissance and Neoclassical Theory

The Renaissance critics believed that the ancient works were considered the surest models for modern greatness. The movement began in Germany and England at the turn of the 16th century, and saw its members regarding the writing of poetry and other literature as an almost transcendentally important activity, which helped uncover depth and meaning in the world. The poet was seen as having almost a God-like power, and his writing as being almost a spontaneous overflow of powerful feelings. Most writers shared an emphasis on individual passion and inspiration, a taste for symbolism and historical awareness.

Neoclassicism signalled towards a tempering of enthusiasm and a sense of propriety. It led to more of a strict orthodoxy about the different dramatic unities and the requirements of texts to belong to distinct genres, to avoid a departure of traditional craftmanship. Many British Romantics rejected Neoclassicism, because they saw it as being too intricate and pedantic in its conventions, especially alongside the rise of the novel. Emphasis was less about meeting fixed criteria but more on the state of the reader and the author himself.

Key ideas

Castelvetro: He reformulated some of Aristotle's unities of time and place in drama, but also had views about the purpose and audience of poetry. Unlike Horace, he believed that the sole purpose of poetry was to cause pleasure. He also claimed that poetry wasn't divinely inspired but instead, a poet had to study and train to create a poem. He also believed that history and the arts and sciences are not suitable topics for poetry as the common people are incapable of understanding these topics. Instead, they should be about the everyday common happenings that humans talk about.

Corneille: He was a playwright who caused much controversy by writing a play called *Le Cid*, which flouted all the traditional conventions of the theatre, set out by Aristotle and Horace, such as the classical unities. He wanted to adapt classical precepts to modern requirements of the stage and to provide a broader and more liberal interpretation of those precepts than had previously been done and wanted to stress the importance of performance as well as conventions.

Dryden: Sometimes called the father of English criticism, Dryden attempted to strike a compromise between the claims of ancient authority and the concerns of the modern writer. Unlike earlier critics, he believed that the primary purpose of poetry was to delight the reader, saying that wit is the biggest talent of a poet and advocating rhyme in drama. He believed however, that all poetry and prose was probably based on imitation of nature. But that the poem can decide to differ from the classics should he desire, and that context and time should vary the content also, so that it suits the audience. He was a supporter of classicism but also against strict boundaries.

Giraldi: He was in favour of the use of vernacular languages and against the classical notions of literature, even advocating the new genre of the romance poem – a longer narrative poem combining elements of the classical epic with conventions of medieval romances. Giraldi viewed literature in a historical context and rejected some of Aristotle's prescriptions for tragedy. He insisted that poetry must praise virtuous actions and censure the vicious overtly, rather than just hint at this like the Greeks and Romans. He called for poets to write about what is fitting for time and place, to be moderate in their use of allegory and to not cloud the meaning. Overall, he attempted to strike a compromise between the virtues of the classics and modern artistic needs.

Romantic Theory

Romanticism focused on emotions and the inner life of the writer, with writers often using events from their own lives and autobiographical material to inform their work. Romantic literature used ordinary people as their subjects, and they were often celebrated alongside the fixation of nature as a powerful and ancient force. Romantic literature was also marked by characteristics, such as a focus on spirituality and the individual, the celebration of melancholy and isolation, personification and pathetic fallacy, and the exaltation of women. Nature was viewed as a teacher and a source of infinite beauty, with seasons often being personified. Yet, nature was also seen to be powerful and dangerous, so much that it could take people's breath away – this feeling was coined as 'the sublime.'

Key ideas

Schleiermacher: He is generally credited with having laid the foundations of modern systematic textual interpretation. His book, *Hermeneutics and Criticism*, was the first text to establish hermeneutics as a discipline. Hermeneutics is the art of understanding the written discourse of another person correctly, and judging and establishing the authenticity of texts. This includes the central role of language in human understanding, the relationship between individual speech and the structure of language as a whole, the interdependence of the various elements in language, and the understanding of the differences between our own culture and that of the text we are interpreting. Schleiermacher offered a formula for interpretation, where readers can identify with the author's overall meaning, so that the reader can understand the meaning of the text just as well as the author, as we attempt to make conscious elements which the writer himself may have been unconscious of.

  Coleridge: He completed detailed studies of Shakespeare and Milton, and many critics see Coleridge as the first English critic to build literary criticism on a philosophical foundation. He believed that writers ought to assimilate the events of their own age to those of the ages that had come before. He also saw the Bible as the universal principle of truth and morality. He believed that the language of poetry is different from that of prose, and that it is untranslatable into prose. He sees the difference as lying in the different combinations of language and the differences of purpose, and that poems were all about giving pleasure, not finding truth. Coleridge saw the unity of a poem as shaped from within, through internal connections of its different elements. He called this a kind of poetic faith which the reader enters into willingly, through a suspension of disbelief. The images in poetry have a force and logic of their own, which urge the reader to enter the world of poetic illusion and to suspend judgment as to whether the images of that poetic world have a real existence. Poetry does not have to mirror reality, and because of this, the reader's gaze becomes more focused on the poetic world, which is temporarily isolated from all contexts and has a unifying power on the imagination.

von Schiller: He developed some of Kant's aesthetic ideas and was a Romantic in many of his sensibilities. He saw art and letters as the solution to the malaise of a world corrupted by the principles of mechanism and utility, and was a strong advocate for freedom, staunchly opposed to authoritarianism of any kind. Von Schiller urges artists to elevate themselves above reality and place beauty before freedom, as aesthetics will lead to freedom. Primarily, he urged artists to turn away from reality and seek inspiration from an ideal world or from a bygone golden age, and to recreate the world in the artistic image of such ideality.

Marxism

Marxism originated from the teachings and philosophies of Karl Marx and focus on the structure of societies a text is written or read in, which are somewhat determined by the economic foundation of that society. It also posits that literary texts themselves are a reflection of the economic foundations of the society they are written in, and that the social institutions and human relationships portrayed in texts are products of these foundations. In fact, even the literature texts themselves would be seen as an institution, with its own ideological function, which can be traced back or connected to the ideology and life experiences of the author themselves. Marxist critics not only focus on the portrayal of the working classes in their interpretations, but also analyse the form, style and meanings of texts in relation to class struggles and the means of production, which can be analysed by looking at the social and material conditions in which they were constructed. Therefore, the social situation of the author determines the plot, style and character choices made.

Key ideas

Althusser: Althusser was a structuralist Marxist, who combined structuralism with ahistorical and asocial analysis – quite a unique position to take! He did this by focusing on the relationship between the state and its subjects, and questioned why people don't revolt against oppression and capitalism, when the state is formed by capitalists in a way which protects their own interests, and democracy only gives the illusion that all people are equal, while actually masking exploitation. He believed that one of the mechanisms the state uses to keep people obedient is 'Ideological State Apparatuses' – institutions which generate ideologies, which are internalised and acted upon by both individuals and groups. His focus on ideologies highlighted that they work unconsciously and give the illusion that we are acting of our own free will, but that actually it is a structure which is controlling us. He felt this is due to the fact that people distance themselves from the truth, as they are unable to cope with the harsh reality of our alienation from the means of production. Thus, literature is always a representation of our relation to the world and the stories we tell ourselves about our relation to the world.

Bakhtin: Bakhtin focused on an interesting philosophy of language and a theory of the novel. He insisted that the language and discourse used in prose is a social phenomenon, unlike other stylistics theorists who analysed language as separate from the historical, political and ideological struggles of the age it was written. Indeed, he claimed that traditional stylistics categories were not even applicable to analysing the discourse in a novel. His broader view about language in a novel was that it is dialogic, for example religious discourse does not exist in isolation, it may be orientated as it could be acting as a reply to political discourse, therefore it doesn't exist in neutrality. These examples of types of discourse might encourage loyalty to the state or church and do not solely come from a writer's brains, he may be writing in response to other works or traditions so that his dialogue intersects with others. It is through this relation to other texts or art that the language becomes dialogic. Therefore, any meaning we assign to a word is not composed in a vacuum, instead, it is invested with many layers of meaning, and our use of the word must accommodate those other meanings and, in some cases, compete with them.

Jameson: Jameson recognised the need to see objects of analysis within their broader historical context. Rather than just analysing through the ideology of the superstructure of the economic base of the time, Jameson critically analysed texts through their historical and social context alongside their economic production. This was termed the Hegelian concept of immanent critique, which suggested that texts must be criticised in the same terms as they were written in and analysed in light of their own times.

Formalism

This movement emerged in Russia during the early 20th century and emphasised the autonomous nature of literature, which didn't necessarily reflect the life of the author or have a connection to the historical or social context in which it was written. As such, critics from this school instead attempted to isolate and define the more formal properties of language and devices and how effects have been created. Therefore, they were much more concerned with form than the content, in terms of the techniques used to create the images being more important than the images themselves, sometimes referred to as the literariness. Fundamentally, the Formalists insisted that the study of literature be approached by means of a scientific and objective methodology, as opposed to the more symbolist approach favoured by the Romantics. In essence, the critical approach interprets and evaluates the text through its grammar, syntax and literary devices, placing less emphasis on the importance of a text's historical, biographical and cultural context.

Key ideas

Wellek: Wellek was inspired by Kant to view literature as an autonomous aesthetic phenomenon, which acts as a linguistic sign system, which is related to historical norms and values. He advocated a more synthesised approach to literary criticism, where critics must consider literary theory – including previous works of criticism, the history involved in an author's creation of a work and the author's personal history. He saw all of these as of equal importance, and that to elevate any one of these in importance as being wrong.

    Warren: Warren frequently refused to approach literature from any one set of theoretical methodology, but seemed often to analyse works in the contexts of spirituality and Christianity. He classed himself as a general practitioner, who is open to using any method available to him to suit the literature in question, be that biographical or stylistic.

Psychoanalysis

The psychoanalytical way of interpreting texts argues that literary texts express the secret unconscious desires and anxieties of the author, as well as the author's own neuroses. Psychoanalysing a particular character within a text also became popular in this movement, as well as seeing the characters as representing something about the author's own psyche. As well as this, psychoanalysts might also seek evidence of the author's own childhood traumas or fixations, which might be traceable within the behaviour and motivations of the characters in the text. So, in essence, it is less about what the author intended than what is repressed and censored by the conscious mind.

Key ideas

Freud: Freud, who was greatly influenced by psychiatrists, highlighted the idea of the unconscious mind, which became somewhat of an antidote to rationalism. He analysed literary texts as being somewhat of a symptom of the artist, where the relationship between the author and the text is similar to that of dreamers and their dreams. He stressed that the unconscious has a decisive role in the lives of human beings, as it can act as a repository for traumatic experiences, emotions, desires and fears. Freud claimed that the unconscious comes into being at an early age and involves a repression of unhappy memories from the conscious mind into the unconscious. By repressing these thoughts, experiences, fears and desires, it effects our everyday experiences by becoming drivers for our behaviour and the way people act.

Perhaps Freud's most well-known concepts are the Id, Ego and Superego, which have often been used to analyse characters in literature. The Id resides in our unconscious mind and is the most obscure part of our personality, which exists to fulfil the pleasure principle, with little rationality. Whereas the Ego is the rational governing force of the psyche in the conscious mind and protects the individual from the Id. It acts as an intermediary between the world within (Id) and the world outside (Superego). The Superego can be seen as the conscience of the individual and acts in a moral way to repress the Id, compelling us to move towards perfection. Freud also wrote about psycho-sexual stages in children's development and the significance of dreams – which are all innovative and interesting ways of analysing literature. However, they are not within the scope of this very brief explainer to delve into these in more detail.

Bloom: Bloom established the Anxiety of Influence style of literary criticism, which suggests that when they write, authors enter a psychological struggle with their literary antecedents, which then causes anxieties. He claimed that this anxiety is most noticeable in the Romantic poetry of the early 1800s but that it can also be seen in later literature. Essentially, Bloom believed that there is no such thing as an original poem and that all writers inevitably assimilate elements from their predecessors. He sees this as a negative force, which creates a sense of unease and anxiety in younger writers, as they psychologically struggle to their own success with something original. This idea links to some of Freud's work on the often complex relationships between father and son, with the younger writer acting in the role of the son and the writing predecessor cast as a father-figure. The young writer here feels that he must take the work of his predecessor and re-mould it into something different and revolutionary, yet this can also act as a kind of prison.

Cixous: Cixous developed some of Freud's ideas, by highlighting that there are binary oppositions at work everywhere. She claimed that these binary oppositions always portray a relationship of some kind of violence, and that as part of this, the feminine thing is always terminated. Whereas the male is seen to be creative and have authority, which she termed logocentrism, as all origins are linked back to the phallus. As part of this, she observed that women are seen as possessions, to be passed down from fathers to husbands as gifts, which then maintains the patriarchy. This is also reflected in writing, which Cixous claimed is governed by male laws and creates a hierarchy of sexual differences within language and discourse. She attempted to search for a feminine writing practice, which she stated can never be theorised and coded in the same way that men's writing can be, as it presents an opportunity to escape the oppressive binaries women writers are subjected to. Due to this, she concluded that a feminine text is always subversive. It doesn't seek to fit into the mould of phallocentric writing, with its orders and systems. Instead the stories have a fluidity which falls outside of the oppressive logic of patriarchal society.

Archetypal Theory

Archetypal theory and criticism can be traced back to Plato's ideas about form but was developed to be about archetypes – processes and phenomenon which are intertextual and recurring, almost becoming a convention. Archetypal theory searches for universals in texts, often ignoring genre and language and the reader's own role in the act of reading and understanding. Instead, critical evaluation was based solely on a text's contribution to the advancement of the reader's individuation process, positioning reading as a kind of therapy.

Key ideas

Frazer: Frazer was concerned with cultural mythologies, particularly the death-rebirth myth, which he claimed is present in almost all cultural mythologies. He wrote about the differences between rituals and myths and the symbolic life, death and rebirth cycle, which he claimed has obsessed many poets and passed through spheres of culture over time.

    Jung: Jung believed that there is a far deeper level of Freud's concept of the unconscious, which he called collective unconsciousness. Collective unconsciousness is shared by all the individuals in a particular culture, and the repository of these are called archetypes. Thus, he saw literature as an expression of the collective unconscious, as it gives readers access to the archetypal images which help them to understand. He linked this to the prevalence of myths in some cultures, which help people to redefine history and assert their group cultural identity.

    Frye: Frye introduced the archetypal approach called Myth Criticism, which claims that literary history is a repetitive and self-contained cycle where symbolic myths recur. Frye's Myth criticism regarded the creation of myth as the collective attempt of people in different cultures to establish a meaningful reason for human existence. He argued that literature drew upon transcendental genres such as romance and tragedy and further codified these genres to uncover their basic archetypal structures.

New Criticism

New Criticism sought to oppose the approaches that saw a text as making a moral or philosophical statement or as an outcome of their autobiographical or contextual times. New Criticism claims that a text must be evaluated apart from its context; failure to do so causes confusion of a text's meaning with the emotional or psychological response of its readers or to conflate it with the objectives of the author. Instead, New Criticism critics see a text as an isolated entity, which can only be understood through close reading, because what a text says and how it says it are inseparable. It seeks to take the separate components of a text and understand and analyse them as a thematic whole.

Key ideas

Ransom: Ransom aimed to make literary criticism more precise and systematic, by moving away from consideration of historical scholarship towards a more aesthetic appreciation and understanding. He saw the critic's role as to be studying the literature, not about literature, this included not giving personal impressions, like the effect on the reader, ignoring the biography of the author and not wasting time on the meanings and allusions of the words. He wanted critics to focus on the words on the page and the text itself.

Wimsatt and Beardsley: These two critics refuse to accept authorial design or intent as a form of critical interpretation, as a critic may have no means of really knowing what the writer's intention was. Instead, they believed that a poem can only be understood as an autonomous verbal structure, which can only be understood through the dramatic speaker or persona in the poem, not the author. This is due to their belief that once a poem is published, it no longer belongs to the author, but instead belongs to the public, who then interpret it. A poem does not echo the soul of its author, their psychology or biographical history. Instead, the internal evidence the poem gives has less chance of distorting the meaning than other considerations, and resorting to our knowledge on some of the allusions in the poem to be able to understand the meanings. If conducted in this way, criticism changes from a subjective to an objective process and does not lose sight of the poem itself.

Structuralism

Structuralism focused on how human behaviour is determined by cultural, social and psychological structures. Structuralist critics perceive the world in terms of structures, as things cannot be understood in isolation; instead they have to be seen in the context of the larger structures which they are part of. These larger structures are also formed by our way of perceiving the world, which moves analysis away from the interpretation of the individual literary work and towards understanding the larger structures which contain them, such as genre. Structuralism suggests the interrelationship between units and rules and in literature, units are words and rules are the forms of grammar which order words.

Key ideas

Levi-Strauss: He believed that every system, including a social system, has a particular structure. The structure of a system determines the position of the whole, as well as the position of each part of the whole. The structural laws which are in place then affect the position of the whole and its parts, in the event of changes in society, which encourage coexistence with external systems. Levi-Strauss considered structures to be real, living things, which have meaning and importance outside of being a simple strategy for organising. He also believed that the basic elements of all cultures are the same, and that the systems of societal structures are meant to bring about the same events or preserve the same institutions. Change is avoided unless completely necessary. That is why he believed that despite cultural differences, the human brains of all individuals have the same priorities and viewpoints, which means that the basic elements of all societies are the same, regardless of the external symbolism of individual cultures.

Jakobson: Jakobson was responsible for the development of semiotics as a critical practice. In contrast to his peers, who studied the development of words across time, he developed an approach focused on the way in which language's structure communicated information between speakers. He distinguished six communication functions, all part of the process of communication: referential contextual information, aesthetic/poetic auto-reflection, emotive self-expression, conative addressing of receiver, phatic and metalingual. He proposed that one of the six functions is always the dominant function in a text and usually related to the type of text, for example, in poetry, the dominant function is the poetic function – the message itself.

Lacan: Often referred to as the 'French Freud,' he used Freudian concepts in structural linguistics, underscoring the emphasis on language, rather than the human mind in self-determination. Unlike Freud, who assumed the human consciousness as pre-existent to language, Lacan instead proposed that human consciousness is constituted by language. He took Freud's concept of the psychosexual development and the Oedipus complex and reformulated it into the pre-linguistic 'Imaginary' stage and the linguistic 'Symbolic' stage. What this highlighted, is that in the 'Imaginary' stage, the distinction between the Self and the Other doesn't exist and that before the 'Symbolic' stage occurs, there is a 'Mirror' stage where an infant begins to identify with and recognise his own image. This also coincides with the beginning of the identification of the Self with respect to the Other. As the infant moves into the 'Symbolic' stage, they learn to accept their position in the system of linguistic oppositions, for example adult/child. According to Lacan, this is the realm of the law of the father, where the phallus becomes the privileged signifier and establishes the modes of the other signifiers.

Semiotics

Semiotics, sometimes called Semiology, is the study of signs and has been seen as the foundation for many types of literary theory. Structuralism, Poststructuralism, Lacan's form of Psychoanalysis and Foucault's ideas about power all have their roots in Semiotics. Although theorists studied signs in the literary realm, their ideas also spanned across a wide range of human activities which convey common meanings to members of a particular culture. They explored how symbols can become signs, through the relationship between the signifier and the signified and its socially constructed meaning, for example, a red light meaning 'stop.' Semioticians also believe that signs can be classified by their modality or way they are transmitted. Although the meaning they convey is reliant on codes, such as the letters used to form words, or body language to convey emotion. When people refer to something, the community must have agreed on a denotive meaning for that thing for it to be understood within that culture. The codes also represent the values of the culture, and then more connotative meanings can be understood and convey meaning.

Key ideas

Saussure: He founded his own branch of semiotics, which he termed semiology. He believed that the role of signs is caught up in social life and a part of social psychology, and explored the nature of signs as well as the cultural and social laws governing them. He also believed that linguistics has a clearly defined place in the field of human knowledge due to his concepts of the 'signified' and 'signifier.' He suggested that words do not simply refer to objects in the world for which they stand and that they only become a word when they are linked with a concept. The relationship between signifier and signified is capricious, as it is a matter of social convention, based on the community who are using it. Therefore, signifiers do not refer to things in the world but to concepts in our mind, as our perceptions of the world result from the innate structures we have created within the human mind.

Propp: Propp analysed 100 folktales and identified 31 basic structural functions of all fairy tales. This focus on the events of a story and the order in which they occur is in contrast to some other semantic scholars, as it suggests that the linear structural arrangement of narratives is irrelevant to their underlying meaning. Propp proposed that after the initial situation established in a fairy tale, the rest of the action will consist of a selection of the 31 functions in a consecutive order. These include interdiction and reconnaissance towards the beginning and transfiguration and punishment towards the end. His work on characters also concluded that all characters in fairy tales had functions and categorised them into seven types: the villain, the dispatcher, the helper, the princess or prize, the donor, the hero and the false hero.

Greimas: Greimas sought to analyse all forms of discourse and emphasised that language cannot be given in advance but must be taken on by the person who is speaking. He suggested the existence of a semantic universe, which contained the sum of all possible meanings and is produced by the value systems of the entire culture of the community. He transposed the text into another level of metalanguage, as meaning is only apprehensible if it is articulated or narrativised. Greimas' semiotics is both generative and transformational, and has three phases of development: a semiotics of action, a cognitive semiotics and a semiotics of passion – how belief and knowledge modify the performance of subjects. His work on myth, based on Propp and Strauss' work, positioned myth as a form of knowing. This knowing can be understood in two ways: as a cultural construct, which is limited to the experience of the reader, and as a special ability or skill of the mythical gods. He explained the similarities and differences between these two types of knowing as being related to the narrativity and believing being used. The narrative structures used imply the fundamental patterns of thinking about existence and action and transform individual understanding into a collective one.

Shklovsky: He developed the concept of 'ostranenie' or defamiliarization in literature, which is the need to turn something that has become over-familiar in the literary canon, into something revitalised. He suggested that 'enstranging' objects and forms, makes perception long and that this perceptual process ought to be extended to the fullest. The form isn't important, it is the art itself. He challenged novelistic realism by drawing the reader's attention to the strangeness of what is most familiar, calling into question the illusionary function of language. He also contributed to the plot/story distinction, which aimed to separate out the sequence of events in the story from the plot. He was particularly interested in what distinguished the language of prose from ordinary language and aimed to demonstrate the autonomy of prose.

Post-Structuralism

Post-Structuralists attacked the scientific pretensions of structuralism which emphasised that there is a centre that organises and regulates the structure. Instead, Post-Structuralism emphasised the indeterminate nature of semiotic codes and the constructed foundations of knowledge. It stressed the effects of ideology and power on human subjectivity, and the connection between thought and reality are seen as linguistic terms, not as pre-existent to language. Derrida claimed that there is nothing outside the text that established the reality and that human subjectivity is constructed. Post-Structuralists discard the concept of interpreting literature and the world within pre-established, socially constructed structures and instead propose that culture can be understood by a structure which is modelled on language. This categorises concrete reality, as opposed to abstract ideas about reality and a mediator between these two dichotomies. However, it is false to assume that the definitions of these categories are fixed. To build meaning, the conceptions of reality need to be based on the mediation between the interrelationship of them.

Key ideas

Barthes: Barthes focused on the importance of language in writing and examined the relationship between the structure of a sentence and that of a larger narrative, which situated narratives as something to be viewed along linguistic lines. He proposed that there are three stratified levels: functions, actions and narrative.

Barthes used these to evaluate how certain key 'functions' work in forming characters, such as the words used to describe them, for example, words like 'dark,' 'captivating' and 'weird,' when taken together, make us imagine a specific type of character or action. Breaking things down like this helped Barthes to analyse the degree of realism these functions have in forming their actions and whether a narrative can be said to reflect on reality. He was not completely anti-formulisation when it comes to literature but didn't believe that it had to be so strict or scientific.

Derrida: He was a proponent of deconstructive criticism, by challenging the distinctions of philosophies of presence and questioning the basis of the distinction – particularly by focusing on what philosophies supress. Derrida disputed the distinction between expressive and indicative signs. Expressive signs were seen as meaningful, for they express conscious lived experience. Whereas, indicative signs, such as written signs are only meaningless marks, unless they refer to some expressive meaning. Earlier work from theorists such as Husserl made a distinction between these two signs, yet Derrida disputes this. Instead he argued that the entanglement of expression with indication is there from the outset, as expressive meanings must be identifiable and recallable over time as having the same meaning. This implies that expressive meaning must involve indicative signs from the outset, otherwise they would not be recallable and meaning would be singular, falling short of meaning.

Foucault: Foucault believed that our ways of understanding the world are not stable or unchangeable through time. He suggested that our ways of thinking are historically formed, and that even our own self-recognition is not stable. Furthermore, he stressed that even the things that we take for granted as simple truths are actually embedded in complex and historically contained systems of understanding and the worlds that people experience themselves in are vastly different. Foucault also analysed power and argued that if we really want to understand power, we need to abandon the analytical frameworks we might usually use, as these are too focused on state institutions and power is more subtle than that – it is everywhere. Instead, power must be explored at the micro-level, as it is here that systems of power or knowledge are produced, reproduced or even disrupted and overthrown. Power exists only in relation and the power relations must be constantly repeated if it is to be maintained, making the institutions and dominations power dynamics support somewhat vulnerable.

Deconstruction

Deconstruction was strongly influenced by Edmund Husserl and Martin Heidegger. The main concern is that the philosophy of thinking is worldly, and that language is fluid rather than static and easily definable; it does not refer in a stable and predictable way to the world outside it, it designates its own relationships of internal difference. Unlike Saussure's earlier work, which held that there is an essential link between the words (the sign) used in a text and the things they signify, but that the sign is of arbitrary significance. Deconstruction suggests that the signifier is just as important as the signified and that language, as a system of signs, only has meaning because of the contrast between these signs and the contrast-effects between them. Deconstructive analysis calls our attention to the failure of philosophy to describe presence and suggests that it is not the more authentic register of discourse. Instead, it focuses on the way in which language constitutes meaning through a play of differences.

Key ideas

de Man: Paul de Man developed the mode of analysis termed 'rhetorical reading,' which suggested that language is always figurative and not referential and that there is no unrhetorical language. He also claimed that tropes allow the writer to say something and mean something else, as there is a tense relationship between the referential and figurative meaning. He believed that all language, not just literary texts, works through metaphors and relies on it to convince us. De Man analysed rhetorical figures in a text to prove that the text is actually aware of itself as a rhetorical construct and that the text's literal/narrative level actually repeats the figurative/rhetorical structure. He also suggested that texts have an element of unreadability because so much in their interpretation depends upon the way they are said. Sometimes, the things that are left unsaid in texts can return when read. However, this doesn't mean that either the unsaid or repressed should be privileged, but that instead there is an impasse of undecidability and the testing of the impossible.

    Derrida: He believed that language is hierarchical, that one term always governs the other and that deconstructionists ought to aim to find and overturn these oppositions but that they are also necessary to make sense of a text. Derrida's view of Deconstruction then makes these language decisions and hierarchies more explicit and create new terms, by noticing their differences and the way they interplay.

Post-Modernism

Post-modernism coincided with the power shifts of the post-Second World War era and the rapid rise of consumer capitalism. Linked to some of the ideas of Modernism, Post-Modernism rejects the boundaries between genres and high and low art, and creates a pastiche of incongruous elements, which remind the reader that the text is both fictional and constructed, while also being consciously ambiguous in nature, giving rise to multiple possible interpretations. This uncertainty is celebrated by Post-Modernists, who do not see it as tragic but celebrate its fragmentary nature as being the only logical way of existence. It has similarities with Post-Structuralism in that both schools of thought recognise that it's not really possible to have a coherent centre which is completely powerful. Instead, Post-Modernism celebrates difference – indeed, it claims that this mimics life. Consequently, Post-Modernists both question and deconstruct metanarratives and highlight that grand narratives hide, silence and negate differences which are inherent in any social system. Instead, they advocate mini narratives that instead explain small practices without claiming some kind of universality. When it comes to language also, they claimed that language has surfaces but no depths as there is no agreed reality to signify. Later Post-Modern theorists also stated that there are no originals only simulations – that the world is artificial and we have lost the ability to recognise it.

Key ideas

Jameson: Jameson described Post-Modern culture as being depthless because people are inundated with information, which means we struggle to understand what is real and what is not. His analysis is linked to the commodification culture, and he even suggests that all art forms are commodities in themselves, and that due to this, the signifier has become more important, so the linguistic sign has lost its value. Appearance is all that matters and due to this, the subject loses its uniqueness and becomes pastiche – a copy of what has come before.

Lyotard: Lyotard claimed that technology transforms knowledge and that computers will link knowledge to exchange value and privilege scientific knowledge above all else. He suggested that actually, scientific knowledge is not a totality but that there are also other forms of legitimate knowledge which are sometimes excluded, despite them being essential to actually understanding scientific knowledge, such as more empirical evidence. This led to Lyotard questioning the legitimacy of such knowledge, demonstrating that it may be futile to try to construct grand narratives as they can never describe the totality of all experience. Simply, knowledge is always rooted in unprovable assumptions, so it is much more effective to look for multiple truths or interpretations. This idea also linked with his work on phases and genres, where he argued that it's impossible to comment on the rules of a genre from outside of that genre, as those commenting are not subject to the cultural conditions within which these genres were constructed and formulated.

Reader Response

Reader Response criticism is derived from some of Aristotle and Plato's work on literature's effect on the reader but also has links to French structuralism and semiotics. However, unlike other schools of thought, reader-response criticism is less unified, with no one set of critical principles that guide thinking. What they do have in common is their rejection of the New Critical principles, which disregards the reader as a decisive factor in literary analysis. Some Reader Response critics see the reader as an abstract or hypothetical being, who the narrator is addressing in the story, or are controlled by the text itself. Whereas the intended reader is more presumed than implied in the text and can be discovered mostly by exploring them in terms of the context of the text. In addition, there are postulated readers, where the meaning of the text emerges from perceiving it through the eyes of a reader – although, the characteristics the reader possesses here are assumed by theorists. Then of course, many Reader Response critics also focus on real readers and how they negotiate meanings with themselves and amongst others, such as in classrooms. While it is clear that what Reader Response critics mean by the 'reader,' they do mostly agree that the act of reading needs to be contextualised and that meaning is somewhat context dependent.

Key ideas

Fish: Fish aimed to situate the Reader Response process within a much broader context of interpretive communities, where institutions have an important role in the construction of meaning. Thus, he argued that meaning is not contained in the text itself but is created by the reader's experience. However, he also argued that these interpretative communities and experiences of the reader exist prior to the act of reading and that they in turn also shape what is read, and that facts do not exist independently of the interpretations and viewpoints that construct them.

    Iser: Iser believed that when readers consider a literary work, they need to take into account not only the actual text but also the response to a text. He highlighted that texts have two poles: the artistic pole is the text created by the author, and the aesthetic pole refers to meaning created by the reader. Therefore, the realisation of a text lies somewhere between the two poles, as reading is very much both a creative and active process. His point here is that reading is an active and dynamically creative process. It is the act of reading which brings the text to life, as the reader works out the unwritten implications and gaps, using their own imagination.

    Jauss: Jauss argued that the history of a work's reception by readers played an important role in the text's status and significance. He claimed that the audience of literature does not merely play a passive role and that to understand a work, we must explore the history of a text's reception and their experiences of that work. This is because he doesn't see a literary work as something which offers the same view to all readers, throughout the ages. Instead it is dialogic in nature and the meanings are modified and shaped from one generation of readers to the next.

New Historicism

New Historicists suggested that texts should not be consigned to the realm that they were written in and that texts did not reflect a dominant and coherent world view, which was held by the whole population. This approach called for the analysis of texts to be delineated from the institutions, practices and beliefs that constituted that culture – particularly the Renaissance. Although the New Historicists received criticism from other critics, who accused them of having a disingenuous relationship to literary theory, they posited that art and society are intertwined and that this can't be deeply understood by using a single theoretical stance or approach, particularly when it comes to understanding capitalist aesthetics. This attempt was to stop New Historicism turning into a doctrine or method, like other theoretical approaches. Consequently, this approach deals more with questions about a text than a paradigm of interpretation.

Key ideas

Greenblatt: Unlike earlier critics of Formalism and Historicism, Greenblatt isn't as concerned with treating texts from the same era as united in the same concerns and views, but instead suggests that within each era, there are complex networks of beliefs. He sought to move beyond the traditional terminology used in literary criticism, especially when analysing the relationship between art and society. Instead, he sought to explore the way ideas and meanings changed as they go from one discursive sphere to another and the contradictions and tensions in a given literary text become apparent.

    Montrose: Montrose made a distinction between New Historicism, which he claimed deals with the textuality of history and the historicity of texts, and the Historicity of Texts, which refers to the cultural specificity of writing. He claimed that the rootedness of a text in the social-historical, political and cultural milieu of its production is fictitious, as history is constructed and complies with the dominant ideology of the state. History is a narrative, so objective history does not exist; it is produced in context and is governed by dominant institutions and groups.

Cultural Studies

Literary studies, prior to the advent of a Cultural Studies approach, focused mainly on the literary canon. Whereas Cultural Studies focuses on more popular culture, such as newspapers, magazines, radio, film, television and popular songs. From the 1980s though, Cultural Studies academics began to challenge the binary opposition between high and popular culture, as all texts are discursive practices that are shaped through their contexts and cultures. Theorists also see discourses as being composed in a hierarchy, including language – linking both Structuralism and Semiotics. For example, what the characters in the novel say to each other is separate from the metalanguage of the narration stands outside the dialogue and reveals more of the truth. Cultural Studies is also interested in how cultural artefacts, such as music and events, are organised by power relations, seeing them as politically engaged and analysing not only the artefact but the means of production also.

Culture itself is seen as an instrument of both social and political control, striving for hegemony, with some groups resisting this subordination. Therefore, to find the meanings of texts, they must be studied within social and material perspectives, such as analysing the publishing industry and the other machinery which helps to sell the text.

Key ideas

Hall: Hall focused on the way that messages are produced, circulated and consumed, and that the messages that are sent are distorted, so that what is received is different from what is sent, because different audiences generate different meanings. Essentially, the audience is not a passive recipient of meaning, rather they construct and distort messages and decode meaning and can have any effect. He also suggests that denotation and connotation are false dichotomies, as in reality all signs are connotative, and they wrestle for significance amid ideological intervention. Consequently, language is multi-accentual because decoding involves a struggle over meaning, which depends on the reader's or viewer's social position, so more than one connotation can legitimately exist. But the meanings that are created are hierarchical as they will reflect the dominant cultural order of either the institution, or political or societal ideology. However, essentially meanings are always contested and open to both interpretation and transformation.

Hoggart: Hoggart was the forefather of working class studies and held a magnifying glass over working class culture and what social attitudes informed their daily practice and what moral categories they deployed. He claimed that those who rise into academia from working class origins will always feel a sense of dislocation and discomfort, being at once celebrated and cut off by their own communities. Although Hoggart deplored prejudice against the working class, he also never fully celebrated working class culture, such as rock and roll, being assimilated into the mainstream. Other critics sometimes labelled him as a cultural conservative, as he believed that literary criticism should be made more relevant to all and assimilated into popular culture, privileging it over other forms of analysis. Fundamentally, Hoggart believed that everybody has the right to transcend social class and be heard, to speak their truth about the way that they see the world, regardless of any social barriers that are put in their way by the most privileged in society.

Williams: Williams explored literature by relating books and authors to the broader historical and social development of ideas. He saw culture as something that is embedded in everyone's everyday experience, not just the preserve of the cultural elite. Culture, for Williams, was a constant tension between the dominant higher, more privileged culture, such as literary criticism and the popular culture, which was seen as less civilised. He called these conflicts lived experiences, as they captured people's lived experiences in that particular time in history.

Consequently, he claimed that any analysis of literature or text must be read in terms of three types of cultures and the interplay between them; not only the dominant culture but also any residual and emergent cultures too. This positioned literature as a site of political contest, which is entwined with life experiences.

Post-Colonialism

The Post-Colonialist movement challenged the traditional Western fabrication of the other, questioning the problematic way Western anthropology and history depicted the colonised in literature. It suggests that the scapegoating of the colonised helps the West cling to its power and cause the colonised to rebel, thus giving seeming legitimisation to the idea of imperialism as being for the good of the colonised. Theorists focused on how the colonised had been removed from history and had to fight their way into the more dominant European history through a mixture of both correction and dialogue. Post-Colonialist criticism focuses on colonial experiences outside of Europe but also more widely on the internal colonialisation that goes on within countries to minority groups, such as black women, who become doubly colonialised. It has given rise to incredible texts which give a voice to minority discourse and expresses new perceptions in a hegemonized Western literary landscape. Instead, Post-Colonial approaches focus more on the totality of texts and seek to undo the whitewashing of Western hegemony, by unpicking the inherent problems in clinging to Eurocentric views. In this way, Post-Colonial writing is situated as a form of resistance, which aims to point out what was missing in previous analyses and facilitate change in academic debates.

Key ideas

Fanon: Psychologist Frantz Fanon was actively involved in the Algerian liberation movement and wrote about the psychological effects of the colonised, who have been subjected to colonial domination and social and economic control. He suggested that the colonial domination didn't necessarily have to come from the white dominant class but could also come from a comprador class who swapped roles with the white elite, becoming complicit in their powers and failing to restructure society. Fanon did not have a naïve view of pre-colonial societies as being homogenous and agreed that they were still prejudicial and needed reform – but not by a coloniser, by the colonially educated elite within the country, who could act as national liberators, in conjunction with the people.

Said: Said viewed texts as being ensconced within concrete social and ideological constraints. In addition, he suggested that texts are related to one another through both their cultural location and their positions in a hierarchy of power relations. Thus, textuality is a cultural matter, and dominant forms try to control other forms which lie outside of their conception of culture. To evidence this thesis, Said used the example of the Western portrayal of oriental culture and the way academic study has sought to construct it as somehow alien, in order to exercise control. This alienisation positions the West as rational, while the oriental is construed as irrational and in radical opposition to dominant Western tendencies. In his later work, he also posited that literary works such as the works of Jane Austen were implicit in the domination of colonial forms of power.

Spivak: Spivak coined the term 'writing under erasure,' which she suggested allows writers to cross out problematic worlds but still include some details which allow readers to make sense of systems of thought. Through critical essays, she sought to deconstruct the positioning of Third World subjects, by articulating her position clearly, in relation to the marginalised groups she writes about. She also critiques other theorist's work on subaltern voices as being too focused on their differences to elites, which further displaces them as it positions them as a heterogeneous voice. Spivak focused particularly on the voices of marginalised women, whom she felt are defined solely through the identity of their husbands. As a consequence of this, when the husband dies, the widow has no identity which is worth continuing without his presence. This places women's identity as firmly attached to patriarchal law and colonial oppression. Due to this positioning, universal definitions of women are dominantly constructed through a Western Orientalist vision of the Other. Instead, she suggests that feminist work needs to continue by learning from Third World subjects, not by imposing false interpretive models upon them. Fundamentally, Spivak's approach to literary studies is a resistance to homogenisation and she calls for a reorientation towards a more truly global perspective.

Feminism

Feminist literary theory critiques male dominated language and offers re-readings of seminal texts, which question how they reflect and support patriarchal social systems. This kind of literary criticism can be seen to originate from the obstacles that women writers faced, which Virginia Woolf wrote about. She suggested that in order for women writers to be successful, they needed to get rid of the angel in the house view of women. De Beauvoir built on this to state that woman is a socially constructed concept, as male and female gender roles are created by the culture they live in.

These ideas led to women's liberation movements which became visible in public consciousness during the 1960s and '70s. These movements split into a French and Anglo-American bifurcation, with the British feminists focusing on women and class, as well as how women are represented in misogynist ways in canonised literary works. This also led to an attempt to re-analyse female writers' work, such as Mary Shelley and to examine the many obstacles female writers of this era faced.

French feminism, however, focused more on the language and the binary logic of language acquisition which seems to connect oppression and language, grouping positive qualities with the masculine. They argued that this then results in women feeling alienated from linguistic structures and seeking a different discourse, which dissolves generic boundaries and stable perspectives and turns to more allusive writing. This writing of one's own body was not seen as only the preserve of women though, as the writer James Joyce was also said to transgress the margins of dominant culture in this way.

Both the Anglo-American and French feminist critics have been attacked for their underlying assumption that all women share the same oppression. Later feminists have argued that this forced homogeneity actually strengthens the hierarchies that feminists are criticising. Even more recent critics have interrogated the assumption of everyone having an innate biological sex, suggesting that this might be a strategy to justify gender attributes. This calls for a more critical approach to identities as things that are entwined with ethnicity, sexual orientation and social status, among other characteristics.

Key ideas

First wave feminism

Wollstonecraft: She analysed the way that women were discriminated against by being excluded from important discussions. She strove to promote gender equality, in an expansion of Rousseau's ideal democratic society and argued that this could only be achieved if women were allowed to be educated properly and break away from their traditional gender roles. The Suffragettes were greatly influenced by her ideas as they campaigned for votes for women.

Woolf: She focused on what women needed to be able to overcome the barriers and obstacles they faced so they could have a voice and fulfil their potential. Woolf investigated gender roles and societal expectations to define how female experience was dogged and shaped by male perceptions and the misogyny that permeated society, through its patriarchal structures. She highlighted how women's potential was often constrained by gender role and society's expectations about their behaviour and gender norms. Woolf invited women to pursue education and professional careers and was committed to progress and the advancement of human rights.

Second wave feminism

De Beauvoir: She believed that gender differences are a socially constructed concept, so that women had to battle with their ideological positioning to change things. Second wave feminists such as de Beauvoir were committed to building a body of knowledge which specifically addressed the ways in which women have historically been marginalised, both culturally and socially. Due to the way huge social change that disturbing patriarchal realities would bring, second wave feminists often spoke about the obstacles to realising the change they called for.

That being said, de Beauvoir argued that women are as capable as men, and they should strive to elevate themselves and reach for transcendence, where they can choose their own freedom. Her thesis was that men had made women 'other' by creating a false air of mystery around them, which acted as an excuse for them not to even attempt to understand them, instead creating stereotypes which placed women at the bottom of a hierarchy.

Friedan: Friedan highlighted that some women felt a dissatisfaction in their role of being a mother and a wife. She compared this to the way the happy house-wife was romanticised on television and in magazines and called this the 'feminine mystique.' She also claimed that women were not encouraged to have their own personalities and that they were always seen as somehow relational to other people, such as their husband or children. However, her work was later criticised for focusing on largely white middle class women, who were not expected to also work outside of their role in the home.

Greer: Greer argued that a male-dominated world affects a female's sense of self, and how sexist stereotypes undermine female rationality, autonomy, power and sexuality. She claimed that women have to look within themselves for personal liberation before trying to change the world. Greer also described the stereotypes, myths and misunderstandings that combine to produce the oppression that women experience. One of these forms of oppression, she claimed, is the nuclear family, as it can be demeaning and confining and can cut off women's capacity for action. Interestingly, Greer often castigated women for being the creators of their own misery, as they cannot love themselves and sometimes despise one another in a displaced anger.

Third wave feminism

Walker: Walker aimed to reevaluate feminism in the 1990s, by focusing on the varied perspectives and experiences of women, who are challenging gender roles and stereotypes. Instead of focusing on collective women's experiences, she explored how personal narratives can help analyse gender injustice. In her later work, she encouraged women that it was possible to be a mother alongside a career, and that it doesn't need to be a trade-off, despite sometimes society making women believe that they need to make this choice.

Wolf: Wolf argued that the normative value of beauty is socially constructed by the patriarchy, to subjugate women. She described these extreme beauty standards as being like an iron maiden to women, as they are punished for being unable to reach and maintain them. Not only did she condemn the beauty and fashion world for this exploitation, but that judgements on women's looks permeate every facet of society, from religion, hunger and violence. She suggested that even though women have more freedoms and power than ever before, but that the iron maiden of beauty standards means we may be more unliberated in how we feel about our physical appearances than women fifty years ago or more.

Queer Theory

Queer Theory questions how cisgender and heterosexual identities are perceived as the standard, and theorists revisit literature and studies through evaluating the binaries and languages which are portrayed and how they consider essentialist views of sexuality. Queer Theory does not define what is queer as such, as gender and sexuality can be difficult to define but it celebrates the visible transgression from norms. Essentially it seeks to analyse queer people's lived experience and how it is perceived by others, including how they are marginalised. These repressive structures in society police the discourse concerning sex and sexuality and position heterosexuality as normal and homosexuality as stigmatised. Due to this, homosexuality can be seen as a historical construct, as it is performed through repeated actions, rather than being a biological reality.

Key ideas

Sedgwick: Sedgwick analysed homoerotic subplots in the work of writers like Charles Dickens, as she aimed to make readers more alert to the queer nuances of literature, encouraging them to instead seek out queer idioms. In addition, she also analysed sentence structures, rhythm and syntax and their queer implications.

Butler: Butler argued against the labelling of women as a homogenous group with the same common characteristics, as this view just reinforces the binary view of gender relations. Instead of trying to define women, Butler believes feminists should break the links between sex and gender, and analyse how power functions shape how womanhood is perceived within the feminist movement. Instead, gender, Butler argues, shouldn't be seen as flexible, as gender is a performance, not an essence.

This whistlestop tour is by no means a detailed deconstruction or exploration of every literary movement throughout history. As stated earlier, that's way out of the scope of this book and actually, English teachers don't have time for that on top of busy teaching timetables. What it aims to do instead, is to serve as a reminder that different ways of looking at literature exist and this is what makes our subject so fascinating!

Some theoretical lenses and *A Christmas Carol*

Busy English teachers may struggle to read academic papers which explore *A Christmas Carol* through these different lenses. Therefore, this handy table sets out some basic ideas for how different lenses may reinterpret some of the themes, characters and events in the novella.

Classical Theory	Medieval Theory	Renaissance and Neo-Classical Theory	Romantic Theory	Marxism
A Christmas Carol is an example of mimesis, as the plot and themes explored in the novella imitate the huge gap between the rich and poor in Victorian London, as well as the rise in capitalist attitudes and commodification of Christmas in the industrial revolution.	The view that knowledge of truths will make a person happy can easily be applied to Scrooge's quest. Scrooge has to seek his happiness within his mind, although in contrast to Medieval theory, which might suggest he can do this without sensory experiences, the ghosts need to help him along the way.	Although A Christmas Carol has fantasy elements, such as time travel and supernatural visitations, it largely follows Castelvetro's teachings. This is because it also tells the stories of ordinary people like the Cratchits and the other poor and destitute inhabitants of London, seeking to show Christmas through a lens of poverty, warts and all.	Romantic writers often used events from their own lives and autobiographical material to inform their work, and we know that Charles Dickens himself was heavily influenced by the poverty he lived through when his father went to a debtor's prison. There is a focus on spiritualism in the novella, as readers are encouraged to think of their immortal souls and acting in a Christian way in their mortal lives. Individualism is also highlighted as Scrooge's own spirituality and lack of feeling become the focus of the story. However, his melancholies are not a cause for celebration, unlike some poets in the Romantic era. Instead, his loneliness is seen as a catalyst for his unfeeling nature. However, the focus on nature and particularly pathetic fallacy is used to represent Scrooge's cold nature. As Romanticism often explored authenticity, Carol has remained an authentic text as its themes of poverty and kindness are relevant to audiences throughout the ages. Yet readers are asked to enter a phase where they suspend their disbelief about ghosts – as Coleridge discussed.	A Christmas Carol can be seen as Marxist, as it intends to arouse indifferent people from their selfishness and obsession with capitalism. The novella not only sets out to transform Scrooge, but also a particular brand of people who resemble him and worship his materialistic virtues. Scrooge's disposition was representative of the spirit among the bourgeoisie at the time. It is written in the aftermath of events like the Plug Plot riots, where the masses, condemned to live in squalor, rose up against their oppressors. Seething hatred of the ruling classes pervaded Britain and talk of revolution was everywhere.
Dickens also drew on influences from earlier texts, such as the religious symbolism in Dante's work and the Book of Job in the Bible. Dickens also employs diegesis, as a narrator tells us the story, and although he is not a character in the novel, the way he tells the story influences the way we see Scrooge.	Medieval theory was largely used as an analysis on religious texts and Carol has many religious motifs. The novel has five staves, but these can also be seen as five staffs, in the sense of sticks to walk with, as a staff is a stick carried in the hand as an aid in walking. This points to the motif of the pilgrimage of life, a reference that is particularly relevant to A Christmas Carol.	If Dryden's claims about literature's purpose being to delight the reader, then Scrooge's metamorphosis to kind and generous gentleman at the end can certainly be said to provide this enjoyment and sense of catharsis for the reader.		Victorian capitalists had few qualms about using whatever methods they could to increase profits and squeeze more labour out of the working class. One of the most shocking examples of this was the use of child labour and the Poor Laws. Scrooge highlighted his draconian attitude, that punishing the 'deserving poor' by starving them back to work is the way to do things – which echoes the interests of the rest of his class.
Socrates' ideas about the complexity of characters certainly highlights the complexity of Scrooge's character and the mixed feelings the reader has for him as we witness his transformation.	Carol's main message and themes are also quite faithful to the scriptures, as it promotes the idea of kindness and feeling towards fellow man and corroborates biblical teachings that those who do not live good, Christian lives will be doomed to a restless afterlife, forced to pay for their selfishness for eternity.	Giraldi's claims that literature must overtly praise virtuous actions and censure the vicious is evident in Carol. Marley's fate is an obvious symbol of this, alongside the threats of the grim reaper like Ghost of Christmas Yet to Come, whose bony hand points towards Scrooge's untended, neglected grave. When Scrooge becomes generous, we at once see his happiness.		
In addition, Horace's ideas about literature being both sweet and useful could certainly match Dickens' objective for Carol to not just be enjoyed at Christmas but to also drive home the message that charity and benevolence should be shown to society's most vulnerable throughout the year.				

Psychoanalysis	Archetypal Theory	New Criticism	Structuralism	Semiotics
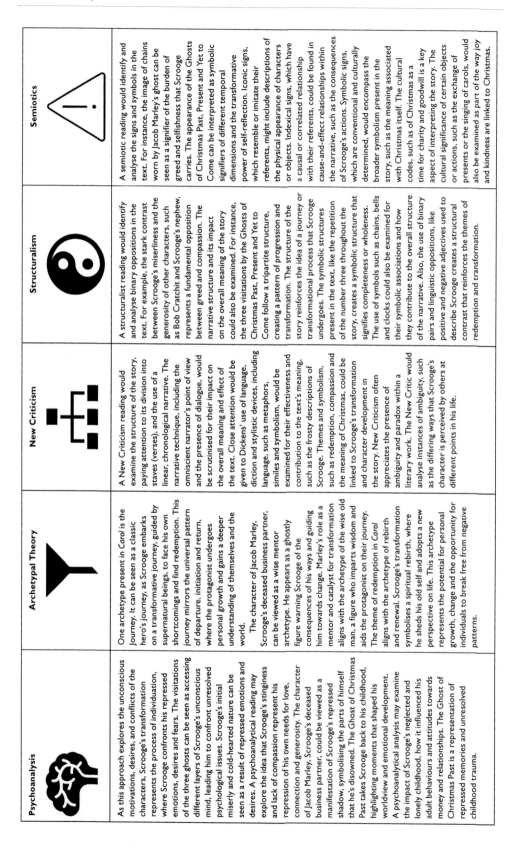				
As this approach explores the unconscious motivations, desires, and conflicts of the characters, Scrooge's transformation represents the process of individuation, where Scrooge confronts his repressed emotions, desires and fears. The visitations of the three ghosts can be seen as accessing different layers of Scrooge's unconscious mind, leading him to confront unresolved psychological issues. Scrooge's initial miserly and cold-hearted nature can be seen as a result of repressed emotions and desires. A psychoanalytical reading may explore the idea that Scrooge's stinginess and lack of compassion represent his repression of his own needs for love, connection and generosity. The character of Jacob Marley, Scrooge's deceased business partner, could be viewed as a manifestation of Scrooge's repressed shadow, symbolising the parts of himself that he's disowned. The Ghost of Christmas Past takes Scrooge back to his childhood, highlighting moments that shaped his worldview and emotional development. A psychoanalytical analysis may examine the impact of Scrooge's neglected and lonely childhood, how it influenced his adult behaviours and attitudes towards money and relationships. The Ghost of Christmas Past is a representation of repressed memories and unresolved childhood trauma.	One archetype present in *Carol* is the Journey. It can be seen as a classic hero's journey, as Scrooge embarks on a transformative journey, guided by supernatural beings, to face his own shortcomings and find redemption. This journey mirrors the universal pattern of departure, initiation and return, where the protagonist undergoes personal growth and gains a deeper understanding of themselves and the world. The character of Jacob Marley, Scrooge's deceased business partner, can be viewed as a wise mentor archetype. He appears as a ghostly figure warning Scrooge of the consequences of his ways and guiding him towards change. Marley's role as a mentor and catalyst for transformation aligns with the archetype of the wise old man, a figure who imparts wisdom and aids the protagonist on their journey. The theme of redemption in *Carol* aligns with the archetype of rebirth and renewal. Scrooge's transformation symbolises a spiritual rebirth, where he sheds his old self and adopts a new perspective on life. This archetype represents the potential for personal growth, change and the opportunity for individuals to break free from negative patterns.	A New Criticism reading would examine the structure of the story, paying attention to its division into staves (verses), and the use of a linear, chronological narrative. The narrative technique, including the omniscient narrator's point of view and the presence of dialogue, would be scrutinised for their impact on the overall meaning and effect of the text. Close attention would be given to Dickens' use of language, diction and stylistic devices, including language, such as metaphors, similes and symbolism, would be examined for their effectiveness and contribution to the text's meaning, such as the frosty descriptions of Scrooge. Themes and symbolism, such as redemption, compassion and the meaning of Christmas, could be linked to Scrooge's transformation and character development in the story. New Criticism often appreciates the presence of ambiguity and paradox within a literary work. The New Critic would analyse instances of ambiguity, such as the differing ways that Scrooge's character is perceived by others at different points in his life.	A structuralist reading would identify and analyse binary oppositions in the text. For example, the stark contrast between Scrooge's miserliness and the generosity of other characters, such as Bob Cratchit and Scrooge's nephew, represents a fundamental opposition between greed and compassion. The narrative structure and its impact on the overall meaning of the story could also be examined. For instance, the three visitations by the Ghosts of Christmas Past, Present and Yet to Come follow a tripartite structure, creating a pattern of progression and transformation. The structure of the story reinforces the idea of a journey or transformational process that Scrooge undergoes. The symbolic structures present in the text, like the repetition of the number three throughout the story, creates a symbolic structure that signifies completeness or wholeness. The use of symbols such as chains, bells and clocks could also be examined for their symbolic associations and how they contribute to the overall structure of the narrative. Also, the use of binary pairs and linguistic oppositions, like positive and negative adjectives used to describe Scrooge creates a structural contrast that reinforces the themes of redemption and transformation.	A semiotic reading would identify and analyse the signs and symbols in the text. For instance, the image of chains worn by Jacob Marley's ghost can be seen as a signifier of the burden of greed and selfishness that Scrooge carries. The appearance of the Ghosts of Christmas Past, Present and Yet to Come can be interpreted as symbolic signifiers of different temporal dimensions and the transformative power of self-reflection. Iconic signs, which resemble or imitate their referents, might include descriptions of the physical appearance of characters or objects. Indexical signs, which have a causal or correlated relationship with their referents, could be found in cause-and-effect relationships within the narrative, such as the consequences of Scrooge's actions. Symbolic signs, which are conventional and culturally determined, would encompass the broader symbolism present in the story, such as the meaning associated with Christmas itself. The cultural codes, such as of Christmas as a time for charity and goodwill is a key aspect of interpreting the story. The cultural significance of certain objects or actions, such as the exchange of presents or the singing of carols, would also be examined as part of the way joy and kindness are linked to Christmas.

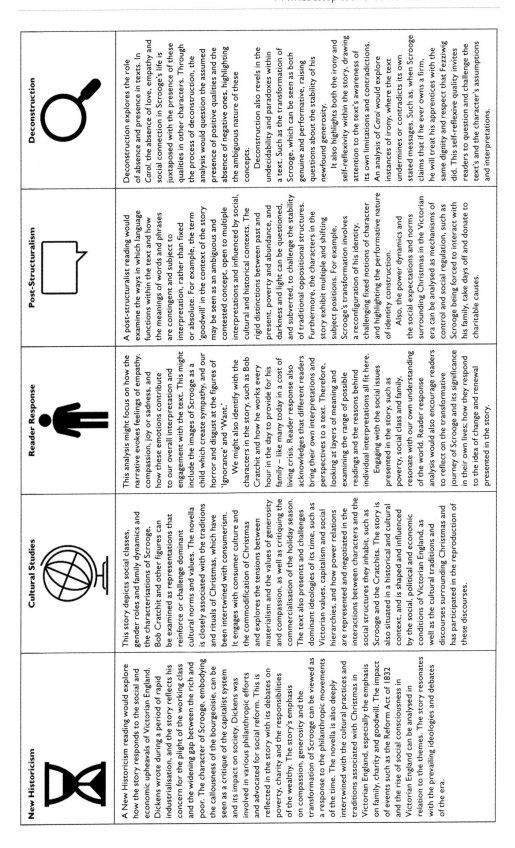

New Historicism	Cultural Studies	Reader Response	Post-Structuralism	Deconstruction
A New Historicism reading would explore how the story responds to the social and economic upheavals of Victorian England. Dickens wrote during a period of rapid industrialisation, and the story reflects his concern for the plight of the working class and the widening gap between the rich and poor. The character of Scrooge, embodying the callousness of the bourgeoisie, can be seen as a critique of the capitalist system and its impact on society. Dickens was involved in various philanthropic efforts and advocated for social reform. This is reflected in the story with its debates on poverty, charity and the responsibilities of the wealthy. The story's emphasis on compassion, generosity and the transformation of Scrooge can be viewed as a response to the philanthropic movements of the time. The novella is also deeply intertwined with the cultural practices and traditions associated with Christmas in Victorian England, especially the emphasis on family, charity and goodwill. The impact of events such as the Reform Act of 1832 and the rise of social consciousness in Victorian England can be analysed in relation to the themes. The story resonates with the prevailing ideologies and debates of the era.	This story depicts social classes, gender roles and family dynamics and the characterisations of Scrooge, Bob Cratchit and other figures can be examined as representations that reinforce or challenge dominant cultural norms and values. The novella is closely associated with the traditions and rituals of Christmas, which have been intertwined with consumerism. It engages with consumer culture and the commodification of Christmas and explores the tensions between materialism and the values of generosity and compassion, as well as critiquing the commercialisation of the holiday season. The text also presents and challenges dominant ideologies of its time, such as Victorian values, capitalism and social hierarchies, and how power relations are represented and negotiated in the interactions between characters and the social structures they inhabit, such as Scrooge and the Cratchits. The story is also situated in a historical and cultural context, and is shaped and influenced by the social, political and economic conditions of Victorian England, as well as the cultural traditions and discourses surrounding Christmas and has participated in the reproduction of these discourses.	This analysis might focus on how the narrative evokes feelings of empathy, compassion, joy or sadness, and how these emotions contribute to our overall interpretation and engagement with the text. This might include the images of Scrooge as a child which create sympathy, and our horror and disgust at the figures of 'Ignorance' and 'Want.' We might also identify with the characters in the story, such as Bob Cratchit and how he works every hour in the day to provide for his family – like many today in a cost of living crisis. Reader response also acknowledges that different readers bring their own interpretations and perspectives to a text. Therefore, looking at layers of meaning and examining the range of possible readings and the reasons behind individual interpretations all fit here. Engaging with the social issues presented in the story, such as poverty, social class and family, resonate with our own understanding of the world. Reader response analysis would also encourage readers to reflect on the transformative journey of Scrooge and its significance in their own lives; how they respond to the idea of change and renewal presented in the story.	A post-structuralist reading would examine the ways in which language functions within the text and how the meanings of words and phrases are contingent and subject to interpretation, rather than fixed or absolute. For example, the term 'goodwill' in the context of the story may be seen as an ambiguous and contested concept, open to multiple interpretations and influenced by social, cultural and historical contexts. The rigid distinctions between past and present, poverty and abundance, and darkness and light can be questioned, and subverted, to challenge the stability of traditional oppositional structures. Furthermore, the characters in the story exhibit multiple and shifting subject positions. For example, Scrooge's transformation involves a reconfiguration of his identity, challenging fixed notions of character and highlighting the performative nature of identity construction. Also, the power dynamics and the social expectations and norms surrounding Christmas in the Victorian era can be analysed as mechanisms of control and social regulation, such as Scrooge being forced to interact with his family, take days off and donate to charitable causes.	Deconstruction explores the role of absence and presence in texts. In *Carol*, the absence of love, empathy and social connection in Scrooge's life is juxtaposed with the presence of these qualities in other characters. Through the process of deconstruction, the analysis would question the assumed presence of positive qualities and the absence of negative ones, highlighting the ambiguous nature of these concepts. Deconstruction also revels in the undecidability and paradoxes within a text. Such as the transformation of Scrooge, which can be seen as both genuine and performative, raising questions about the stability of his newfound generosity. It also highlights both the irony and self-reflexivity within the story, drawing attention to the text's awareness of its own limitations and contradictions. An analysis of *Carol* would explore instances of irony, where the text undermines or contradicts its own stated messages. Such as, when Scrooge claims that if he ever owns a firm, he will treat his apprentices with the same dignity and respect that Fezziwig did. This self-reflexive quality invites readers to question and challenge the text's and the character's assumptions and interpretations.

Queer Theory

A queer analysis would explore the potential subversions and alternative readings of relationships in the novella. It would consider the possibility of queer interpretations, such as examining the close bond between Scrooge and Jacob Marley as a non-conventional relationship that challenges traditional notions of friendship or business partnerships.

It also might highlight the fluidity and ambiguity of desire, for example, instances in the text where characters exhibit complex desires or emotional connections that defy heteronormative expectations. For example, the nostalgia and longing that Scrooge feels towards Belle could be examined as a multi-faceted emotional attachment that goes beyond the boundaries of a heterosexual romantic relationship.

Queer theory also challenges rigid gender norms and explores non-binary or gender queer possibilities. An analysis would examine how characters in the story might transgress or challenge traditional gender expectations, such as Tiny Tim, who embodies vulnerability and tenderness that goes beyond conventional expectations of masculinity. In addition, the idea of the closet and the pressures individuals face to conceal their non-normative desires or identities, can be considered, when Scrooge hides aspects of himself due to societal expectations or fear of social repercussions. This can be seen when he shows emotion in front of the spirits and is ashamed to admit it.

Feminism

As feminism explores the gender roles and expectations depicted in literature, we might examine how characters like Mrs Cratchit, Belle and Mrs Fezziwig are situated within traditional gender norms of the time, often confined to domestic roles and limited agency. We would consider how these roles perpetuate gender inequalities and restrict women's opportunities for self-determination. It might also involve exploring the power dynamics between male and female characters in the story and analysing the dominance of male characters like Scrooge and the ways in which they exercise control and authority over female characters. This is highlighted when Belle's life becomes unhappy as like Scrooge, she is being forced to care only about money and greed. Yet she shows resistance and subverts the Victorian norms by calling off the engagement to Scrooge, which sheds light on her agency and challenges patriarchal power. We might also analyse the economic conditions and challenges faced by female characters such as Mrs Cratchit, who struggle with poverty and limited resources. Economic inequalities intersect with gender here and women's financial dependence on men perpetuates their subjugation. Often, the portrayal of female characters and their roles in fostering empathy and moral growth can be highlighted. There are parts of the book where the story reinforces traditional gendered expectations of women as nurturing and self-sacrificing, such as Fred's wife showing sympathy to Scrooge. Yet Mrs Cratchit challenges these stereotypes when she speaks out about his cruelty.

Post-Colonialism

A post-colonial analysis would explore the power dynamics represented in *Carol* and how they relate to colonialism. For example, Scrooge's position of power as a wealthy businessman and the ways in which he wields economic control over others reflects the colonialist ideologies of exploitation and dominance. Marginalised voices are also usually amplified in Post-Colonial texts, so characters like Bob Cratchit and the impoverished Londoners could be examined, by analysing how their experiences and perspectives are portrayed in the story, plus how their marginalisation is linked to broader structures of power and economic inequality.

In *Carol* the cultural hegemony of Victorian England can be analysed, as the story reflects the dominance of Victorian values, traditions and customs, which are presented as normative and superior. This analysis would consider how these dominant cultural elements shape the characters' actions and interactions. A Post-Colonialist reading might also explore acts of resistance and subversion against oppressive systems. For example, the transformation of Scrooge can be seen as a subversion of the colonialist capitalist mindset and a rejection of the values that perpetuate social inequality.

Post-Modernism

Postmodernism emphasises the fragmented nature of experience and identity, like how the narrative disrupts linear chronology and presents fragmented moments in time. The fragmented structure can be seen in the episodic visits of the ghosts, which disrupt Scrooge's sense of a coherent reality. It also emphasises intertextuality, the referencing and reworking of other texts within a work. These include the influence of Christian morality and the Christmas traditions of Victorian England. The text's self-awareness, metafictional elements and direct address to the reader also highlight its playfulness and the blurring of boundaries between fiction and reality. In addition, hyperreality can be seen, where reality becomes indistinguishable from its representations. *Carol* engages with the idea of simulacra, where the idealised version of Christmas presented in the story becomes more real and significant than the actual lived experiences of the characters. The text's emphasis on spectacle, illusion, and performance underscores this theme. The story also subverts the dominant narratives of Victorian society, such as the idealised view of the wealthy as morally superior and the notion of progress tied to industrialisation. The story's emphasis on personal transformation and the critique of social inequality disrupts these grand narratives. Victorian social norms are also parodied, such as the portrayal of Scrooge as a caricature of greed and the subversion of traditional morality through the redemption of a seemingly irredeemable character.

Again, this table is not exhaustive but it can be used by teachers who may want to improve their subject knowledge, or different ideas and sections can be used with pupils. This may act as a helpful introduction to critical theory, which could be followed by deeper analysis.

2 Critical Theory journey through the English curriculum

Curriculum used with permission of Gaurav Dubay of Handsworth School, Birmingham.

Year 7

Focus Area	Autumn Term	Spring Term	Summer Term
Core Areas	English Language and Poetry	Shakespeare and Pre 20th Century Fiction/ Non-Fiction	Genre and Modern Novel
Unit Title	The History of the English Language	Oral Speech – The Art of Persuasion	Detective Fiction
Main Text(s)	'Beowulf', 'The Canterbury Tales: The Prologue', Anthology of texts e.g. slang and text speak	'Henry V'	'The Number One Ladies…' or 'Enola Holmes' & Anthology of Detective Fiction
End Point Assessment (Reading/ Writing)	Reading: What does the pilgrimage reveal about life in Chaucer's England?	Writing: Construct a rousing war speech.	Writing (opinion piece): Should writers be able to write outside their lived experience?
Conceptual ideas/ Critical theory	Presentation of gender in literature, nouns, adverbs, verbs, article, figurative language, inflection, grapheme, received pronunciation, stress and word family.	Colonialist presentations/ tropes in Shakespearean literature, word family, verse, blank verse, figurative language, Chorus, prosody, standard English, register, punctuation, clause and cohesion	Feminist literary movement, figurative language, adjectives, tentative language, conjunctions, morphology/etymology and root word.

Figure 2.1 A grid detailing the units of study for a year 7 English group and how conceptualised/ critical theory could be included.

DOI: 10.4324/9781003453468-3

Year 8

Focus Area	Autumn Term	Spring Term	Summer Term
Core Areas	Modern Novel and Genre	Poetry and Pre 20th Century Fiction and Non-Fiction	English Language and Shakespeare
Unit Title	Dual Narrative & Dystopian Fiction	The Romantics: Poetry and the Language of Protest	The Art of Rhetoric
Main Text(s)	'Stone Cold' (reading lessons) & Dystopian Fiction Anthology of Extracts	Anthology of Romantic Poetry & 'Jane Eyre' or 'Oliver Twist' (post Romantic protest fiction)	'Julius Caesar' - "Friends, Roman, Countrymen" or 'MAAN' (rhetorical speech & 'Lord of the Flies'
End Point Assessment (Reading/ Writing)	Writing: Write a letter to a newspaper arguing against John Major's stance towards the homeless.	Reading: How is Coleridge's 'submerged politics' (Patrick J Keane) presented in 'The Rime of the Ancient Mariner'?	Writing: Election speeches
Conceptual ideas/ Critical theory	Character analysis using cultural studies. New Historicist view of the culture and socio-economic issues surrounding homelessness. Reader response analysis of Dystopian fiction.	Analysing language, form, structure, caesura, enjambment, figurative language, narrative, verse and epic through a lens of Romanticism and its historical contexts.	Using Classical Theorists ideas to analyse prosody, enunciate, triplets, epithets, appositives, subordination, standard English, register, punctuation, morphology, etymology and cohesion

Figure 2.2 A grid detailing the units of study for a year 8 English group and how conceptualised/ critical theory could be included.

Year 9

Focus Area	Autumn Term	Spring Term	Summer Term
Core Areas	Modern Novel & Poetry	Shakespeare and Pre 20th Century Fiction and Non-Fiction	Genre and English Language
Unit Title	American Renaissance: Literary Movement and Poetry	Autocratic Success and Failure	Subverted Gothic
Main Text(s)	'Punching the Air', 'OMaM', 'Roll of Thunder…' or 'To Kill a Mockingbird'	'Romeo and Juliet'	Gothic extracts and 'The Woman in Black'
End Point Assessment (Reading/ Writing)	Reading: How does the writer use language, structure and form to present societal concerns?	Reading: How does Shakespeare present autocratic rule in 'Romeo and Juliet'?	Reading/Writing: Explorations in subverted gothic fiction.
Conceptual ideas/Critical theory	Post-structuralist approach of deconstruction analysing figurative language, extended metaphor, caesura, enjambment, sonnet, etymology, morphology, tense and emotive language	Analysis of text through a Marxist lens, looking at power and control. Including text features such as: blank verse, figurative language, prose, tentative language and conjunctions.	Analysis through a Post-Modern lens looking at character development through: language, verb, structure, form, shift, foreshadowing, evaluation, etymology, morphology, tense, tentative language, conjunction, description, narration and word class

Figure 2.3 A grid detailing the units of study for a year 9 English group and how conceptualised/ critical theory could be included.

Year 10 or 11

Focus Area	Autumn Term	Spring Term	Summer Term
Core Areos	Pre & Post 20th Century Fiction & Modern Texts	Shakespeare and Language (not GCSE qualification)	Poetry & Genre (Form)
Unit Title	Social Commentary	Symbols and Motifs	Pattern Spotting and Comparison
Main Text(s)	'An Inspector Calls' and 'Jekyll & Hyde'/'A Christmas Carol'	'Macbeth'/ 'The Merchant of Venice'	Conflict and Power Poetry and Unseen Poetry
End Point Assessment (Reading/ Writing)	Reading: AQA Literature question	Reading: AQA Literature question	Reading: Mock Examination (Papers 1 and 2)
Conceptual ideas/ Critical theory	Drama, stage directions, narrative, epistolary form and structure. Context – social, political, religious and cultural, feminist and queer theory	Drama, stage directions, narrative, subverted tragedy form and structure. Context – social, political, religious and cultural, feminist theory, symbolism, motif and Aristotelian Tragedy	Imagery and subverted forms. Context – social, political, religious and cultural, feminist theory, symbolism, motif, language of comparison and form

Figure 2.4 A grid detailing the units of study for a year 10 or 11 English group and how conceptualised/critical theory could be included.

As is evidenced from these medium-term plans, key theories and terms are bumped back into and revisited, so that students are able to develop mastery in these concepts and use the ideas and approaches as a springboard to stimulate their own conceptualised ideas.

3 Case studies from English teachers

Elaine McNally, Head of English

(@mrsmacteach33)

Integrating an exploration of literary criticism with textual study at GCSE is an excellent way to deepen students' knowledge of a text, generating fresh ideas through discussion and building connections. I've noticed that introducing critical perspectives creates a classroom environment that encourages open discussion and the sharing of diverse viewpoints as students realise that there are many ways to read a text. Not only can this be a satisfying lesson activity at GCSE, but the structure and implementation of the lesson can give students an insight into the rewarding study of Literature at A Level as they move away from the idea of a 'right' answer to the flexibility of debate.

I started by identifying critical perspectives on *Romeo and Juliet* that I felt offered an opportunity for rich discussion. Without this careful planning and preparation, critical perspectives can become a source of confusion rather than a valuable tool for deepening students' understanding of a text. I was confident in my students' robust knowledge of the whole play, and I used this activity to synthesise ideas and generate new, more sophisticated interpretations. I also had a clear goal in mind, and formalised this with a big picture question that I added to each resource. I also appreciate that critical perspectives can be quite abstract; they use academic language and concepts that may be unfamiliar for some students which means I decided to begin, where appropriate, with definitions, breaking quotations into chunks to deal with them carefully and slowly.

One of the best things about a lesson that deals with critical perspectives on a text is that conversation is encouraged. I like the fact that talk can be tentative, speculative and relatively unplanned, and that knowledge is cooperatively created. There is joy to be found in those moments when students get to really think for themselves. Yet, I had some pre-planned questions on the resource, using these to redirect discussion and to ensure that my intentions for coverage were met. Additionally, if students are familiar with accountable talk, then their contribution

DOI: 10.4324/9781003453468-4

is likely to be more significant. Using simple, but effective strategies like: think, pair, share or A, B, C (agree, build on, challenge) give talk a meaningful structure. I included key quotations, but to encourage students to reason and explain, they could be given time to select their own quotations from the text.

I really wanted the lesson to be driven by the students' engagement with the critical perspectives. There is a risk that this activity could be perceived as just more criteria that students need to meet to succeed in their exams. For me, the exam essay wasn't really the point: seeking insight and developing personal understanding was the focus. At the end of the lesson, a couple of students asked 'should we include this in an essay?' and this is where a writing task accessed through that final big picture question can help consolidate and refine understanding. It is also a valuable opportunity to model how to summarise and utilise these ideas in a paragraph, maybe by selecting key sentence stems, and making use of critical perspectives in a way that is non-threatening, low stakes and uncomplicated.

Emma Sheppard, Founder of MTPT Project and English teacher

(@emma_au_soleil)

In January 2017, following the return from my first maternity leave, I was fortunate enough to inherit a small top set class who were conceptually very able. By the Easter holidays, we had addressed the trauma of their February mocks by spending a lot of time working on essay technique, and we had discussed, planned or written timed essays on all the *Macbeth* questions I could muster. What more could we do to ensure they hadn't used up all their reserves and developed repetitive strain in their writing hands ahead of their exam in May?

This was the point at which I shared two academic sources with them: one of my own university essays on the theory of evil in *Macbeth*, and small extracts from A. C. Bradley's lectures, *Shakespearean Tragedies*.

Our use of the resources was simple: in separate lessons, I asked students to read the essays and extracts and highlight the parts that they *did* understand. They discussed this in 'safe' partnerships and groups, and once I had an understanding of what they had taken from the essays, I provided them with a set of scaffolded questions as a bridge to even deeper understanding. When students had no idea what the essays were saying, they asked me, and I provided them with a mini-lecture that became a more accessible talking point. This approach meant that the students were in charge of instigating the higher level discussions, rather than me wading in with complicated ideas that would either confuse or intimidate them just before their exams.

The essays were also useful for 'magpie-ing' more sophisticated phrasing and essay wording, which was helpful both for the students already writing articulately – almost the final polish on their writing – as well as providing an impressive crutch for those students who had the ideas, but were a little clumsier in their expression.

When students came across a word or phrase they liked, but weren't yet confident enough to use – for example, Lady Macbeth's 'failure of nature' or 'agency' – this once again provided an opportunity for explicit vocabulary teaching and discussion around higher level concepts. As we were a small class with a lot of space, students were able to spread their highlighted essays and notes on the table in front of them when we continued with our last few essay practices, trying these words and phrases out in their own work.

This class had been subjected to a three year GCSE and so there was the risk that, by the Easter of Year 11, they would have been sick to death of hearing about *Macbeth*. As well as the positive impact that this approach had on their ideas and written expression therefore, it also enabled me to maintain this class's engagement all the way until the exam. The psychological impact of having 'nothing left to teach' this class, and therefore turning to A Level and undergraduate stimuli, was also a huge boost to their confidence. In their minds, they went into the exam already thinking and writing far beyond what they thought was required of them and – whether this was an accurate self-perception or not(!) – it meant that they enjoyed sitting their Shakespeare paper.

Gemma Fincham, Head of English

The catalyst for adding critical theory at GCSE was the new AQA Literature spec and the introduction of *Frankenstein* to the syllabus. I had previously taught *Frankenstein* at A level and this led me to design our school's new GCSE scheme of learning with an A level mindset. I realised it was possible to take the core tenets of the main taught theories at A level and open up the top level responses at GCSE – giving students the opportunity to create more exploratory answers. So, initially, I had my top set year 10 class in mind when I started the process.

I decided to link the theory to some specific points and characters in the text and break it down into more easily digestible chunks. I considered postcolonial theory when discussing Walton's attitude to exploration, feminist theory when analysing *Frankenstein*'s view of Elizabeth and Marxist theory intersected with feminist theory to consider the double oppression of Justine.

I pre-taught some key vocabulary such as marginalisation and the male gaze, and focused on discussion of very specific quotations to tease out the ideas with the whole class. I supported this with some extended reading of essays from sources such as the English and Media Centre.

I wrote these lessons for the use of the whole department and found that, with small adaptations, the core ideas of the theories worked across the ability spectrum and engaged the interest of all learners. They found that this approach made some of the classical texts such as *Frankenstein* more rather than less accessible, as it linked it to a more modern view of the world that they recognised and they could connect it to their own thinking about race, gender and class. It certainly helped to further engage those who were more interested in the social sciences and humanities, as it provided another way into discussing the literature and sometimes a clearer purpose for the close analysis of language and structural features.

It also gave rise to wider useful discussions on political change which helped the students understand elements of Romanticism more effectively. From this point I began exploring how I could engage further with critical theory in all the GCSE Literature texts and have found it has also prepared my current students much more effectively for some of the expectations of the A Level curriculum.

Yasmin Bansal, Second in English

With Shakespeare's *Macbeth*, the features of tragedy very quickly enable students to engage with the idea of the character as a construct: from war hero to dead butcher, students have a tangible framework to apply. They track the titular character's hamartia, debating whether his fate is pre-determined, catalysed by the witches, or thrust upon him by his emasculating wife.

What I wasn't seeing, however, was the same level of sympathy and will to dig deeper into the motivations of Lady Macbeth. All too quickly, she was branded a bully to blame for her husband's downfall. As a feminist, standing before a generation of post-Tate teens, I couldn't help but be troubled by the ongoing demonisation of women who wield power, particularly the lack of any nuance when rationalising their motivations. Objective? Humanise the scapegoat.

Returning to her first scene, and arguably the most polarising, with the infamous 'unsex me' soliloquy, she asks spirits to replace her femininity with 'direst cruelty' ahead of the regicide plot. I selected three extracts from critical essays on the character and challenged students to apply to find new interpretations of her language:

- *Masking Femininity: Women and Power in Shakespeare's Macbeth, As You Like It, and Titus Andronicus* by Kelly Sorge

- *Shakespeare's Heroines: Characteristics of Women, Moral, Poetical, & Historical* by Anna Brownell Jameson

- *Simone de Beauvoir and The Second Sex* by Nasrullah Mambrol.

With less able students, we use reciprocal reading to question, clarify and summarise key arguments together, paragraph by paragraph. With more autonomous students, I gave them feminist theory not directly about the play (e.g., de Beauvoir) to encourage them to make links to Lady Macbeth's life independently. For example, if the female reproductive system was consistently used to justify the patriarchy, how can this help us to understand her desperation to 'stop' her 'blood' and 'milk'?

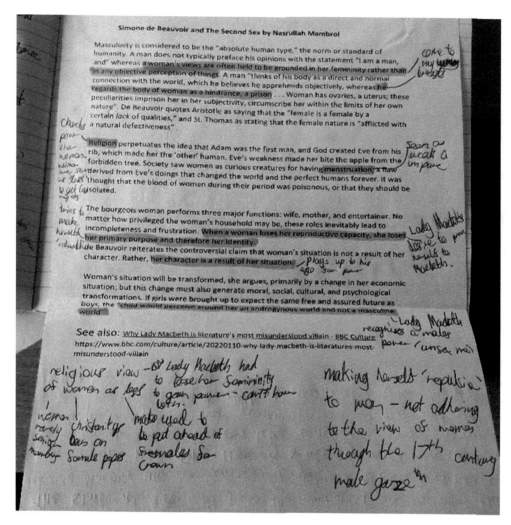

Figure 3.1 A student's initial annotations of a key scene in *Macbeth*.

Having discussed and summarised the key arguments in each group's texts, students are then challenged to return to the quotations in their books to see if they can unlock any new meanings, seen below in green and red pen.

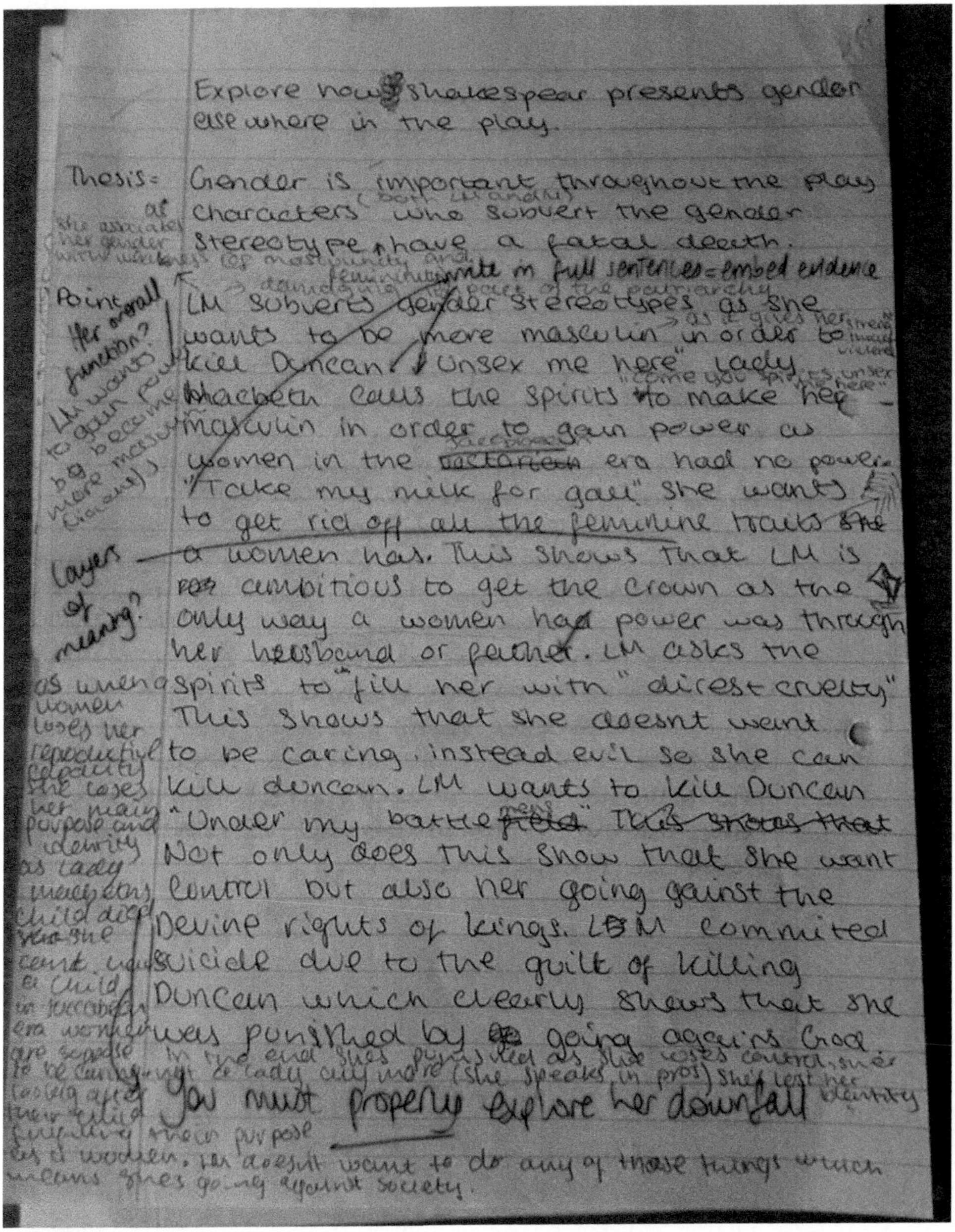

Explore how Shakespear presents gender else where in the play.

Thesis = Gender is important throughout the play characters (both LM and LM) who subvert the gender stereotype have a fatal death.

as she associates her gender with weakness

write in full sentences = embed evidence

Point all LM subverts gender stereotypes as she wants to be more masculin in order to kill Duncan. "Unsex me here" Lady Macbeth calls the spirits to make her masculin in order to gain power as women in the victorian era had no power. "Take my milk for gall" she wants to get rid off all the feminine traits a women has. This shows that LM is too ambitious to get the crown as the only way a women had power was through her husband or father. LM asks the spirits to "fill her with" "direst cruelty" This shows that she doesnt want to be caring, instead evil so she can kill duncan. LM wants to kill Duncan "Under my battlefield" This shows that Not only does this show that she want control but also her going gainst the Devine rights of kings. LM committed suicide due to the quilt of killing Duncan which clearly shows that she was punished by going agains God. You must properly explore her downfall.

Point of her action? LM wants to gain power to become masculin. (to be more masculin?)

Layers of meaning?

as when women loses her reproductive capacity she loses her main purpose and identity as lady macbeth child died, yet she cant, in victorian era women are suppose to be caring by looking after their child fulfilling their purpose as a women. she doesnt want to do any of those things which means shes going against society.

in the end shes punished as she loses control, she loses her lady identity

Figure 3.2 A student's red and green annotations on the same scene after reading the critical sources.

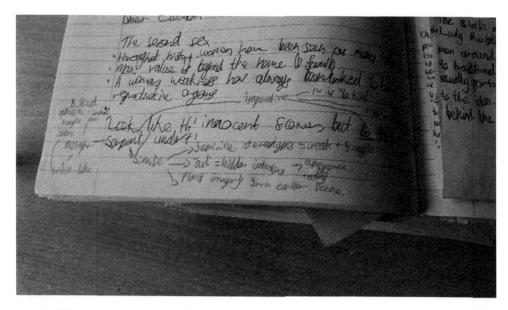

Figure 3.3 A close-up of a student's red annotations on the same scene after reading the critical sources.

We reframe the character within a theatrical lineage of subversive women: Shakespeare creates a framework for his audience to question, challenge and debate the morality of his characters. The EMC's 'Everybody Dies' infographic works wonderfully in tandem to demystify the typicality of Shakespeare's female character arcs, with one year 11 brilliantly summarising: 'so in a comedy they have to get married, and in a tragedy they have to die.' We have found this application of context much more helpful than the classic bolt-on: 'this would shock the audience because women weren't powerful.'

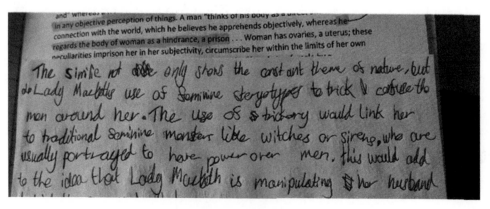

Figure 3.4 A student's work on gender stereotypes.

Sentence stems such as 'Not only...but also...' or 'A X reader would argue ...' help students to articulate layers of nuance, where there would have been otherwise a straightforward interpretation of her actions. Embedding critical theory and wider readings as additional 'layers of meaning' means that when re-calling high scoring scripts from the summer exams, for *Macbeth* and increasingly across different questions, I can clearly recognise where students have drawn on alternative readings to achieve top band marks for authorial intent, and that 'mature and thoughtful' interpretation we strive for as lovers of literature.

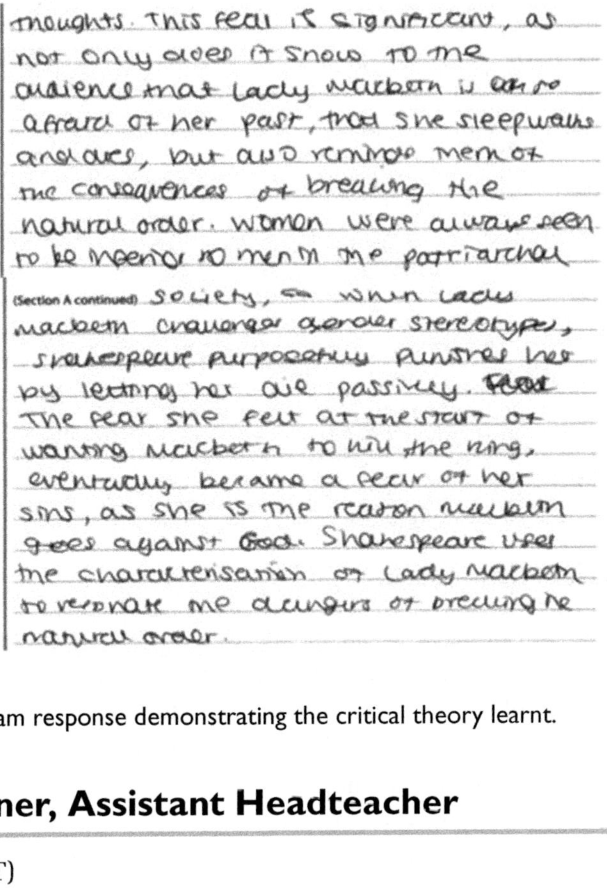

Thoughts. This fear is significant, as not only does it show to the audience that Lady Macbeth is also afraid of her past, that she sleepwalks and does, but also reminds them of the consequences of breaking the natural order. Women were always seen to be inferior to men in the patriarchal (Section A continued) society, so when Lady Macbeth challenges gender stereotypes, Shakespeare purposely punishes her by letting her die passively. The fear she felt at the start of wanting Macbeth to kill the king, eventually became a fear of her sins, as she is the reason Macbeth goes against God. Shakespeare uses the characterisation of Lady Macbeth to resonate the dangers of breaking the natural order.

Figure 3.5 Exam response demonstrating the critical theory learnt.

Alex Trainer, Assistant Headteacher

(@0captainAT)

I have been teaching a wonderful year 11 class this year, but I noticed that they were afraid to trust their own voices and instincts when it came to analysis of texts. Not only did this limit their analysis in literature, but it also meant that they felt intimidated by the unseen nature of the language papers.

In an attempt to broaden their thinking, and explicitly show them how to conduct additional research, I decided to set some flipped learning by setting critical reading for homework. There were two key processes that I wanted students to go through when reading the text – making efficient Cornell notes and learning how to read from an evaluative standpoint. Each of these processes is discussed in turn below.

Using Cornell notes

Below is an example of Cornell notes taken in response to 'Sponging the Stone: Transformation in *A Christmas Carol*' (Patterson, 1994).

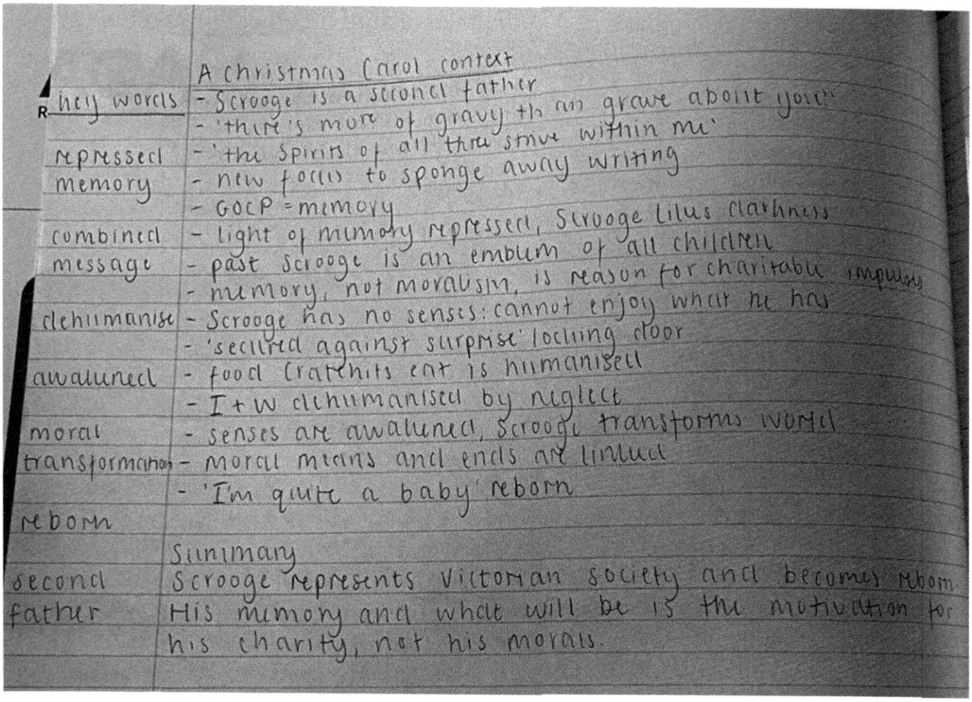

Figure 3.6 An example of Cornell notes.

Instead of merely reading the essay and highlighting it, which is a low impact reading strategy, the aim of using Cornell notes is for students to process the information a number of times with a slight delay in between to increase the possibility of the ideas moving into long-term memory.

We can then use these notes in several ways across subsequent lessons to build strong connections between the arguments of the essay and students' understanding of the text. I tend to do this by using the key words that students have identified as a springboard to developing their ideas.

Examples:

● 'Scrooge's memory becomes the motivation for his transformation.' Prove that this is true.

- Write down everything that you know about the moral transformation of Scrooge.

- What is the significance of the Ghost of Christmas Past in the transformation of Scrooge?

- Discuss the significance of 'I am quite a baby' in Stave 5. Use the following terms in your response: memory, moral transformation, rebirth.

- Why is humanisation and dehumanisation so integral to the text of *A Christmas Carol*? Give an example of each.

Evaluative questions

The evaluative questions were designed to help show students that the primary function of literary criticism to put forward an argument or thesis. This was something they need to understand in order to develop their own critical writing. For example, what key arguments does Patterson propose when discussing the significance of the transformation of Scrooge?

I also wanted them to have the confidence to evaluate the validity of the argument so the questions always required an element of reflection. Therefore, the second question would be how far do you agree with these arguments?

Finally, I wanted them to become curious about the texts so I always posed a third question that required them to identify further areas for exploration – what additional research would you now like to explore?

As a result of these activities, students have shown an increase in confidence in exploring texts in both literature and language. I have seen the ideas of the wider reading undertaken begin to take shape in a more nuanced appreciation of the texts studied. Perhaps most importantly, students have really engaged with the process and have said that they have enjoyed this additional reading.

Rebecca Slatter, Assistant Head of English

Teaching a top set year 10 Literature class comes with its many challenges; will they be able to complete in depth word analysis? Will they be able to effectively explain the writer's intentions? Will they be able to thoughtfully consider their reader responses? After teaching them for only a few months, I knew that none of this would be a problem for my class.

To effectively stretch and challenge this class, I had to consider my own experiences and where my own education had taken me. I thought back to my time at college and during my A level studies I had been taught to use literary criticism. Would they be able to rise to this challenge? There was only one way to find out.

I spent a whole lesson teaching them about four key literary theories: formalism, new historicism, feminist theory and psychoanalytic theory. Once this had been understood, I challenged them to put it into practice.

My lesson was as follows. The question for the starter activity was: In *Macbeth*, how does Macduff respond to King Duncan's murder? Students were required to find key quotations and provide inferences about what they revealed about Macduff. My students engaged well with this task and were able to select relevant quotations to support their ideas, demonstrating clear links to their prior learning and that routines are clearly in place. I then shared the key skills for the lesson and made links to why this, why now, the curriculum intent statement and our learning journey.

Next, I introduced a new word (foil) that was going to be pivotal for the lesson. I was able to cold call my students to explain this word and I asked open ended questions (how could Macduff be described as a foil to Macbeth?), which allowed me to stretch and challenge my students as they were able to apply the new vocabulary to offer a response to the question. During this activity I effectively used cold calling to share feedback and encouraged my students to use green pen work to record additional ideas from other pupils – making their engagement with the feedback clear. I encouraged my students to extend their verbal responses through questions such as: can you say that better/with more detail? I also 'bounced' the question to other students to ensure the responses were extended. Furthermore, I questioned my students to encourage links to contextual factors (why would it shock them?)

What? How? Why? (YOU DO)

		In Act 2 Scene 3, Shakespeare presents Macduff as a foil to Macbeth as his morality is used to show how

How does Shakespeare present Macduff in Act 2 Scene 3?

How is Macduff a foil to Macbeth?

You are going to attempt a what, how, why paragraph on the same question but using a quotation of your choice.

This will be completed on the blank bit of the page using the scaffold strip to help you.

In Act 2 Scene 3, Shakespeare presents Macduff as a foil to Macbeth as his morality is used to show how immoral Macbeth is. This is evident when he says, "O horror, horror, horror! Tongue nor heart cannot conceive nor name thee!' The use of the repeated noun 'horror' demonstrates Macduff's intense feelings of fear, shock and disgust because he cannot comprehend that such a horrendous act could take place in Macbeth's castle. Also, the emotive phrase 'tongue nor heart' implies that Macduff cannot put into words what he has just witnessed and he cannot comprehend his feelings regarding the crime because he viewed Duncan as a benevolent King. Furthermore, this is heightened by the alliterative phrase 'cannot conceive nor name' as it suggests that Macduff cannot believe that someone would do this to Duncan as he was perceived as a exemplary leader. Analysing this quotation through the viewpoint of formalism highlights how the exclamation mark demonstrates Macduff's disbelief and his tone during this line is one of confusion that shows he is possibly feeling guilt regarding not being there to protect the king. The act of regicide links to a new historicism viewpoint as men were strong physically and mentally yet the audience would recognise that this act shares some similarities with the gunpowder plot and the treason committed, therefore foreshadowing that Macbeth will face the consequences of his actions later on in the play. Through the viewpoint of feminist theory, an audience is able to see that Macbeth and Macduff are in conflict because Macbeth tried to challenge the divine right of kings and the great chain of being. Within this quotation, Macbeth upholds the traditional views of men by resorting to violence rather than dealing with his emotions. In direct contrast to this, Macduff challenges the traditional views of men as he is overcome with emotion upon discovering Duncan's body. It is also dear to see that through the viewpoint of psychoanalytic theory, Macduff's conscious behaviour is to seek revenge for the murder yet his unconscious behaviour is his emotions surrounding the murder. There is therefore a conflict between Macduff's conscious and unconscious and this amplifies Macduff's psychological state as he is not demonstrating equilibrium.

Figure 3.7 Academic vocabulary model answer.

I introduced the big question for the lesson: How does Shakespeare present Macduff in Act 2 Scene 3? We deconstructed a model answer to create a structure strip of sentence starters that my students could use to scaffold their analytical paragraphs, and I included high challenge with the use of literary criticism. My students were then encouraged to create their independent paragraph utilising all the information that they had learned within the lesson.

Gaurav Dubay, Windsor Academy Trust, Director of English

Whilst outcomes in English were above national average, we felt that our students' experiences of English did not always allow them to effectively demonstrate the vision we had for them: cultured, engaged and informed. We wanted this strapline to underpin our approach in building an effective curriculum where students not only achieved the highest academic outcomes, but were able to assess the opinions of others, review them and develop their own unique interpretations as a result; the role literary criticism could play in seeing that happen was a strong one.

Each unit of work begins with an orientation lesson, which seeks to explore the following:

● Where does this unit fit in with what we learnt before?

● Where does this unit fit in with what we're learning now?

● How will this unit act as an enabler of future learning?

Critical reading hooks are used in the orientation lesson to encourage students to engage with literary lenses, sharpen and develop views, and ultimately shape their own opinions. Students engage with these hooks throughout the unit. For instance, our opening unit in year 9 looks at problematic literature and literature as protest building on the unit on Romantic Poetry and Protest that they experienced in year 8. Through the lenses of identity and post-colonial interpretations of texts, students are encouraged to look at the role literature played as part of the Black Arts Movement, develop an awareness of the role literature plays in disrupting societal attitudes and norms, and create imitative works whereby they develop their own written agency – be that academic or personal.

Year Group	Autumn: Critical Reading Hook and Lens	Spring: Critical Reading Hook and Lens	Summer: Critical Reading Hook and Lens
7	English Timeline: https://www.bl.uk/ englishtimeline Lens: Literary criticism as the imitation of art	Shakespeare's Quartos: https://www.bl.uk/ treasures/shakespeare/ ho mepage.html Lens: The role of the chorus as an unreliable narrator	Murder: https://www. bl.uk/romantics-and-victorians/articles/ murder-as-entertainment Lens: Detective fiction and othering of marginalised groups
8	Freedom and Oppression in Literature: https://www. bl.uk/20th-century-literature/articles/ freedom-or-oppression-the-fear-of-dystopia Lens: Introduction to literary political criticism e.g. Marxism	The Romantics – Protest Fiction: https://www. bl.uk/romantics-and-victorians/articles/ the-romantics Lens: Cementing awareness of political criticism e.g. Marxism	Rhetoric and Imitation: https://www.bl.uk/ collection-items/ the-arts-of-logic-and-rhetoric-by-dudley-tenner Lens: Literary criticism as the imitation of art
9	Harlem Renaissance – Problematic Readings of Texts: https://literariness. org/2020/07/10/ harlem-renaissance/ Lens: Post colonial theory and identity criticism	Shakespeare – Tracking Autocracy: https://literariness. org/2020/07/10/ harlem-renaissance/ Lens: Foucault's concept of power	Gothic Motifs: https://www.bl.uk/ romantics-and-victorians/articles/ gothic-motifs Lens: Subversion of power in fiction

Figure 3.8 Examples of critical reading hooks at Key Stage 3.

Year Group	Autumn: Critical Reading Hook and Lens	Spring: Critical Reading Hook and Lens	Summer: Critical Reading Hook and Lens
10	Othering in Fiction: https://journals.sagepub.com/doi/10.1177/1077800411433546 Lens: Othering of marginalised groups	Supernatural Symbolism: https://www.bl.uk/shakespeare/articles/witchcraft-in-shakespeares-england Lens: Power structures presented through the supernatural	Conflict Literature: https://www.bl.uk/20th-century-literature/articles/broken-mirrors-the-first-world-war-and-modernist-literature Lens: Art as imitation
11	Multiculturalism in Literature: https://www.bu.edu/africa/outreach/teachingresources/literature-language--arts/selection_guide/ Len: Language and structure in presenting power structures	Exploitation Meeting Non-Fiction: https://www.jstor.org/stable/20107261 Lens: Language and stricture in presenting power structures	

Figure 3.9 Examples of critical reading hooks at Key Stage 4.

The role literary criticism plays in empowering our students is undeniable. Introducing critical reading hooks from the onset of one's secondary schooling gives students the tools to effectively develop knowledge, form views and shape judicious conclusions.

4 The forgotten ghost – the importance of Marley: How is Marley an integral part of the plot of *A Christmas Carol?*

Ask anybody how many ghosts there are in *A Christmas Carol* and chances are that they will quickly answer 'three.' Of course, many people forget about the first and arguably most macabre of all of Dickens' spectres, the one who starts the ball of self-discovery rolling for Ebenezer Scrooge: Jacob Marley. It is foolish for readers to discount Scrooge's old business partner, whose life and dealings with mankind mirror so closely those of Scrooge. Perhaps it is due to the fact that Marley's part in the novella is so short and comes so early on, or that unlike the other spirits, he doesn't physically take Scrooge on a journey and so is left behind. In addition, the other spirits represent Christmas in their various forms and so are easier for the audience to relate to. Yet, Marley's importance cannot be underestimated, as he inspires the fear in Scrooge which begins his transformation, by demonstrating to 'Scrooge how one who shared his ideals and commitments fared in the afterlife.'[1] When faced with this hellish vision, his Victorian obsession with the afterlife comes to the fore and he begins the slow process of being galvanised into action.

Scrooge's reactions to the spirits

Orford[2] argues that the fear Marley inspires in Scrooge actually leaves no need for the visitation of the third spirit. He charts the reaction that Scrooge has to the three spirits, noting that he begins by reacting contrarily to the first child-like spirit, remarking that it is far too early for him to be woken for such 'pedestrian purposes.'[3] For the second spirit, his attitude softens as he speaks 'timidly.'[4] Yet by the time the third spirit arrives, whose hooded cloak and skeletal appearance resembles the

Grim Reaper, he has already changed and is happy to accompany the spirit with a 'thankful heart.'[5] Although, he goes on to say that Scrooge needs the last spirit, as it is then that he demonstrates that he is capable of being pro-active and realising what the consequences will be if he doesn't change his ways. However, without the initial ghostly demonstration by Marley, would these consequences have seemed as real and terrifying? I think not.

A supernatural connection

Much has been written about the importance of there being the three spirits and the way the number links to the Holy Trinity, cementing *A Christmas Carol* as a religious allegory. Marley is not the same as the other spirits though, so his inclusion as a character of great importance does not disturb this connection. A spirit is much more symbolic and associated with feelings and the soul, hence the three in the story used as manifestations of the symbolism surrounding Christmas. But it could be argued that Marley was portrayed as more of a traditional ghost, as much is made of his mortal life and his personal connection to Scrooge during his lifetime, including the business sign that still bears his name. He was an active participant in Scrooge's past and therefore reaches Scrooge in a way that the other three allegorical spirits cannot.

Through Marley, Scrooge sees his own fate in gory realism and the desire for self-preservation in his long afterlife haunts him the most. What is more, he experiences Marley's frustrations himself, while witnessing the Cratchit's despair at the death of Tiny Tim. Unable to reach out and comfort his clerk, he has a taste of what it must be to walk the earth and be unable to positively affect the lives of those who you should have cherished in life, and unsurprisingly, he doesn't like it.

The visitation of Marley also gives readers an inkling that there may be something in Scrooge worth saving and that deep in the icy caverns of his heart, he is capable of tender feeling. When asked whether his business is 'Scrooge and Marley' he answers that it isn't but replies that his business partner died seven years ago, that very night. Marley was Scrooge's friend, and he tells Marley as much when he arrives for his ghostly visitation; he remembers the date of his death and mourns it in his own way. Therefore, although Scrooge is filled with fear at the sight of his friend, he is also pleased to see him and asks him for some tenderness, imploring him to 'speak comfort to me Jacob.'[6] Which seems to imply that Marley has been there to help Scrooge before, as a friend, confidante and paternal figure, which Scrooge lacked after leaving Fezziwig's. This importance to Scrooge makes Marley a key character in the novella as it is him that really speaks to Ebenezer and opens his eyes fully to the possibility for change, making him more receptive to the three spirits to come as he appreciates their potential powers for his rebirth. He may get the chance that Marley never did.

Biblical connections

Finally, the description of Marley's ghost and the way Scrooge reacts to him, renews the biblical connections afresh, with its links to The Gospel of St. Mark. He is 'fettered' and wears a 'chain'[7] just like Legion, who seems fated to forever cry and cut himself with stones, until Jesus appears, filling him with his grace and releasing him from his bondage.[8] Could this man be Scrooge? Is Marley his saviour, come to free him from his metaphorical bonds he has built for himself and is now unable to escape from? It is perhaps Scrooge's acceptance of receiving this grace, along with that offered from the other spirits, which seems to disintegrate the chains and offers him a freedom he can envisage…and it all begins with Marley.

Summed up in six

- Marley is an important character in the novella who inspires Scrooge to begin his transformation, through fear.

- Some critics argue that Marley's visitation negated the need for the third spirit.

- However, the third spirit gave Scrooge the chance to be pro-active and show he had changed.

- Marley is more of a ghost than a spirit as he still has physical links with Scrooge's life on earth.

- Through the character of Marley, we learn that Scrooge is capable of tenderness.

- The way that Marley is described links him to the description of Legion in the Bible, therefore cementing *A Christmas Carol*'s place as a religious allegory.

Ideas for teaching

AO2: Photocopy the pages where Scrooge implores Marley to speak comfort to him and tells him he was always a good man of business (Charles Dickens, *A Christmas Carol* (London: Wordsworth Classics, 2018), 21–22) and place it on an A3 sheet next to the passage where he is dismissive to Fred (Charles Dickens, *A Christmas Carol* (London: Wordsworth Classics, 2018), 10–11.). Ask pupils to annotate both passages, with a focus on the way Scrooge speaks to them and his body language. What does this show about how Scrooge felt about Marley? Does it foreshadow his later resurrection as somebody who is now capable of warmth of feeling to others? Ask students to write an analytical paragraph juxtaposing Scrooge's reaction to Fred and Marley and how this might demonstrate Scrooge's strong relationship with Marley.

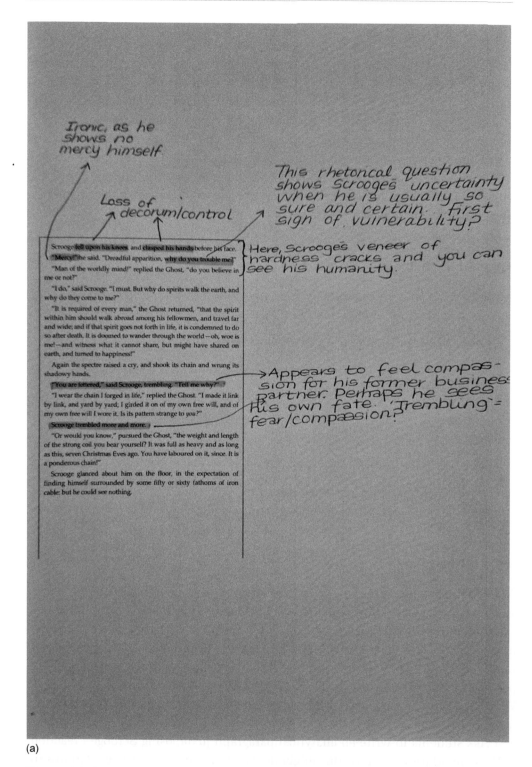

(a)

Figure 4.1 (a, b, c) A student's annotations of the key Marley scene. *(Continued)*

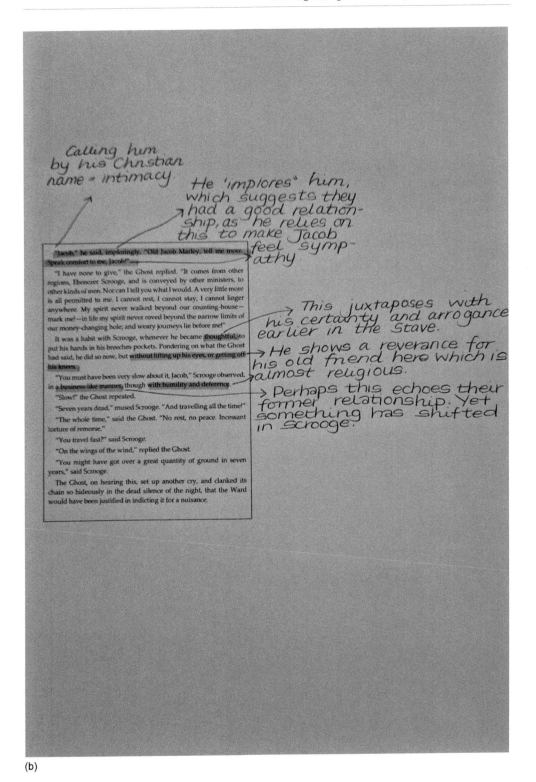

Calling him by his Christian name = intimacy

He 'implores' him, which suggests they had a good relation- ship, as he relies on this to make Jacob feel symp- athy

"Jacob," he said, imploringly. "Old Jacob Marley, tell me more. Speak comfort to me, Jacob!"

"I have none to give," the Ghost replied. "It comes from other regions, Ebenezer Scrooge, and is conveyed by other ministers, to other kinds of men. Nor can I tell you what I would. A very little more is all permitted to me. I cannot rest, I cannot stay, I cannot linger anywhere. My spirit never walked beyond our counting-house— mark me!—in life my spirit never roved beyond the narrow limits of our money-changing hole; and weary journeys lie before me!"

It was a habit with Scrooge, whenever he became thoughtful, to put his hands in his breeches pockets. Pondering on what the Ghost had said, he did so now, but without lifting up his eyes, or getting off his knees.

"You must have been very slow about it, Jacob," Scrooge observed, in a business-like manner, though with humility and deference.

"Slow!" the Ghost repeated.

"Seven years dead," mused Scrooge. "And travelling all the time!"

"The whole time," said the Ghost. "No rest, no peace. Incessant torture of remorse."

"You travel fast?" said Scrooge.

"On the wings of the wind," replied the Ghost.

"You might have got over a great quantity of ground in seven years," said Scrooge.

The Ghost, on hearing this, set up another cry, and clanked its chain so hideously in the dead silence of the night, that the Ward would have been justified in indicting it for a nuisance.

This juxtaposes with his certainty and arrogance earlier in the Stave.

He shows a reverance for his old friend here which is almost religious.

Perhaps this echoes their former relationship. Yet something has shifted in Scrooge.

(b)

Figure 4.1 (Continued) (a, b, c) A student's annotations of the key Marley scene.

(Continued)

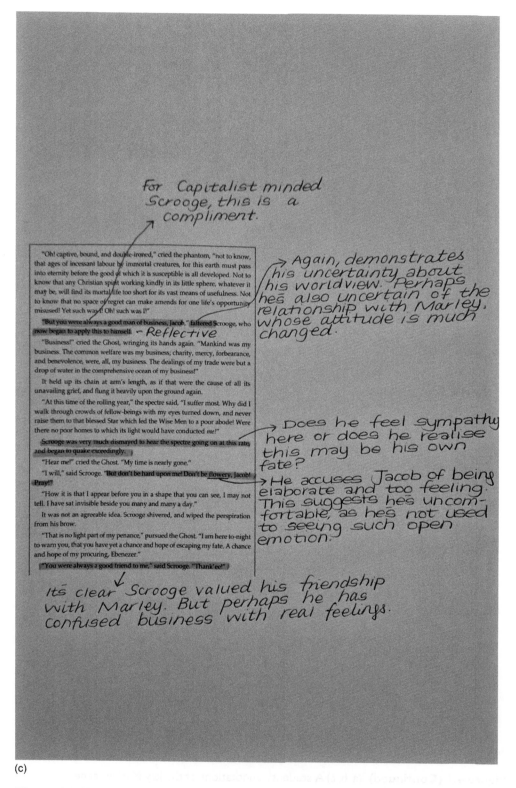

For Capitalist minded Scrooge, this is a compliment.

"Oh! captive, bound, and double-ironed," cried the phantom, "not to know, that ages of incessant labour by immortal creatures, for this earth must pass into eternity before the good of which it is susceptible is all developed. Not to know that any Christian spirit working kindly in its little sphere, whatever it may be, will find its mortal life too short for its vast means of usefulness. Not to know that no space of regret can make amends for one life's opportunity misused! Yet such was I! Oh! such was I!"

"But you were always a good man of business, Jacob," faltered Scrooge, who now began to apply this to himself. ~ Reflective

"Business!" cried the Ghost, wringing its hands again. "Mankind was my business. The common welfare was my business; charity, mercy, forbearance, and benevolence, were, all, my business. The dealings of my trade were but a drop of water in the comprehensive ocean of my business!"

It held up its chain at arm's length, as if that were the cause of all its unavailing grief, and flung it heavily upon the ground again.

"At this time of the rolling year," the spectre said, "I suffer most. Why did I walk through crowds of fellow-beings with my eyes turned down, and never raise them to that blessed Star which led the Wise Men to a poor abode! Were there no poor homes to which its light would have conducted me!"

Scrooge was very much dismayed to hear the spectre going on at this rate, and began to quake exceedingly.

"Hear me!" cried the Ghost. "My time is nearly gone."

"I will," said Scrooge. "But don't be hard upon me! Don't be flowery, Jacob! Pray!"

"How it is that I appear before you in a shape that you can see, I may not tell. I have sat invisible beside you many and many a day."

It was not an agreeable idea. Scrooge shivered, and wiped the perspiration from his brow.

"That is no light part of my penance," pursued the Ghost. "I am here to-night to warn you, that you have yet a chance and hope of escaping my fate. A chance and hope of my procuring, Ebenezer."

"You were always a good friend to me," said Scrooge. "Thank'ee!"

Again, demonstrates his uncertainty about his worldview. Perhaps hes also uncertain of the relationship with Marley, whose attitude is much changed.

Does he feel sympathy here or does he realise this may be his own fate?

He accuses Jacob of being elaborate and too feeling. This suggests hes uncomfortable, as hes not used to seeing such open emotion.

Its clear Scrooge valued his friendship with Marley. But perhaps he has confused business with real feelings.

(c)

Figure 4.1 (Continued) (a, b, c) A student's annotations of the key Marley scene.

"A merry Christmas, uncle! God save you!" cried a cheerful voice. It was the voice of Scrooge's nephew, who came upon him so quickly that this was the first intimation he had of his approach.

"Bah!" said Scrooge. "Humbug!"

He had so heated himself with rapid walking in the fog and frost, this nephew of Scrooge's, that he was all in a glow; his face was ruddy and handsome; his eyes sparkled, and his breath smoked again.

"Christmas a humbug, uncle!" said Scrooge's nephew. "You don't mean that, I am sure?"

"I do," said Scrooge. "Merry Christmas! What right have you to be merry? What reason have you to be merry? You're poor enough."

"Come, then," returned the nephew gaily. "What right have you to be dismal? What reason have you to be morose? You're rich enough."

Scrooge having no better answer ready on the spur of the moment, said, "Bah!" again; and followed it up with "Humbug."

"Don't be cross, uncle!" said the nephew.

"What else can I be," returned the uncle, "when I live in such a world of fools as this? Merry Christmas! Out upon merry Christmas! What's Christmas time to you but a time for paying bills without money; a time for finding yourself a year older, but not an hour richer; a time for balancing your books and having every item in 'em through a round dozen of months presented dead against you? If I could work my will," said Scrooge indignantly, "every idiot who goes about with 'Merry Christmas' on his lips, should be boiled with his own pudding, and buried with a stake of holly through his heart. He should!"

"Uncle!" pleaded the nephew.

"Nephew!" returned the uncle sternly, "keep Christmas in your own way, and let me keep it in mine."

Scrooge is not pleased to see his nephew. He forgoes social expectations by using mono-syllabic replies, punctuated by exclamation marks, demons-trating his annoyance. 'Humbug' suggests his nephew is talking nonsense.

Repeated rhetorical questions, like an interrogation. Insults Fred - 'poor'.

Not willing to engage.

The lists and short sentence at the end of this monlogue shows Scrooges annoyance. The adverb 'indignantly' portrays an arrogance in Scrooge, as he believes hes right.

This imperative almost signals the end of the conversation for Scrooge. He expects his nephew to give up on him like so many others previously.

(a)

Figure 4.2 (a, b, c) A student's annotations of the Fred scene. *(Continued)*

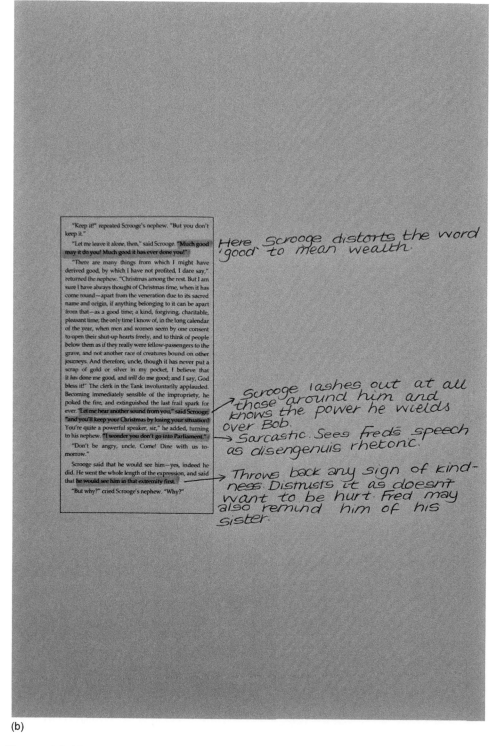

"Keep it!" repeated Scrooge's nephew. "But you don't keep it."

"Let me leave it alone, then," said Scrooge. "Much good may it do you! Much good it has ever done you!"

"There are many things from which I might have derived good, by which I have not profited, I dare say," returned the nephew. "Christmas among the rest. But I am sure I have always thought of Christmas time, when it has come round—apart from the veneration due to its sacred name and origin, if anything belonging to it can be apart from that—as a good time; a kind, forgiving, charitable, pleasant time; the only time I know of, in the long calendar of the year, when men and women seem by one consent to open their shut-up hearts freely, and to think of people below them as if they really were fellow-passengers to the grave, and not another race of creatures bound on other journeys. And therefore, uncle, though it has never put a scrap of gold or silver in my pocket, I believe that it *has* done me good, and *will* do me good; and I say, God bless it!" The clerk in the Tank involuntarily applauded. Becoming immediately sensible of the impropriety, he poked the fire, and extinguished the last frail spark for ever. "Let me hear another sound from you," said Scrooge, "and you'll keep your Christmas by losing your situation! You're quite a powerful speaker, sir," he added, turning to his nephew. "I wonder you don't go into Parliament."

"Don't be angry, uncle. Come! Dine with us tomorrow."

Scrooge said that he would see him—yes, indeed he did. He went the whole length of the expression, and said that he would see him in that extremity first.

"But why?" cried Scrooge's nephew. "Why?"

Handwritten annotations:

Here, Scrooge distorts the word 'good' to mean wealth.

Scrooge lashes out at all those around him and knows the power he wields over Bob.
Sarcastic. Sees fred's speech as disengenuis rhetoric.

Throws back any sign of kindness. Dismusts it as doesn't want to be hurt. Fred may also remind him of his sister.

(b)

Figure 4.2 (Continued) (a, b, c) A student's annotations of the Fred scene. *(Continued)*

> "Why did you get married?" said Scrooge.
>
> "Because I fell in love."
>
> "Because you fell in love!" growled Scrooge, as if that were the only one thing in the world more ridiculous than a merry Christmas. "Good afternoon!"
>
> "Nay, uncle, but you never came to see me before that happened. Why give it as a reason for not coming now?"
>
> "Good afternoon," said Scrooge.
>
> "I want nothing from you; I ask nothing of you; why cannot we be friends?"
>
> "Good afternoon," said Scrooge.
>
> "I am sorry, with all my heart, to find you so resolute. We have never had any quarrel, to which I have been a party. But I have made the trial in homage to Christmas, and I'll keep my Christmas humour to the last. So A Merry Christmas, uncle!"

Odd reply. Perhaps demonstrates Scrooges jealousy and bitterness at his own broken engagement.

Mimics and ridicules Fred. Due to his experience with Belle, hes lost faith in love.

His lack of feeling makes him seem inhuman.

Freds talk of marraige brings back painful memories and he wants to get rid of him. He can then repress the memories again.

(c)

Figure 4.2 (Continued) (a, b, c) A student's annotations of the Fred scene.

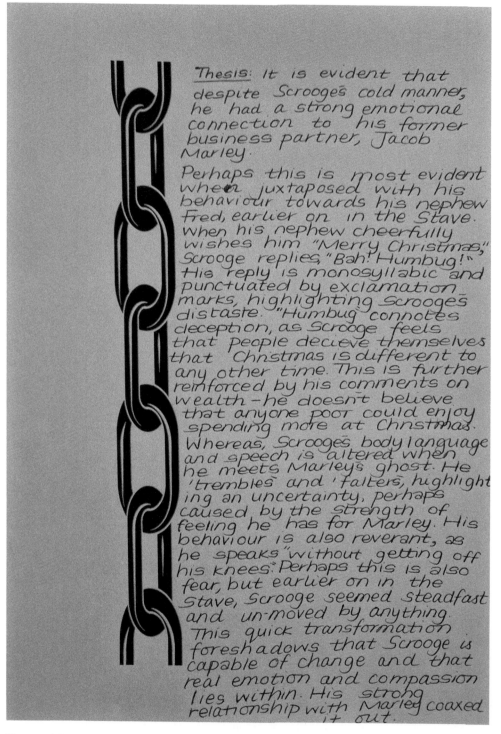

Thesis: It is evident that despite Scrooge's cold manner, he had a strong emotional connection to his former business partner, Jacob Marley.

Perhaps this is most evident when juxtaposed with his behaviour towards his nephew Fred, earlier on in the Stave. When his nephew cheerfully wishes him "Merry Christmas," Scrooge replies, "Bah! Humbug!" His reply is monosyllabic and punctuated by exclamation marks, highlighting Scrooge's distaste. "Humbug" connotes deception, as Scrooge feels that people decieve themselves that Christmas is different to any other time. This is further reinforced by his comments on wealth – he doesn't believe that anyone poor could enjoy spending more at Christmas. Whereas, Scrooge's body language and speech is altered when he meets Marley's ghost. He 'trembles' and 'falters', highlighting an uncertainty, perhaps caused by the strength of feeling he has for Marley. His behaviour is also reverant, as he speaks "without getting off his knees." Perhaps this is also fear, but earlier on in the Stave, Scrooge seemed steadfast and un-moved by anything. This quick transformation foreshadows that Scrooge is capable of change and that real emotion and compassion lies within. His strong relationship with Marley coaxed it out.

Figure 4.3 A student's analytical paragraph exploring the thesis.

AO3: Research Victorian beliefs about the afterlife and find links to the way Jacob Marley's ghost has been presented.

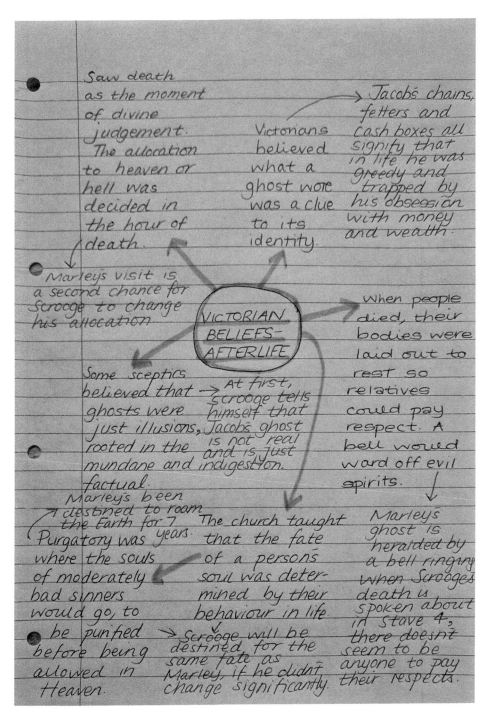

Figure 4.4 A student's research on Victorian beliefs about the afterlife and highlighted quotations from the text to link context to Dicken's descriptions.

Notes

1 Kathleen Poorman Dougherty, 'Habituation and Character Change,' *Philosophy and Literature* 31, no. 2 (January 2007): 294–310.
2 Pete Orford, 'To Begin With: Justifying Marley in A Christmas Carol,' *Dickensian* 110, no. 2 (June 2014): 145–153.
3 Charles Dickens, *A Christmas Carol* (London: Wordsworth Classics, 2018), 30.
4 Ibid., 47.
5 Ibid., 72.
6 Ibid., 21.
7 Ibid., 19.
8 Song Cho, 'Charles Dickens' Jacob Marley and the Gospel of St. Mark,' *Notes and Queries* 61, no. 4 (December 2014): 547.

References

Song Cho. 'Charles Dickens' Jacob Marley and the Gospel of St. Mark,' *Notes and Queries* 61, no. 4 (December 2014): 547. https://doi.org/10.1093/notesj/gju134
Charles Dickens, *A Christmas Carol*, (London: Wordsworth Classics, 2018).
Pete Orford, 'To Begin With: Justifying Marley in A Christmas Carol,' *Dickensian* 110, no. 2 (June 2014): 145–153.
Kathleen Poorman Dougherty, 'Habituation and Character Change.' *Philosophy and Literature* 31, no. 2 (January 2007): 294–310. https://doi.org/10.1353/phl.2007.0025

5 Religious ideology and Dante in A Christmas Carol: Is *A Christmas Carol* a religious text?

Whilst there is no concrete proof that Dickens' *A Christmas Carol* was inspired by Dante, G. K. Chesterton claims that he actually wrote the novella while he was on a tour of Italy[1] in 1843, but even if this is not the case, it seems that Dante's influence would have been impossible to escape in the extremely religious Mediterranean surroundings Dickens found himself in. In fact, this claim seems even more likely when you read his book *Pictures from Italy*, where he mentions Dante,[2] and academic Susan Jhirad claims that he possessed volumes of Dante in his library.[3] When furnished with these facts, it is easy to start drawing parallels between Dante's *Divine Comedy* and *A Christmas Carol* and noticing the influence it may have had on Dickens' plot in *Carol*.

To begin with, both texts start in a dark place befitting of the sombre mood and events depicted in them: for Dante in Canto 1 of *Inferno*, it takes the form of The Dark Forest, where 'this forest savage, rough, and stern, which in the very thought renews the fear.'[4] Whereas, the gloominess of the industrial revolution takes centre stage in *A Christmas Carol*, where the weather is 'cold, bleak, biting' and the 'fog came pouring in at every chink and keyhole, and was so dense without, that although the court was of the narrowest, the houses opposite were mere phantoms.'[5] These ghostly openings make it clear that both characters have lost their way and they serve as the backdrop for their mystical journey to reclamation.

The road to redemption

To achieve this redemption, the pilgrim Dante has to travel through Hell, Purgatory and Heaven, while our miser Scrooge must be dragged kicking and screaming into his own Past, before he explores his Present and Future. The experiences both characters have in these places, will contribute to their understanding of how they have ended up in their present circumstances, and the guides they meet will impart wisdom, which should they listen to it, will set them on the path to redemption. For Dante, it is Virgil who was sent by Beatrice to be Dante's guide who tells him after he cries for pity, 'you must journey down another road if ever you hope to leave

DOI: 10.4324/9781003453468-6

this wilderness.'[6] Dickens' Marley serves as Scrooge's first guide who warns him that if Scrooge does not change, he will be condemned to wander the earth dragging his own chains behind him, filled with the cash boxes and accoutrements of capitalism that he held so dear in his mortal life. However, like Virgil to Dante, he offers Scrooge a slither of hope: 'I am here to-night to warn you, that you have yet a chance and hope of escaping my fate. A chance and hope of my procuring, Ebenezer.'[7]

The similarities don't end there, however, as the three beasts that Dante meets in the wood serve a similar function to the three omens that Scrooge experiences before Marley's appearance: the hearse, the door knocker transformed to Marley's face and the clanging ringing of the bell. The three beasts are allegories of three different sins: the leopard represents lust, the lion pride, and the wolf avarice. While the hearse could be interpreted as a symbol of Scrooge's impending doom, if he does not change, the face of the dead Marley and the loud peal of the bell, moving of its own accord, are surely a sign that Scrooge needs to be woken up from the reverie of his current selfish existence if he is to avoid the same fate as his old friend.

Medieval morality play?

Yet perhaps the most striking similarity between the two works is the religious imagery and the spirit of the Medieval morality play which permeates the novella. Chesterton stated that although Dickens saw a lot that was bad in Medievalism and was deeply aware of the flaws of his own age,[8] he rejected the idealised medievalism of Thomas Carlyle and John Ruskin, as he thought that they had antidemocratic political views based on feudalism.[9] However, despite these reservations, he fought for all that was good in the concepts of good and evil in Christianity through most of his works of literature and some of the religious imagery used in the *Comedy* also make their way into *Carol*.

Firstly, in *Inferno*, when people sin, they are punished 'by a process either resembling or contrasting with the sin itself.'[10] This process is known as a contrapasso and it wasn't invented by Dante, he took inspiration for it from various theological and literary sources, including the Medieval *Summa Theologica* by Thomas Aquinas. Surely then, there is no clearer contrapasso than Marley's cumbersome chain he carries around, whose heavy burden resembles the hoarding of material wealth and greed he embodied when alive.

Characters as the agents of change

Both stories need a character, who after their explorations, will move them towards their final redemptions and compel them to change. For Dante, it is his muse Beatrice, who symbolises divine love, and also illuminates the way for Dante to find the spiritual salvation he has been seeking. When Dante nears the top of the mountain, he sees Beatrice, who admonishes him and excoriates him. But she then calls his name, and as he has not heard it uttered on his long journey, he is moved to look into a stream where he sees his own reflection and feels ashamed. Scrooge's Beatrice is the less aesthetically pleasing Ghost of Christmas Yet to Come. Although he succeeds in illuminating the way for Scrooge, he doesn't do so through divine love, but instead he represents the mortal fear of death and his reaper-like qualities help refract Scrooge's lessons about empathy and generosity, which are essential if he wants to avoid this fate. This dark and faceless spectre points to a grave with his bony finger and Scrooge is forced to see his own name engraved there. In this moment, his self-realisation is as powerful as Dante's, it forces him to accept who he is and what he has done and most importantly, to repent of his sins in the good Christian way. Both Scrooge and Dante weep heartily for all of their sins and they are forgiven.

In style, *The Divine Comedy* presents a horrifically scathing examination of conscience, as does *A Christmas Carol*. Most pointedly perhaps, when the Ghost of Christmas Present pulls back his cloak to reveal the ragged forms of Ignorance and Want – a symbol for the innocent exploitation of children during the Industrial Revolution. This graphic description and caustic comment on mankind's neglect and oppression of society's poor, is a reminder that Scrooge needs to change his misanthropic behaviour and embrace more philanthropic ways. Neither Scrooge nor Dante are irrevocably damned. In *The Divine Comedy*, Dante faints and wakes up feeling a new level of peace and joy. Similarly, Scrooge awakes on Christmas morning, proclaiming that he is 'as light as a feather' and as 'merry as a school boy.'[11] Scrooge's journey ends there and he says he 'will honour Christmas in my heart, and try to keep it all the year.'[12] But for Dante, he has an entire canticle to come – where he will meet saints and God himself. Perhaps this can be explained by Dickens' more domestic views about Christianity, which differed somewhat from Dante's beliefs in the fuller mystical church.

Writers as social reformers

It is difficult to separate Dickens' political views from his spiritual ones, as he was such a prolific social critic and reformer. For him, the injustices of the day, such as child poverty and cruelty towards the poor, were not only unfair but they were also sinful. The messages from the Bible to 'love thy neighbour'[13] highlight his belief that our role as humans is to look after one another. Although Dante was a Catholic from the Middle Ages, he and Dickens have much more in common than first appears, with both authors delving into human nature and their struggles of good and evil in their work. They were also great believers in God, sin and redemption and were critics of the corruption in their societies. Although both texts track the spiritual journey of one flawed character, both stories encourage all of us to rise above selfishness, so we can lead a more Christian life and thereby attain personal salvation.[14]

Of course, Dickens liked to criticise organised religion in his works, and in later life, he temporarily turned towards Unitarianism, leading some to declare that he was not a true Christian. Yet in a letter to the Reverend D. Macrae, Dickens declared that 'all my strongest illustrations are derived from the New Testament; all my social abuses are shown as departures from its spirit.'[15] Indeed, there are Christian themes woven through many of his books, and although they are not overt theological texts, they have much in common with the Medieval morality plays, where the selfish protagonist Scrooge represents humanity as a whole and characters such as Fred and Tiny Tim are symbols of all that is good. For Dickens, 'good' represented simple kindness and love,[16] and actions spoke louder than words, so if Scrooge changes, humanity is sure to follow. His redemption didn't need to be drawn out and prolonged, the tripartite structure of past, present and future sufficed. On the other hand, Dante's ideas of redemption take much more time for the protagonist to go through, and it is only when he comprehends how the circles fit together that his soul is able to become aligned with God's love. Like Scrooge, he can go forth as a changed man from his moral experience, with an understanding of what it truly means to be a good Christian.

Summed up in six

- There is evidence to suggest that Dickens may have been influenced by Dante while he was writing *A Christmas Carol* in Italy.

- There are similarities between *The Divine Comedy* and *A Christmas Carol* in terms of the opening setting, tripartite structure and the characters of Virgil and Marley.

- Religious symbolism, such as the chain Marley carries being a contrapasso, cements the two texts together further.

- Both Scrooge and Dante have a character who compels them to change and moves them towards their final redemptions: In *Comedy* it is Beatrice and in *Carol* it is the Ghost of Christmas Yet to Come.

- Dante and Dickens are similar in that they both explore human nature and people's struggle with good and evil. They differ, however, in their view of the church, as Dante has a more mystical outlook of spirituality, whereas for Dickens it is the more practical message of kindness which is important.

- *A Christmas Carol* is most like a Medieval morality play as its protagonist Scrooge represents the greed of humanity, and if he changes, humanity are sure to follow.

Ideas for teaching

AO3: Split an A3 piece of paper into four and write a moral from the list below in the centre of each square. Around it, mind map any quotes or characters which link to that moral along with reasons why. Highlight the key words in the quote and annotate them, exploring connotations and linking to the author's intention in including that message. The morals are: 1) Money doesn't bring happiness 2) Give back to the community 3) It is never too late to change 4) Human connections are more important than physical wealth.

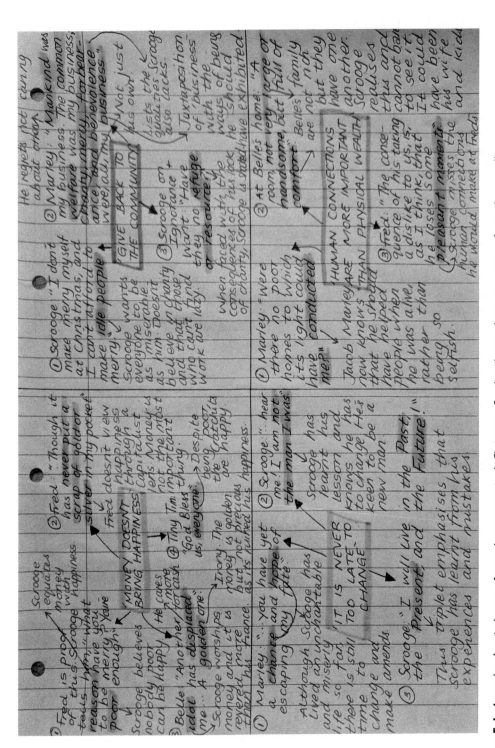

Figure 5.1 A student's mind map of moral messages in A Christmas Carol with matching quotations from the novella.

Notes

1 Charles Dickens, Gilbert Keith Chesterton, Bertram Waldrom, *A Christmas Carol: A facsimile of the original edition. With an introduction by G. K. Chesterton and a preface by B.W. Matz* (London: Cecil Palmer, 1922), 13.
2 Charles Dickens, *Pictures from Italy* (London: Penguin Classics, 1998).
3 Susan Jhirad, *Dickens' Inferno: The moral world of Charles Dickens* (South Carolina: Create Space, 2013).
4 Dante Alighieri, *The Divine Comedy*, Project Gutenberg, https://www.gutenberg.org/files/1001/1001-h/1001-h.htm#CantoI.
5 Charles Dickens, *A Christmas Carol* (London: Wordsworth Classics, 2018), 9.
6 Dante Alighieri *The Divine Comedy*.
7 Charles Dickens, *A Christmas Carol* (London: Wordsworth Classics, 2018), 25.
8 Charles Dickens, Gilbert Keith Chesterton, Bertram Waldrom, *A Christmas Caro* (London: Cecil Palmer, 1922).
9 George Landow, 'Dickens Satirizes the Mediæval Revival,' *Victorian Web*, January 8, 2021, http://www.victorianweb.org/authors/dickens/antimedieval1.html.
10 Mark Musa, *Commentary Notes in The Divine Comedy. Volume 1: Inferno* (London: Penguin, 1984), 37–38.
11 Charles Dickens, *A Christmas Carol* (London: Wordsworth Classics, 2018), 88.
12 Ibid., 93.
13 *The Holy Bible* (London: Oxford University Press, 1898), 31.
14 Stephen Bertman, 'Dante's Role in the Genesis of Dickens' A Christmas Carol,' *Dickens Quarterly* 24, no. 3 (September 2007): 167–175.
15 Charles Dickens, Kathleen Tillotson, Graham Storey, *The Pilgrim Edition of Letters of Charles Dickens Version 3* (Oxford: Clarendon Press, 1974), 29.
16 Susan Jhirad, 'Charles Dickens and the Notion of Evil,' *UU World*, March 8, 2021, https://www.uuworld.org/articles/charles-dickens-the-notion-evil.

References

Stephen Bertman, 'Dante's Role in the Genesis of Dickens A Christmas Carol,' *Dickens Quarterly* 24, no. 3 (September 2007): 167–175, 198.
Bible, *The Holy Bible* (London: Oxford University Press, 1898).
Charles Dickens, *Pictures From Italy* (London: Penguin Classics, 1998).
Charles Dickens, Gilbert Keith Chesterton, Bertram Waldrom, *A Christmas Carol: A facsimile of the original edition*. With an introduction by G. K. Chesterton and a preface by B.W. Matz (London: Cecil Palmer, 1922), 13.
Charles Dickens, Kathleen Tillotson, Graham Storey, *The Pilgrim Edition of Letters of Charles Dickens Version 3* (Oxford: Clarendon Press, 1974), 29.
Dante Alighieri, *The Divine Comedy*, Project Gutenberg, (January 12, 2022), https://www.gutenberg.org/files/1001/1001-h/1001-h.htm#CantoI
Susan Jhirad, 'Charles Dickens and the Notion of Evil,' *UU World*, (March 8, 2021), https://www.uuworld.org/articles/charles-dickens-the-notion-evil
Susan Jhirad, *Dickens' Inferno: The Moral World of Charles Dickens* (South Carolina: Create Space, 2013).
George Landow, 'Dickens Satirizes the Mediæval Revival,' *Victorian Web*, (January 8, 2021), http://www.victorianweb.org/authors/dickens/antimedieval1.html
Mark Musa, *Commentary Notes in The Divine Comedy. Volume 1: Inferno* (London: Penguin, 1984), 37–38.

6 Scrooge and the parallels between the Book of Job: Was Dickens influenced by biblical writings in his portrayal of Scrooge?

At the beginning of *A Christmas Carol*, it seems impossible that somebody as miserable and melancholic as Ebenezer Scrooge is capable of the monumental change in temperament which comes upon him by the end of the novella. Indeed, this radical transformation seems so incredible that it is unrealistic and leaves the more cynical reader unconvinced.[1] However, this would be doing the wider messages in Dickens' story a disservice, as it is a tale that we can all empathise with and recognise ourselves in, as it documents the self-development of Scrooge, demonstrating that no matter what our former transgressions, we are all able to alter the course of our fate.

Ultimately, *A Christmas Carol* is a monologist story, where Scrooge defines himself through his expositions of self – not just through his relationships with other characters. In fact, Frank Kermode[2] went even further than this and stated that many of Dickens' novels showcase aspects of metaphysical despair, as they reflect on the inner spiritual and transcendental aspects of human experience, highlighting an individual's movement towards self-actualisation. This is certainly true of Scrooge, who acts as a mirror the audience can hold up to reflect on their own behaviour and attitudes; it may help them to gain insight and reflect on their own spiritual journey. If we are to label Dickens as a metaphysical writer, then it is important that 'every central character must...be relatively innocent at the beginning: that is, he must be more innocent early in the story than he is later.'[3] This is exemplified clearly when the Ghost of Christmas Past, in his almost child-like form, returns Scrooge to his more innocent childhood self. As soon as Scrooge recognises his former home, the reader witnesses his whole demeanour soften: 'Your lip is trembling,'[4] the spirit tells him, as Scrooge is clearly overcome by the rush of memories which confront him as he looks upon his past.

DOI: 10.4324/9781003453468-7

Scrooge facing his past

In this expedition to the past, we witness a lonely boy – 'a solitary child, neglected by his friends'[5] who has been abandoned by his family and left to stay at school over Christmas. The effect on Scrooge is swift and palpable. Within minutes of witnessing his former life of loneliness and regret, he wishes to travel back in time and relive the moment where a boy came to his door the evening before, singing a Christmas carol, and confides to the benevolent spirit that he should have liked 'to have given him something.'[6] In a way, Scrooge mourns for his own innocence and laments that he no longer possesses it. The visits that follow in the rest of the novella can be seen as his quest for the rediscovery of his own innocence. In this way, the story of *A Christmas Carol* can be seen as cyclical in its nature, just like life; it is not a linear mechanical process, but is a process by which we leave innocence behind due to events and experiences in our lives and then return back to it after we realise that it offered a better existence or mode of being. This realisation is similar to the religious experience of grace, as it offers sinners salvation through divine favour, offering them the chance for regeneration and sanctification.

Religious and moral themes

Many critics have commented on Charles Dickens' fondness for 'religious and moral themes'[7] with Hanna stating 'one does not have to read very far in either the major or the minor works of Dickens to learn lessons contained in both the New and Old Testaments.'[8] Some of these comparisons are obvious, such as the similarities between the money grabbing Scrooge and Belshazzar, or the parallels between the three spirits and the Holy Trinity. However, one connection which is perhaps less well explored are the parallels between the character of Ebenezer Scrooge and the Old Testament's *Book of Job*. This comparison is less obvious, as Dickens was often more oblique and subtle than 'many of his drum-beating peers,'[9] but when examined, *A Christmas Carol*'s parable like qualities sharpen into focus.

Parallels with the Book of Job

The *Book of Job* tells the story of Job – a wealthy man living in a land called Uz with his large family and extensive flocks. Like Scrooge, he enjoys the privilege of money, but unlike Scrooge at the beginning of the novella, he is a 'blameless' and 'upright'[10] man who tries to live a good life and avoids doing evil. One day, Satan challenges God about Job's apparent goodness and claims that he will punish Job to test him and ascertain whether his goodness can withstand challenges, or whether it simply exists because God has been good to him. He claims that if faced with excessive challenges, Job will forsake and curse God. God agrees and over the day, Job is given four messages each telling him that his livestock, servants and children have been murdered or been killed in natural catastrophes. Job is devastated and he tears at his clothing and shaves his head in mourning, yet still he refuses to turn from God. Frustrated, Satan is given permission to test him again, this time by afflicting him with skin sores, yet still Job accepts the struggle and carries on – despite his wife encouraging him to give up and curse God's name.

These messages are like the four messengers that Scrooge meets: Marley, the Ghosts of Christmas Past, Present and Yet to Come. Each of them challenges Scrooge, and although the pain he goes through is not physical, the emotional turmoil is just as real. He is forced to relive his abandonment from his father and estrangement from his old friends and colleagues. He relives the bereavement of his sister Fan and also endures the metaphorical death of his engagement to Belle. Unlike Job, he keeps his emotions inside, choosing to bottle them up and close his vulnerabilities behind his hard oyster-like shell, which is why when he revisits his former experiences, he shows emotion so readily.

Another parallel between the two texts is the advice and wisdom that the protagonists receive from their three visitors. Three of Job's friends, Eliphaz, Bildad and Zophar, come to visit him and each of them shares their thoughts and theological insights on his predicament, just like the three spirits do for Scrooge. Their messages also have a striking similarity, with Job's first friend, Eliphaz, telling him that though he had always comforted other people, he never really understood their pain. This echoes the lack of empathy Scrooge felt for Belle's feelings when he refused to admit to her accusations of his more distanced attachment, as his affection for her had been replaced by 'another idol.'[11] Job's other friends, Bildad and Zophar agreed that Job must have committed evil to offend God's justice and argue that he should strive to exhibit more blameless behaviour. The Ghost of Christmas Present provides this insight for Scrooge as he is faced with the consequences of his poor treatment of his clerk Bob Cratchit, when he is transported to their home and witnesses their meagre Christmas dinner. However, the real evidence of Scrooge's evil is only revealed towards the end of this scene, when Scrooge begs the spirit to tell him whether 'Tiny Tim will live.'[12] For perhaps the first time, Scrooge realises the true ramifications of his miserly attitude is 'overcome with penitence and grief.'[13]

Job's last friend, Zophar, implies that whatever wrong Job has done probably deserves greater punishment than what he has received. His harsh message once again reflects the one delivered by Scrooge's last ghostly visitor, the death-like spectre of the Ghost of Christmas Yet to Come. This ghost delivers the shock and

Keith Hooper, *Charles Dickens: Faith, angels and the poor*, (Oxford: Lion Hudson, 2017), 42.

Keith Hooper, 'The Simple Faith of Charles Dickens,' *The Church Times*, (March 8, 2021), https://www.churchtimes.co.uk/articles/2017/22-december/features/features/the-simple-faith-of-charles-dickens

Frank Kermode, *Romantic Image* (New York: Random, 1964).

Janet Larson, *Dickens and the Broken Scripture*, (Athens: University of Georgia, 1986), 142.

Terry Thompson, 'The Writing on the Wall: Belshazzar in the fiction of Charles Dickens,' *Renascence*, 71, no. 3 (July 2019): 173–185. https://doi.org/10.5840/renascence201971312

7 Ebenezer misunderstood? How can philosophical approaches help us analyse Scrooge's character?

Studying the character of Scrooge through a philosophical and ethical lens can be a challenging undertaking, as his ideologies and motivations can seem complex and intangible from the often contradictory information we are given about his feelings in the novella. When discussing ethics, we are exploring the standards of what humans ought to do and the way they should behave; this is usually based on well-founded standards of right and wrong. These choices and un-written rules were something which fascinated Dickens, and in 1843, he planned to write a non-fiction pamphlet which would present the hellish conditions endured by child labourers in Britain to a Victorian audience. He hoped this would publicise the immoral way that children were being treated and galvanise the middle and upper classes into action to prevent it.

This pamphlet instead became *A Christmas Carol*, which Dickens believed would 'come down with twenty times the force—twenty thousand times the force—I could exert by following out my first idea.'[1] It is clear Dickens hoped the reader would embark on their own moral and ethical journey alongside Scrooge, perhaps realising the need to change and consider their own ethical choices. Without sometimes even realising it, they are witnessing a complex ethical wrangling in the actions of Scrooge. This idea led Plourde to describe the novella as a way to enable readers to practice different ethical positions,[2] but what ethical positions might help illuminate Scrooge's metamorphosis, and why might Dickens have considered them when presenting his reformation?

Ethics: A quest for the truth?

To begin, John Bowen has described *A Christmas Carol* as being about a quest for the truth and linked this to Dickens' view that making 'the truth' more widely

DOI: 10.4324/9781003453468-8

known could lead to change.[3] For example, by Dickens exposing how tough life was for the poor and destitute (particularly children), he could drive legislative reform. Yet truth is an abstract concept, as what one sees as the truth depends on key philosophical discussions of ethics and what moral standpoint a person ascribes to. This was a discussion which fascinated the Victorians, as the understanding of how we develop moral codes during a period defined by its rising capitalism and greed was an interesting one.

Ethicists do not decide what qualities and principles characterise a good or bad person; instead, they set out principles about how we as humans define what we consider the most moral action to take. Perhaps the most famous philosophical and ethical viewpoint, which in many ways has gone on to define the Victorian era, is Bentham and Mill's Utilitarianism.

Scrooge as a Utilitarian

Utilitarianism is based on the principle of choosing an action which will 'maximise the overall happiness or pleasure for all people'[4] as happiness is the fundamental value for any Utilitarian. This value is known as the 'Greatest Happiness Principle,' and each person's happiness counts as much as anyone else's; there is a gradation of right and wrong actions, but the best action, the one we should engage in, is the one which maximizes general utility. Essentially, the guiding principle for how Utilitarians ought to act and behave should promote the greatest good for the greatest number. When deciding which course of action to take, Mill recommends using a hedonistic calculus to explore a cost/benefit analysis. This includes determining the alternative courses of action available; what the consequences of each alternative may be; how happiness might be produced or destroyed with each alternative and what the net benefits will be, which will then help people choose the course of action with the most optimal benefits.[5] It is a practical moral code, where ethical considerations are measured thoroughly and weightily, in cold hard facts.

It is not difficult to see why critics might label Scrooge as a Utilitarian. He is cold and sceptical and his character is dominated by suspiciousness, which is clear when his nephew, Fred, speaks so passionately about Christmas and he responds, 'You are quite a powerful speaker, sir,'[6] as if he disbelieves his depth of feeling. This scepticism is reinforced when he refuses to believe in the supernatural 'fancy' of Marley's ghost, instead attempting to explain away the spectral vision as an undigested bit of beef. His bitter past experiences perhaps compel him to be naturally predisposed to be mistrustful of others and always to feel like he needs to expose a falsehood and defend himself against those who are more passionate, preferring to concern himself more with facts than feelings. Facts are incredibly important to Scrooge as they determine what can be trusted, and as Mill stated about moral choices, 'we know nothing, except the facts which present themselves to our senses,'[7] as they help us determine 'what is worthy and what is unworthy of belief.'[8]

As mentioned previously, we see Scrooge looking for scientific explanations for his experiences when visited by Marley's ghost, displaying a defensive attitude, almost in self-preservation of his practical approach. Marley asks him, 'Why do you doubt your senses?' and Scrooge replies 'because a little thing affects them. A slight disorder of the stomach makes them cheats.'[9] He suspects he is being tricked, as in the Utilitarian tradition, ghosts should not exist, therefore the phenomenon he is experiencing must be easily and rationally explainable.

Here perhaps, Dickens seeks to ridicule this wholly pragmatic approach as it is well documented that he had his doubts about Utilitarianism as a philosophical approach. He suggested that the over-dependence on fact resulted in a kind of disenchantment[10] and that fantasy ought to be protected and 'preserved in their simplicity, and purity, and innocent extravagance, as if they were actual fact.'[11] It is this rejection of fantasy and obsession with cold hard facts which possibly divides Scrooge from his fellow man, manifesting itself as a blockade between him and the rest of society. As Plourde explains:

> Utilitarianism fools him into believing that one person's role in the world can be isolated from others' while still contributing to some imaginary greater good. He sees himself as uninvolved with everyone else, viewing the world as a mass of data. And, because he cannot see himself as entangled with people around him, he lacks imaginative empathy.[12]

Yet later, Scrooge appears to be softening and empathises with the Cratchits, feeling 'an interest he had never felt before,'[13] he begins to see the family as more human – like himself and starts the process of knocking down the blockades he has built, opening himself up to more than just facts and beginning to allow feelings through too. Seeing Scrooge as a Utilitarian and recognising that Dickens wishes to use his behaviour as a vehicle through which to criticise Mill's approach, may help reduce our disbelief in his rapid transformation, as it demonstrates that even the most ardent follower of the 'Greatest Happiness Principle' can change.

Scrooge through a Kantian lens

However, reading Scrooge through a Utilitarian lens might not be the only philosophical approach that could illuminate Ebenezer's character. Indeed, evaluating Scrooge's character through a more Kantian perspective, with its insistence upon duty at the cost of emotion, may help us to understand Scrooge's coldness towards others. For followers of Kant, the fundamental value revolves around the free will of human beings and their inherent worth and dignity. His concept, the 'Categorical Imperative,' captures the idea that human beings are aware of a general principle of duty – a fundamental rule or precept of morality and what is right, which helps to govern what we choose to do in problematic situations. In Kant's view, when a person freely chooses to do the right thing simply because it is the right thing to do, their action adds value to the world. He stated, 'always treat people as ends in themselves, never merely as a means to one's own ends.'[14] This is commonly referred to as the ends principle and puts the onus for following the categorical imperative on humankind, and not on the divine intervention of a religious doctrine.

Kant is also famously negative about his views on human beings. He claims that human beings are universally and radically evil, which he defends, labelling it as a 'gentlemanly misanthropy,'[15] where people choose to do the right thing as it is the dutiful action to take, not necessarily because they want to. It is through this idea that we may think of Scrooge's reluctance to love his neighbour...he knows he should, as it is expected and seen as the correct thing to do. Yet Scrooge is what Israelsen terms a 'selfish misanthrope'[16] who does not care about the suffering of others, as long as his own life is going well. In order for him to actually change and tear himself out of this selfish existence, he would have to undergo a complete overhaul of his feelings and make an effort to be more benevolent and less selfish, by reflecting on the categorical imperative of how he ought to see his fellow humans.

Kant also claimed that knowledge is not always gained through experience but that it is a combination of a priori and a postiori factors. We learn some things through our experiences in life, but other knowledge is due to information which is pre-programmed into us, and this determines how we interpret moral dilemmas. Therefore, there is a transcendental form of knowledge, because of the way things are known to us through our own personal experiences. An example of this is seen in Tiny Tim, who remains pure and good and wholesome, even in the face of adverse circumstances such as his disability and poverty. Tim's situation highlights the selfishness of the rich capitalist Utilitarians such as Scrooge, who asks 'are there no workhouses?'[17] when confronted with the predicament of some of the poor and destitute. Yet despite this, Tim survives, as Scrooge sees that the right thing to do is change and pay his clerk more. His conception of goodness becomes more shaped by the Kantian a priori structures expected by society, rather than the pursuit of the 'Greatest Happiness Principle.'

Aristotle's virtue ethics

Despite *A Christmas Carol* being a morality tale in many respects, where Scrooge is warned through a direct divine intervention about his fate in the afterlife if he does not change his ways, it is also interesting to consider Aristotle's arguments about the development of character and virtue ethics. For Aristotle, people become virtuous over time, through the habituation of good actions and deeds, 'to sum it up in a single account: a state [of character] results from [the repetition of] similar activities.'[18] Essentially, once somebody has learnt to be good through their actions, their characters would not change rapidly or without some kind of dramatic change in lifestyle. Dougherty posits that 'in becoming virtuous, one learns to frame, perceive, understand, and experience the moral life in certain ways, that is, one learns to engage the world as the virtuous person does.'[19]

Aristotle claims that this kind of transformation can come about through the concept of practical wisdom, which is a more perceptive ability to see the full moral complexity of a situation and enables one to frame a situation, quickly comprehending the kind of moral action required. This practical wisdom can be gained only through experience, and it is easy to see how Scrooge's transformation from selfish miser to benevolent gentleman at the end of the novella could match Aristotle's ideas. Indeed, Scrooge experiences a dramatic change in lifestyle, when he receives visitations from the spirits and he develops his practical wisdom through the omniscient experiences he undergoes, where he is able to see the consequences of his actions and revise his own judgements by reflecting on his failures throughout his life. He can only truly achieve goodness and acquire virtuous traits with repeated experience, which is why one spirit is simply not enough and he needs to be confronted with several moral predicaments to begin the transformation.

However, we only witness Scrooge at the start of his journey, and his character change does seem dramatic and rapid. What we may not be taking into consideration, is the internal struggle which Scrooge may have been dealing with for many years. We see glimpses of this in his conversations with little Fan and Belle during his time with the Ghost of Christmas Past. Although we see little evidence that Scrooge possessed sympathetic character traits in this stave, we do see him begin to tend towards a willingness to change, particularly when discussing the generosity of his old boss Fezziwig, and he even tells the spirit, 'I should like to be able to say a word or two to my clerk just now.'[20] Seeing how the conduct of his former boss affected him and his old colleagues, Scrooge realises the potential he has to make Cratchit's life better.

What Scrooge also gains from his observation of others during the evening is an understanding of what Aristotle terms 'the universal'[21] – what makes the correct moral action right. To comprehend this, Scrooge needs to have an understanding of the world and the way morals function within it; due to the way he had shut himself away and isolated himself, he seemed removed from this understanding. By exposing him to the lives of others, the way Scrooge views the world is reframed and the way he interprets it subscribes to a new world view, due to his life changing experience. Thanks to the ghosts, Scrooge can see what so few of us are given the opportunity to witness: the real human cost of his own moral views. After repeated exposure to these consequences, he realises that his world view must change, but as the world he is now inhabiting seems to him to be an entirely new one, this doesn't seem so radical.

To conclude, as Dickens had such a strong social conscience, it is no surprise that his wrangling with morals and philosophy is evident in his characterisation of Scrooge in *A Christmas Carol*. In a letter to Wilkie Collins he wrote:

> Everything that happens [...] shows beyond mistake that you can't shut out the world; that you are in it, to be of it; that you get yourself into a false position the moment you try to sever yourself from it; that you must mingle with it, and make the best of it, and make the best of yourself into the bargain.[22]

Nowhere is this idea more apparent than in Scrooge's catharsis at the end of Stave Four and his reintegration back into the world he had shut out for so long in Stave Five. Dickens also strongly believed in the ethical potential of novels, using his works as a conduit to flood the Victorian public with the possibilities for social reforms. Therefore, analysing Scrooge's character through some philosophical frameworks of the time helps us to understand his behaviour, and apparent transformation.

Summed up in six

- Ethics explore the idea of what humans ought to do and the ways they ought to behave, based on well-founded standards of right and wrong. Plourde described the novella as a way to enable readers to practice different ethical positions while reading.

- Bowen has described *A Christmas Carol* as being about a quest for truth, and Dickens believed that by exposing the truth, he could drive legislative reform and change the lives of the poor and the destitute.

- Utilitarianism is based on the principle of choosing an action which will 'maximise the overall happiness or pleasure for all people.' It is not difficult to see why critics might label Scrooge as a Utilitarian. This includes determining the alternative courses of action available and what the consequences of each alternative may be; people then choose the course of action with the most optimal benefits. It is a practical moral code, where ethical considerations are measured thoroughly and weightily, in cold hard facts. This is similar to Scrooge as he is cold and sceptical, and his character is dominated by suspiciousness.

- Kantian ethics insists upon duty at the cost of emotion. Kant's fundamental value revolves around the free will of human beings and their inherent worth and dignity. In Kant's view, when a person freely chooses to do the right thing simply because it is the right thing to do, their action adds value to the world. Kant also claimed that knowledge is not always gained through experience but also information which is pre-programmed into us, and this determines how we interpret moral dilemmas. Scrooge's conception of goodness becomes more shaped by the behaviour expected by society, and he begins to change.

- Aristotle believed that people become virtuous over time, through actually doing good actions and deeds. Once somebody has learnt to be good through their actions, their characters would not change rapidly or without some kind of dramatic change in lifestyle. Scrooge experiences a dramatic change when he receives visitations from the spirits and develops practical wisdom through seeing the consequences of his actions. This makes him revise his own judgements and reflect on his own failures.

- Dickens believed in the ethical potential of novels, using his works as a conduit to flood the Victorian public with the possibilities for social reforms. Analysing Scrooge's character through philosophical frameworks helps us to make sense of his behaviour and apparent transformation.

Ideas for teaching

AO1 and AO2: Choose one of the ethical principles of Utilitarianism, Kant's teaching or Aristotle's virtue ethics and match it with some quotes from the novella. Analyse the quotes using a Hexagon analysis template (Webb, 2019), also considering context. What do each of these ethical codes teach us about Scrooge's character?

8 Authorial craft: Dickens the master of his craft: How does Dickens' style influence our understanding of the messages in *A Christmas Carol?*

There is little doubt that Charles Dickens was one of the most prolific writers of the Victorian era. With fifteen novels, five novellas, hundreds of short stories and many non-fiction articles to his name, his influence and legacy are far reaching. From his first novel, *The Pickwick Papers* in 1836, and even prior to this in his Boz days, Dickens was renowned for his humour and satire, which was used to glorious effect in his observations of society and its characters.

A picaresque novella?

While much of Dickens' fiction work can be categorised alongside the popular movement towards the realistic novel in the mid-1800s, there are also clear signs that he was influenced by the picaresque genre. According to the *Encyclopaedia Britannica*, the picaresque novel, was an early form of the serialised novel, which used a first-person narrative to tell the story of an often low-born rogue, as he drifts from adventure to adventure, imparting his wry observations.[1] The picaresque narrative often includes some satirical highlighting of the corruptions and hypocrisies in society, alongside richly descriptive depictions of those in humbler walks of life. Aside from the first-person narrative element (only *David Copperfield* and *Great Expectations* are written fully in first person – but few of the best-selling Victorian novels were[2]), it is clear to see the picaresque influence in Dickens' writing.

DOI: 10.4324/9781003453468-9

Perhaps some of this influence permeated from Dickens' admiration of Henry Fielding, who adopted many of the conventions of the picaresque in his novels – particularly in *The History of Tom Jones, a Foundling*. This admiration was no secret, with Dickens even naming his son Henry Fielding Dickens when he was born in 1849, as he was writing and serially publishing *David Copperfield*. What Fielding did so well was that he opened up the novel to make it more interesting and accessible. They became more egalitarian, as they were no longer solely about the lives of the upper classes, but instead often told the story of the ordinary man – just like Dickens does in *Oliver Twist* and many of his other stories.

Like Dickens, Fielding was also fiercely political; he started out by writing political pamphlets and became a magistrate, later co-founding London's first police force. He used his fiction to openly address political and social issues in a similar way to Dickens, who not only targeted at society's rich capitalists in *A Christmas Carol* but also took aim at the ideas of Thomas Malthus, particularly in his retort to the charity workers who visited his office for a contribution. When he inquires as to whether the prisons and workhouses are no longer open, he is told that many would rather die than go there. 'If they would rather die,' said Scrooge, 'they had better do it, and decrease the surplus population.'[3] The phrase 'surplus population' is a clear link to Dickens' philosophical agenda of criticising Malthas and his ideas of zero-growth.

The picaresque-style surveying of society's corruption is also clearly evident in *Carol* no more so than in the scene displaying the starving and neglected form of 'Ignorance' and 'Want,' who act as a physical reminder of man's avarice. This highlighting of the blight on society that the capitalistic system has imposed is reinforced in Stave 4, where the greedy businessmen discuss Scrooge's death and funeral as they 'hurried up and down, and chinked the money in their pockets… and trifled thoughtfully with their great gold seals.'[4] Here Dickens transports the reader to the very engine room of the financial system in England, where the greedy merchants seem un-affected by the Hungry Forties going on around them. Instead, they benefit from the laissez-faire system and flaunt their wealth through their accoutrements and corpulent bodies, 'a great fat man with a monstrous chin.'[5] A reader couldn't help but get caught up in Dickens' evident disgust for these characters and is swept along in this satirical journey.

Fairy tale influences

Yet as well as being influenced by the work of Fielding and other picaresque novels, Dickens was also enamoured with the fairy tale. He confessed to having a 'very great tenderness for fairy literature,'[6] and this is definitely evident in *A Christmas Carol*. In many of Dickens' books there is a 'hidden relatedness'[7] where seemingly unrelated elements of the plot come together towards the end, usually in a happy culmination to please the reader. This convention is not as evident in *A Christmas Carol*, but Dickens does use some of the favourite fairy-tale character tropes in the novella – particularly the 'fairy godmother,' 'the ill-treated child' and 'the good rich man.'

The 'fairy godmother' is played by either a man or a woman who helps the protagonist along on their journey of self-discovery. In *Carol* the ghosts could be seen to fulfil this function, however unlikely their physical descriptions may be. Yet, fairy godmothers have not always been described as the benevolent grey haired old ladies we associate with Disney-style fairy tales. Indeed, in the original Grimm version of *Cinderella*, her 'fairy godmothers' were the 'tame pigeons... turtledoves, and all birds beneath the sky'[8] who came to assist her. The Ghost of Christmas Present is described as having 'clear and kind' eyes,[9] while the Ghost of Christmas Past has a 'soft and gentle'[10] voice. Even the seemingly immoveable Grim-Reaper-like Ghost of Christmas Yet to Come displays a sliver of tenderness at the end of Stave 4, as he points towards Scrooge's grave and 'for the first time the hand appeared to shake.'[11] This preoccupation with developing 'the character and fortunes of their human protegees'[12] is a common trait in traditional fairy godmothers, and the ghosts certainly fulfil this role. In addition, at the end of the novella, Scrooge is the archetypal 'good rich man' whom Orwell describes as a 'superhumanly kind hearted old gentleman who "trots" to and fro, raising his employees' wages, patting children on the head, getting debtors out of jail, and, in general, acting the fairy godmother.'[13] Although fairy tales seem a little too simplistic to compare to the complex fiction Dickens wrote, the readers may have felt a similar kind of catharsis when reading the novella, as they felt at the end of a fairy tale, where they are able to watch good overcome evil and errant protagonists find their way.

The ghost story genre

A Christmas Carol also belongs to the ghost story genre. Although Dickens saw the ghost story genre as burdensome, with its formulaic conventions, it was also a prop that stirred his creativity.[14] Considering Christmas Eve was traditionally the time to tell ghost stories around the fire in the Victorian era,[15] it seems a work of PR genius to incorporate them into the story. Dickens used a lot of the conventions a reader would expect to see in his descriptions of the ghosts and their appearance in his chambers, from Scrooge's flickering candle as he walks upstairs – which no doubt cast a shadow, to the horror as the 'bell begin to swing,'[16] the arrival of Marley's ghost is shrouded in gothic tropes. This would have been exactly what the audience wanted to read. Although the Victorians were technologically advanced, they delighted in inventing different types of ghost stories and were fascinated by the supernatural. Ruth Robbins, Professor of English Literature at Leeds Metropolitan

University, believes this obsession largely came about due to the science. After all, the carbon monoxide gas lighting emitted could provoke hallucinations![17] It was certainly a genre that Dickens kept returning to, as writing a ghostly tale became almost an annual event for him after *Carol* was published.

What Dickens seemed to rely on most from the ghost story genre was the idea of 'false alarm,' what Tyler refers to as an imagined possibility of something horrific happening, which causes terror then later transmutes to joy once they are shown to be false. When Scrooge cries implores 'Good Spirit…assure me that I yet may change these shadows you have shown me, by an altered life!'[18] his imaginary fears are palpable, but they are short-lived. Only a few lines later he arrives back in his own bedroom, 'Yes! and the bedpost was his own. The bed was his own.'[19] The exclamation and repetition convey his relief and disbelief that it was not real and that in fact, he does have a chance to change. These largely fictitious threats bring a lightness to the story, which separates them from the more traditional ghost stories of the age, allowing Dickens to succeed in his aim of wanting to 'haunt its readers pleasantly.'[20]

Critics have also observed that Dickens' narrator in *Carol* is almost supernatural himself, with Maurice Blanchot calling him 'ghostly, phantom-like.'[21] This is especially evident when Dickens declares:

> The curtains of the bed were drawn aside; and Scrooge, starting up into a half-recumbent attitude, found himself face to face with the unearthly visitor who drew them: as close to it as I am now to you, and I am standing in the spirit at your elbow.[22]

Throughout, the narrator frequently draws attention to their own voice, so that the reader almost imagines him being in the room with them, part of the story but also detached – just like them. His descriptions transform ordinary streets and objects into the extraordinary, creating a dream-like quality over realistic events, what Johnson terms 'the waking dream.'[23] A simple door knocker metamorphoses into the face of Scrooge's dead business partner, the Ghost of Christmas Yet to Come is reshaped from a bed post; even Scrooge himself, who is definitely not prone to fancies, needs to repeatedly convince himself that what he is seeing is imaginary. It seems even some of the objects and rooms have apparitional qualities, with the 'gruff old bell'[24] and 'gloomy old rooms'[25] casting a supernatural shadow over the narrative.

Techniques

In terms of Dickens' writing style, *A Christmas Carol* highlights four main stylistic elements often employed by the writer, to great effect: lists and parataxis, prosopopoeia, paronomasia or puns, and delicious hyperbole. The listing description of Scrooge, 'A squeezing, wrenching, grasping, scraping, clutching, covetous, old sinner!'[26] implies that one verb is simply not enough to describe his abominable frugality. The description of the Ghost of Christmas Present's throne is almost delectable in its imagery, it is formed of:

> turkeys, geese, game, poultry, brawn, great joints of meat, sucking-pigs, long wreaths of sausages, mince-pies, plum-puddings, barrels of oysters, red-hotchestnuts, cherry-cheeke apples, juicy oranges, luscious pears, immense twelfth-cakes, and seething bowls of punch, that made the chamber dim with their delicious steam.[27]

Here, the list succeeds in demonstrating how overwhelmed Scrooge is by the sight in front of him, he is almost disorientated by 'the mass of auditory, visual, and olfactory impressions he receives.'[28] The list is so excessive, it borders on the surreal and absurd, implying a metaphoric meaning as it acts as a reminder of the abundance of food available to those who can afford it, while the poor starve on the streets.

The prosopopoeia, or personification, not only creates the dream-like, fairy tale quality discussed above, but it also suggests that the inanimate world is not separate from the world inhabited by humans. It exists alongside humans, watching over them, ready to serve them in some kind of way.[29] Some of the personification is almost bawdy and pantomime-esque: 'There were ruddy, brown-faced, broad-girthed Spanish Onions, winking from their shelves in wanton slyness at the girls as they went by, and glanc(ing) demurely at the hung-up mistletoe.'[30]

The hyperbolic descriptions are characterised by the superlative – whether imparting the positive or negative. Scrooge's characteristic miserliness is evidenced by Bob's solitary lump of coal in the fire and those who say 'Merry Christmas' are rather harshly told that they should be 'buried with a stake of holly through his heart.'[31] The descriptions from the grocers on Christmas morning are almost theatrical in their hyperbole, 'the raisins were so plentiful and rare, the almonds so extremely white, the sticks of cinnamon so long and straight.'[32] This scene of opulence almost seems to exemplify Christmas and all its excesses. But perhaps Dickens also wanted to make his reader laugh and lighten, the sometimes dark, atmosphere in *A Christmas Carol*, such as at the appearance of Marley's ghost, when Dickens uses a paronomasia for Scrooge's reaction, 'There's more of gravy than of grave about you, whatever you are!'[33]

Linguistics

The study of stylistics may also have something to offer when analysing Dickens' style. Lambert conducted a study where he evaluated his use of the suspended quotation – when a character's speech is interrupted by at least five words of narrator text. These interruptions, which he termed 'suprasegmentals'[34] could be intrusive, but they also represented a lifelike, more realistic dialogue which can often be challenging to capture in linear texts. However, they are also a 'handy place to put information, gestures and facial contortions'[35] in and these were often unflattering!

Two examples can be seen when Scrooge is conversing with his nephew, Fred, in Stave one: 'Scrooge having no better answer ready on the spur of the moment, said, "Bah!" again; and followed it up with "Humbug."' And: '"Because you fell in love!" growled Scrooge, as if that were the only one thing in the world more ridiculous than a merry Christmas. "Good afternoon!"'[36] Both of these examples demonstrate how Scrooge is painted as an aggressive and cantankerous old man, who possesses little warmth or sense of feeling. Surely Dickens aggressively depicts Scrooge in this unflattering way to persuade the audience to also feel coldly hostile towards him, so that we are even more relieved by his thawing later on? Yet the suspended quotation was a stylistic feature which was not as prevalent in Dickens' later works, perhaps when he began to do public readings in 1853, he was more able to connect with his audience without the need for the added suprasegmentals.[37]

Use of verbs

As has been stated, Dickens was very much a master of characterisation, and part of his process of individualising characters came from his use of particular verbs to report speech, which further projected their character traits and fleshed out their personalities. Culpeper posits that 'the way one speaks can trigger information about [...] personality. There is a strong relationship between certain voices and certain personality types.'[38] It is true that Dickens is known for his excessiveness when modelling his character's voices.[39] When comparing the speech verbs used by Scrooge in Stave one, such as 'growled' and 'demanded,'[40] which is later replaced by 'cried,' 'whispered' and 'chuckled,'[41] it serves to reinforce that he is a changed man, making it seem much more believable to the audience. When Marley first appears, Dickens repeats the dour and dull 'returned' and 'said'[42] repeatedly, to imply that Scrooge is seeking to remain rational and un-moved by the spectral vision. At the end of Stave 5, when Scrooge tricks his long-suffering clerk, Bob Cratchit, into believing he will fire him, the speech verb 'growled'[43] is again used by Dickens, perhaps to playfully poke fun at Scrooge, or make the audience complicit in the caricature of his earlier attitude.

Addressing the reader directly

It is this connection with the audience which sometimes makes *A Christmas Carol* seem like a performance, but in the preface, Dickens gets the opportunity to directly speak to the reader – it was an opportunity he always appeared to relish.[44]

According to the Oxford English Dictionary, the word 'preface' means beforehand, which explains why the preface in a novel is usually found before the start of the story. However, the definition then says that the preface often gives 'some explanation of its subject, purpose, and scope,'[45] which makes the preface profoundly important when analysing literature. In this sense, the preface becomes an event in itself and can not only offer an insight into the author's thoughts, ideologies and political sensibilities but can also mark the occasion that they are written for. The preface for *A Christmas Carol* reads:

> I have endeavoured in this Ghostly little book, to raise the Ghost of an Idea, which shall not put my readers out of humour with themselves, with each other, with the season, or with me. May it haunt their houses pleasantly, and no one wish to lay it. Their faithful Friend and Servant, C. D.'[46]

There is a warm tone here, where Dickens directly addresses the reader as a friend, breaking down the barriers between him and his audience, and expressing a desire to have them enjoy his story. Ortiz claims that the prefaces do more than this and that his prefaces correspond to different periods in his life and distinct personas he adopts, which can be categorised as: the Friend, the Truth-Teller, the Advocate, the Professional Writer and the Famous Author.[47] In *A Christmas Carol*, Dickens plays the part of the Friend, who emphasises how hard he has tried to please the reader in that verb 'endeavoured' and lists how much he wants them to enjoy it by imploring them not to get out of humour with 'themselves,' 'each other,' 'the season' or 'with me.' The oxymoron of 'haunt their houses pleasantly' reveals that although *Carol* is a ghost story, its true meaning is one of kindness and generosity in the festive season and the soft, fricative 'faithful friend' followed by the familiarity of just the initials at the end of it seek to open the reader's heart before Scrooge's tale has even begun.

Summed up in six

● *A Christmas Carol* has sometimes been labelled as a 'picaresque narrative' as they often included some satirical highlighting of the corruptions and hypocrisies in society, alongside richly descriptive depictions of those in humbler walks of life.

- There is also fairy tale like elements in the novella, such as favourite character tropes of the 'fairy godmother,' 'the ill-treated child' and 'the good rich man.' The 'fairy godmother' is played by either a man or a woman who help the protagonist along on their journey of self-discovery, just like the ghosts. At the end of the novella, Scrooge subscribes to the character trope of 'the good rich man.'

- Alongside this, Dickens used a lot of the conventions a reader would expect to see in a gothic ghost story, such as Scrooge's flickering candle as he walks upstairs, just before the arrival of Marley's ghost is shrouded in gothic tropes. This also includes the 'false alarm' where perceived terrors do not end up as a reality, and the dream-like sheen which shrouds over the plot of *Carol*. Even the narrator himself possesses a ghostly quality.

- In the novella, Dickens' style is characterised by the excessive use of parataxis, prosopopoeia, paronomasia and hyperbole. This creates rich descriptive imagery and a unique voice which lightens the mood in sometimes dark circumstances.

- Lambert (1981) evaluated Dickens' use of the suspended quotation and concluded that they represented a lifelike, more realistic dialogue which can often be challenging to capture in linear texts. He suggested that they are also a 'handy place to put information, gestures and facial contortions' in which were often unflattering and communicated the author's hostility towards some of his characters. The use of particular speech verbs also help build this picture.

- Dickens addresses the reader as a friend in his preface, which becomes an event in itself, as it offers an insight into the author's thoughts, ideologies and political sensibilities.

Ideas for teaching

AO2: Analyse the speech verbs and suspended quotations used by Dickens when Scrooge is speaking. What do they reveal about his character? Fred has sometimes been labelled as a foil for Scrooge, repeat the process for him. What do you discover?

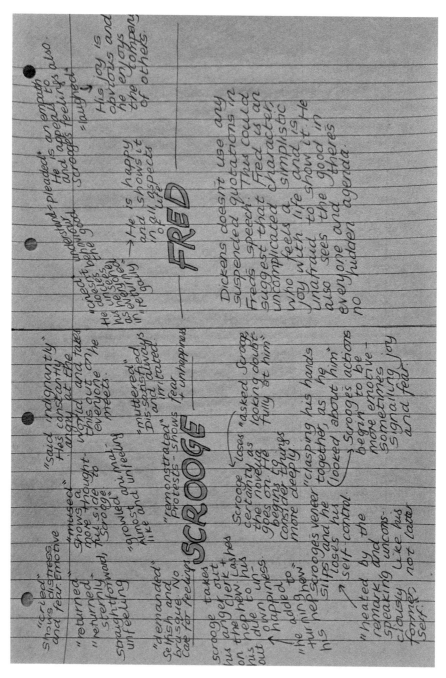

Figure 8.1 A student's analysis of speech verbs and suspended quotations of Fred and Scrooge.

AO3: What genre does *A Christmas Carol* belong to? Produce three paragraphs arguing your response with analysed and evaluated quotations which demonstrate that it conforms to the conventions of that drama. Consider why this matters and how it might influence Dickens' message.

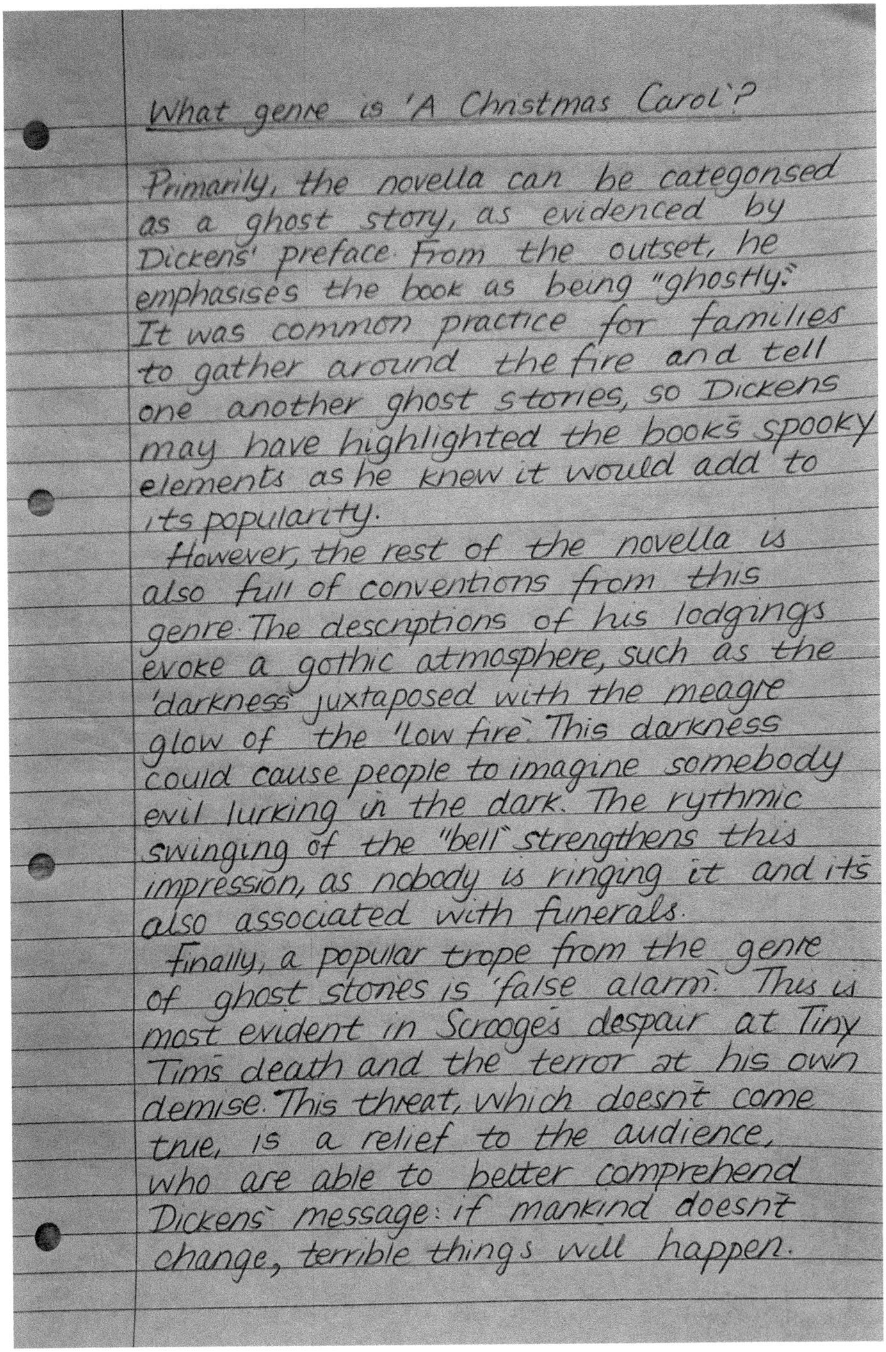

What genre is 'A Christmas Carol'?

Primarily, the novella can be categorised as a ghost story, as evidenced by Dickens' preface. From the outset, he emphasises the book as being "ghostly." It was common practice for families to gather around the fire and tell one another ghost stories, so Dickens may have highlighted the book's spooky elements as he knew it would add to its popularity.

However, the rest of the novella is also full of conventions from this genre. The descriptions of his lodgings evoke a gothic atmosphere, such as the 'darkness' juxtaposed with the meagre glow of the 'low fire'. This darkness could cause people to imagine somebody evil lurking in the dark. The rythmic swinging of the "bell" strengthens this impression, as nobody is ringing it and it's also associated with funerals.

Finally, a popular trope from the genre of ghost stories is 'false alarm'. This is most evident in Scrooge's despair at Tiny Tim's death and the terror at his own demise. This threat, which doesn't come true, is a relief to the audience, who are able to better comprehend Dickens' message: if mankind doesn't change, terrible things will happen.

Figure 8.2 A student's analytical response on the genre of *A Christmas Carol* and how this influences Dickens' message.

Notes

1 Picaresque Novel,' *Encyclopaedia Brittanica*, accessed March 30, 2021, https://www.britannica.com/art/picaresque-novel.

2 Philip V. Allingham, 'First-Person Narration in Best-Selling Victorian Novels, 1837-1861, by Year of Volume Publication,' *The Victorian Web*, April 22, 2021, https://victorianweb.org/authors/dickens/pva/pva91.html.

3 Charles Dickens, *A Christmas Carol* (London: Wordsworth Classics, 2018), 14.

4 Ibid., 74.

5 Ibid., 74.

6 Charles Dickens, 'Frauds on the Fairies,' *Household Words* 8, no. 184 (October 1853), 97.

7 S. Grob, 'Dickens and Some Motifs of the Fairy Tale,' *Texas Studies in Literature and Language*, 5, no. 4 (1964): 567–579.

8 Jacob Grimm, Wilhelm Grimm, 'Cinderella,' University of Pittsburgh, April 23, 2021, https://sites.pitt.edu/~dash/grimm021.html.

9 Charles Dickens, *A Christmas Carol*, 47.

10 Ibid., 30.

11 Ibid., 84.

12 Katherine Mary Briggs, *The Fairies in English Tradition and Literature* (Chicago: University of Chicago Press, 1967), 177.

13 George Orwell, 'Charles Dickens,' In *A Collection of Essays* (New York: Mariner Books, 1954), 5.

14 Daniel Tyler (Ed.), *Dickens's Style* (Cambridge: Cambridge University Press, 2013).

15 Kira Cochrane, 'Ghost Stories: Why the Victorians were so spookily good at them,' *The Guardian*, 23 December, 2013, https://www.theguardian.com/books/2013/dec/23/ghost-stories-victorians-spookily-good.

16 Charles Dickens, *A Christmas Carol*, 18.

17 Ruth Robbins, 'Victorian Ghost Stories,' YouTube, April 23, 2021, https://www.youtube.com/watch?v=Bg94bRJLLj4&t=174s.

18 Charles Dickens, *A Christmas Carol*, 85.

19 Ibid., 87.

20 Ibid., 5.

21 Maurice Blanchot, 'L'Absence de livre', In Harold Bloom, Paul de Man, Jacques Derrida, Geoffrey Hartman, J. Hillis Miller, *Living On: Border lines* (New York: Deconstruction and Criticism, 1979): 88.

22 Charles Dickens, *A Christmas Carol*, 29.

23 Edward Dudley Hume Johnson, *Charles Dickens: An introduction to his novels* (New York: Random House, 969), 133.

24 Charles Dickens, *A Christmas Carol*, 16.

25 Ibid., 17.

26 Ibid., 8.

27 Ibid., 46–47.

28 Monika Fludernik, 'Descriptive Lists and List Descriptions,' *Style* 50, no. 30 (January 2016), 314.

29 J. Hillis Miller, 'The Genres of A Christmas Carol,' *Dickensian* 89, no. 431 (December 1993): 193–206.

30 Charles Dickens, *A Christmas Carol*, 50.

31 Ibid., 10.

32 Ibid., 50.

33 Ibid., 20.

34 Mark Lambert, *Dickens and the Suspended Quotation* (New Haven, CT and London: Yale.

35 Ibid.

36 Charles Dickens, *A Christmas Carol*, 11.

37 Michaela Mahlberg, Catherine Smith, 'Dickens, the Suspended Quotation and the Corpus,' *Language and Literature* 21, no. 1 (February 2012): 51–65.

38 Jonathan Culpeper, *Language and Characterisation: People in plays and other texts* (Harlow: Pearson Education, 2001), 215.

39 Pablo Ruano San Segundo, 'A Corpus-stylistic Approach to Dickens' Use of Speech Verbs: Beyond mere reporting,' *Language and Literature* 25, no. 2 (May 2016): 113–129.

40 Charles Dickens, *A Christmas Carol*, 11.

41 Ibid., 92.

42 Ibid., 21.

43 Ibid., 92.

44 Mario Ortiz-Robles, 'Dickens Performs Dickens,' *ELH* 78, no. 2 (August 201): 457–478.

45 Maurice Waite, Sara Hawker (Eds.), *Oxford Paperback Dictionary and Thesaurus* (Oxford: Oxford University Press, 2009), 718.

46 Charles Dickens, *A Christmas Carol*, 4.

47 Mario Ortiz-Robles, 'Dickens Performs Dickens': 457–478.

References

Philip V. Allingham, 'First-Person Narration in Best-Selling Victorian Novels, 1837–1861, by Year of Volume Publication,' *The Victorian Web*, (April 22, 2021), https://victorian web.org/authors/dickens/pva/pva91.html

M Blanchot, 'L'Absence de livre', In Harold Bloom, Paul de Man, Jacques Derrida, Geoffrey Hartman, J. Hillis Miller, *Living On: Border Lines* (New York: Deconstruction and Criticism, 1979).

Katherine Mary Briggs, *The Fairies in English Tradition and Literature* (Chicago: University of Chicago Press, 1967).

Kira Cochrane, 'Ghost Stories: Why the Victorians were so spookily good at them,' *The Guardian*, (23 December, 2013), https://www.theguardian.com/books/2013/dec/23/ghost-stories-victorians-spookily-good

Jonathan Culpeper, *Language and Characterisation: People in Plays And Other Texts* (Harlow: Pearson Education, 2001).

Charles Dickens, 'Frauds on the Fairies,' *Household Words* 8, no. 184 (October 1853): 97–100.

Charles Dickens, *A Christmas Carol* (London: Wordsworth Classics, 2018).

Monika Fludernik, 'Descriptive Lists and List Descriptions,' *Style* 50, no. 30 (January 2016): 309–326. DOI:10.1353/sty.2016.0011

Jacob Grimm, Wilhelm Grimm, 'Cinderella,' University of Pittsburgh, (April 23, 2021), https://sites.pitt.edu/~dash/grimm021.html

Edward Dudley Hume Johnson, *Charles Dickens: An Introduction To His Novels* (New York: Random House, 969).

Mark Lambert, *Dickens and the Suspended Quotation* (New Haven, CT: Yale University Press, 1981).

Michaela Mahlberg, Catherine Smith, 'Dickens, the Suspended Quotation and the Corpus,' *Language and Literature* 21, no.1 (February 2012): 51–65. https://doi.org/10.1177/09639 470114320

wider families, they become 'a kind of shining language'[5] for others to learn from and emulate. With this portrayal Dickens became 'our great national celebrant of hearth, home and family love,'[6] a status which was only briefly rocked by the Ellen Ternan affair, but regardless, has persisted even today.

The haven of the home

In addition to the importance of family, the Cratchit family also represent the importance of a home base as a site of value in Victorian society. Scrooge is a bystander to the happy homes he inspects – an outsider who sees the warm hearths and cosy spaces with a sense of longing, buried so deep that he probably doesn't recognise it himself. The text describes the inside of some of the homes Scrooge and the Spirit see, as they went along the streets:

> The brightness of the roaring fires in kitchens, parlours, and all sorts of rooms, was wonderful. Here, the flickering of the blaze showed preparations for a cosy dinner, with hot plates baking through and through before the fire, and deep red curtains, ready to be drawn to shut out cold and darkness.[7]

There is sense of desire for this world that Scrooge is shut out from as it depicts a world in which readers may wish to see themselves, as part of a happy family in the safe haven of their home.[8] It is often supposed that the Cratchit's home is based on one of Dickens' childhood abodes, 16 Bayham Street in Camden.[9] His father,

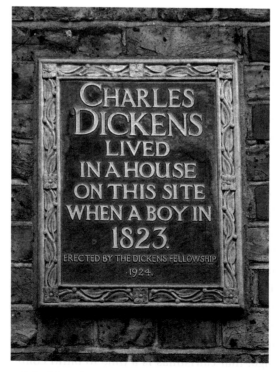

Figure 9.1 An image of the blue plaque in Bayham Street in Camden.

John Dickens, who was a naval clerk, was recalled to London from Portsmouth in 1822 and Charles joined them after his schooling at Chatham. The house was demolished in 1910 but a house a few doors down, which is still standing, now holds a blue plaque commemorating its famous resident.

Figure 9.2 An image of 16 Bayham Street in Camden, before it was demolished.

The house was a simple terraced, four-room dwelling, which would have been typical for a hardworking lower-class family like the Cratchits. It would not have been luxurious but unlike many of the very poorest in society, they at least had shelter and possessions, however meagre they may have been. Today, Camden is in the top twenty-five richest boroughs in the UK[10] and is an incredibly desirable place to live, but it bears little resemblance to the Camden of Dickens' youth. Camden Town only really started to develop at the end of the 1700s and it wasn't until the early 1820s that it really expanded.[11] So, when Dickens was writing *Carol* in the 1840s, it would have been on its way to becoming the vibrant borough it is now, as part of the general urbanisation of Britain which was going on as part of the Industrial Revolution.[12]

Yet it is unlikely that Dickens would have held the happy nostalgic memories of Bayham Street that the idea of him basing the Cratchit's home on it may suggest. Quite the opposite. Dickens' unhappy childhood has been well documented by biographers, including his father's arrest for being in debt and Dickens' subsequent time working in the blacking factory to support the family. Some critics have claimed that this period in Dickens' life was so unhappy that 'it left a wound in him that never healed.'[13] His relationship with his mother also became strained, as it is claimed that even after his father was released from prison, she wanted to keep him at the blacking factory.[14] This suggestion seems to correspond with the dates of Dickens working at the factory, as he remained there for almost a year after his father's release.[15]

The ideal family

Perhaps, instead of his own experiences, the Cratchit family and their togetherness was modelled on the ideal of the family as a stable unit, which was so well modelled by Queen Victoria. Victoria and Albert appeared to be exemplars of traditional family values; like the Cratchits, they had a large family and Victoria acted as a strong matriarch, just like Mrs Cratchit. Victoria had to be resilient and tenacious – after all, she inherited the throne at only eighteen and ruled for many years during a time of intense industrial, cultural, political, scientific and military change.[16] We see Mrs Cratchit as a tough and protective character, who may reflect the shift in some gender concepts of femininity in the Victorian ideal, as she 'challenges the domestic creed.'[17] While Mrs Cratchit clearly maintains the domestic role of caring for her family, she also fiercely defends the family – particularly when Bob proposes a toast to Scrooge, as the 'founder of the feast.' Mrs Cratchit vehemently responds, 'The Founder of the Feast indeed!...I wish I had him here. I'd give him a piece of my mind to feast upon, and I hope he'd have a good appetite for it.'[18] When Bob remonstrates with her, she does not become cowed, replying: 'It should be Christmas Day, I am sure,' said she, 'on which one drinks the health of such an odious, stingy, hard, unfeeling man as Mr. Scrooge.'[19]

Paul Davis has called the women in *A Christmas Carol* 'absent or inconsequential figures,'[20] but Mrs Cratchit leaps out of the novella with a mind and a voice of her own and is a strong and supportive partner to Bob, who appears to be more sensitive. This is evident towards the end of the novella when it appears that Tiny Tim has died. She tries to protect Bob and tells Peter, 'I wouldn't show weak eyes to your father when he comes home, for the world' and makes sure to answer in 'a steady, cheerful voice, that only faltered once.'[21] Yet Mrs Cratchit's portrayal may connect to other depictions of women who are 'defined by their anger and resentment'[22] such as Edith Dombey and Susan Nipper in *Dombey and Son*.[23] For Scrooge, witnessing this united family – who Dickens clearly pits against greed and capitalism – must have really emphasised how truly alone in the world he is. Surely, it was one of the driving factors in his transformation.

We certainly know that part of Scrooge's transformation at the end of the novella involves him becoming an extended member of two families: his nephew Fred's and the Cratchits, where we are told that 'to Tiny Tim, who did not die, he was a second father.'[24] We know that Dickens' relationship with his own father was challenging and this may have manifested in his portrayal of fathers in some of his books, as some of the most likeable father figures are non-biological,[25] such as Joe Gargery in *Great Expectations* and Mr Brownlow in *Oliver Twist*.

Yet, Bob's characterisation as a sensitive man who is at the heart of the domestic sphere of the family, may not have been as unusual as it seems in the Victorian era. Far from the shadowy figure, who was responsible for disciplining, that some may presume, the 19th century father may have seen family time as sacred, with John Tosh even suggesting that 'the domestic sphere ...[was considered] integral to masculinity.'[26] Therefore, Bob's unique mix of provider for the family and sensitive soul at the hearth paints him as an idealised father figure, a foil to the cold and distant Scrooge.

A focus on Bob

However, Bob Cratchit has not always been seen as such a key character in *A Christmas Carol*, and in John Leech's original illustrations which accompanied the novella, he appeared only at the end of the story, as Scrooge discussed his salary with him 'over a Christmas bowl of smoking bishop.'[27]

Figure 9.3 The Christmas Bowl.
https://victorianweb.org/art/illustration/carol/8.html

Fred Barnard's later illustrations seem to expand on Bob's character more, as he is pictured carrying Tiny Tim home from church on his shoulder, the very picture of a kind and loving father, who is completely juxtaposed against the money obsessed Scrooge with his lack of family or friends. Both David Parker[28] and Paul Davis[29] have suggested that the Cratchits are a 19th century depiction of the Holy family, and the absence of the rest of the family in this picture, including Mrs Cratchit, certainly encourage the viewer to focus on the father-son relationship.

Figure 9.4 Bob and Tiny Tim.
https://victorianweb.org/art/illustration/barnard/xmas/1g.html

In Abbey's later illustrations for the American Household Edition in 1876, Bob is presented as more playful, as he is depicted as 'going down a slide on Cornhill, at the end of a lane of boys, twenty times, in honour of its being Christmas Eve.'[30] We see Scrooge repeatedly refuse to engage with society in the novella, and this illustration demonstrates how Bob is so much more at ease with London society, in comparison to his boss' alienation.

Figure 9.5 Bob going down a slide.
Scanned image and text by Philip V. Allingham located at https://victorianweb.org/art/illustration/abbey/3.html.

Attitudes to fertility and the Cratchits

As well as providing rich material when analysing character and examining the juxtapositions between the Cratchits and Scrooge, the family can also be an interesting insight into attitudes to fertility in the 19th century. Dickens often depicted large families in an admiring way; he had eight siblings himself and his wife Catherine had nine. Together they had ten children, not including two miscarriages. Large families like this were not uncommon, in fact, the average married woman gave birth to eight children.[31] Academics have argued that Dickens portrayals of big families as a positive force was not simply because they generate good feelings in the audience, but that they also 'serve as a refutation of the Malthusian and Utilitarian doctrines that he despised, especially as these pertained to the lower classes.'[32]

The multiplying poor, who so terrified Malthus and inspired the Poor Law of 1843, were often presented as a burden on society. Knowledge of birth control was uncertain, and Dickens inverts this prejudice by showing the warmth, generosity and affection large families seem to have for one another. *A Christmas Carol* is ripe with idealised images of the doting mother surrounded by her children, such as Scrooge's ex-fiancé Belle and Mrs Cratchit, who are both encircled by their children. It is clear that Dickens sees the real wealth as lying-in large families, and not in simply reproducing money like Scrooge. Families represent an investment in the future – even the miner, who the Ghost of Christmas Present takes Scrooge to visit, is surrounded by his family. Despite the crude hut of mud and stone they reside in, they find warmth and comfort in the presence of one another:

> Passing through the wall of mud and stone, they found a cheerful company assembled round a glowing fire. An old, old man and woman, with their children and their children's children, and another generation beyond that, all decked out gaily in their holiday attire. The old man, in a voice that seldom rose above the howling of the wind upon the barren waste, was singing them a Christmas song – it had been a very old song when he was a boy – and from time to time they all joined in the chorus.[33]

For large families however, the hungry 1840s were a challenging time. The Poor Law Amendment Act of 1834 sought to eliminate the need for public face-to-face parish pay-table forms of charity, as many reformers objected to how unreliable people's stories could be when they were in need of help. Essentially, many of those seeking help were seen as dishonest and undeserving,[34] and instead of responsibility for the poor being a public obligation, it instead shifted to volunteerism and charities.[35] *A Christmas Carol* clearly denounces these principles as inhumane and draconian, and it would have been families like the Cratchits, who were working hard and struggling to make ends meet, who Malthus so objected to. But Dickens instead flips the narrative, and by providing 'passionate portrayals of the misery of the poor and the presumption and posturing of the rich,'[36] it is the Cratchit family we accept into our hearts and the greedy businessmen like Scrooge that we reject.

Tiny Tim and the plight of children

Despite the enduring power of both Bob and Mrs Cratchit, perhaps the most loved of all the characters in *A Christmas Carol* is the gentle Tiny Tim, whose pure spirit and helpless innocence has captured the imaginations of readers for over 150 years. Dickens himself admitted that he 'wept and laughed, and wept again, and excited himself in a most extraordinary manner' when writing about Tim.[37] Holmes comments that Dickens text here also 'reminds us how often we get to engage in serial weeping about disability through the particular catalyst of crippled children,'[38] and it is a particular brand of pathos which Dickens definitely uses to manipulate the reader. The descriptions of Tim, his good as gold behaviour in church, and active little crutch tapping upon the floorboards as he eagerly joins his family around the table, all paint a picture of 'ennobling sympathy'[39] where we begin to feel an emotional attachment to Tim. This image of the 'afflicted child'[40] was seen by society to be a worthy disabled person, as their 'economic resilience was the product of corruption and whose bodily condition did not signify complete and utter incapacity.'[41] He was designed by Dickens to make us feel pity, so we would open our hearts to innocent children and harden them against the harsh rhetoric of people like Malthus and Scrooge.

At the time of publication, society was becoming more attuned to the suffering of innocent children. Great Ormond Street hospital was founded only a few years after the publication of *A Christmas Carol*, and the novel itself started out as an idea for a political pamphlet titled 'An Appeal to the People of England, on Behalf of the Poor Man's Child,' which Dickens was moved to write after reading the 1843 parliamentary report on Britain's child labourers and visiting his sister Fanny in Manchester, where he witnessed families starving on the streets. He found the breadth of poverty in post-Industrial Revolution Manchester horrifying, and he wanted to write something which would strike 'a sledgehammer blow' on behalf of poor children and have 'twenty thousand times the force' of a government pamphlet.[42] What better way to do this than creating the character of Tiny Tim, who even manages to melt the frosty heart of Ebenezer Scrooge?

But what could possibly have caused Tim's condition? Modern day doctors have analysed the evidence presented by Dickens, and their knowledge of the condition of living for the poor in London, and have suggested he is most likely to have suffered from a combination of tuberculosis (TB) and rickets.[43] The novella tells us, 'Alas for Tiny Tim, he bore a little crutch, and had his limbs supported by an iron frame!'[44] We are later told, as Bob sits by the fire with his son after Christmas dinner, that he held his 'withered little hand in his, as if he loved the child, and wished to keep him by his side, and dreaded that he might be taken from him.'[45]

It is clear that whatever condition Tim had, it was something which could be reversed with the proper treatment and a healthier lifestyle, including fresh air outside of London's smoggy streets and a decent diet. TB was a common disease, which affected around 50% of the population in the 1840s, and around 1% of the population died of TB every year.[46] This huge spread of rickets and TB came after the re-building after the Great Fire of London started and the population started to expand. This was followed by the Industrial Revolution, which was fuelled by coal and helped develop the railroads and steamships. The skies were blackened with soot, which absorbed UV-A and UV-B rays, as well as having a high sulphur dioxide content, which further absorbed UV-B rays. This then prevented the synthesis of vitamin D, which is one of the causes of rickets. The diet of working-class people in London was also low in protein and fat and mostly consisted of starch and carbohydrates, along with a limited intake of vitamin D–containing foods. This poor diet, when coupled with a lack of sunshine, made rickets a very common condition.

Perhaps when Scrooge became a father figure for Tiny Tim, he was able to pay Bob more money, who could provide him with a better diet. Perhaps he took him on trips to the countryside or paid for him to go to a seaside-based convalescence home. It is also possible that he paid for him to be administered cod liver oil, as Dickens wrote about observing children being dosed with it to treat rickets in his journal, *All the Year Round*.[47] Whatever condition Dickens imagined for Tim, it definitely highlighted the plight of children in the eyes of the public, as in 1843, the 'Tiny Tim Guild' charitable trust was formed to attempt to relieve the plight of 'crippled children' in England.[48]

However, to just paint Tiny Tim as a figure to be pitied by the public is to do a disservice to his character. If Dickens' portrayal of Tim is to be analysed through a Bordieuan Capital lens,[49] then his social capital is high, despite his low economic poverty: he has the love of his family and his church and depends on them to secure his movement through life, as he rides on his father's shoulders. When we compare this to the high economic capital and low social capital of Scrooge, it is clear that Tiny Tim possesses a different kind of value to Scrooge, he is 'as good as gold … and better.'[50] Bob was certainly correct in his assertion that 'I am sure we shall none of us forget poor Tiny Tim – shall we?'[51] Both Tiny Tim and the Cratchit family have become iconic symbols of a happier, more nostalgic view of family, which has influenced popular culture for over a century and will continue to do so.

Summed up in six

- The Cratchit family is one of the most repeated motifs in Christmas narratives, as it paints families as 'uncomplicated warm entities,' which creates a nostalgia feeling in readers.

- The home base as a site of value in Victorian society. Scrooge is an outsider in the happy homes he inspects, and the warm hearths and caring environments just emphasise how cold and alone he is.

- The Cratchit's home may have been based on one of Dickens' childhood homes, 16 Bayham Street in Camden. However, the Cratchit family juxtapose Dickens' own unhappy childhood, where his father was imprisoned for debt and Dickens was forced to work in the blacking factory.

- Mrs Cratchit is a strong and fierce character who fulfils her traditional Victorian role of providing for her family but also defends her family against Mr Scrooge and supports Bob when he is suffering after the death of Tiny Tim.

- Bob is depicted to be more sensitive, which may have been more common for a father in the Victorian era than people suppose. His portrayal has changed throughout the ages, and the illustrations which accompany the various versions of A Christmas Carol reflect this.

- Tiny Tim may have suffered from TB and rickets, and Scrooge's money and care could have been instrumental in his recovery. His character is one of the most enduring in the text and his inherent goodness has inspired many to be more charitable.

Ideas for teaching

AO1: Explore how Bob Cratchit's depiction has developed using the illustrations and evidence from the text.

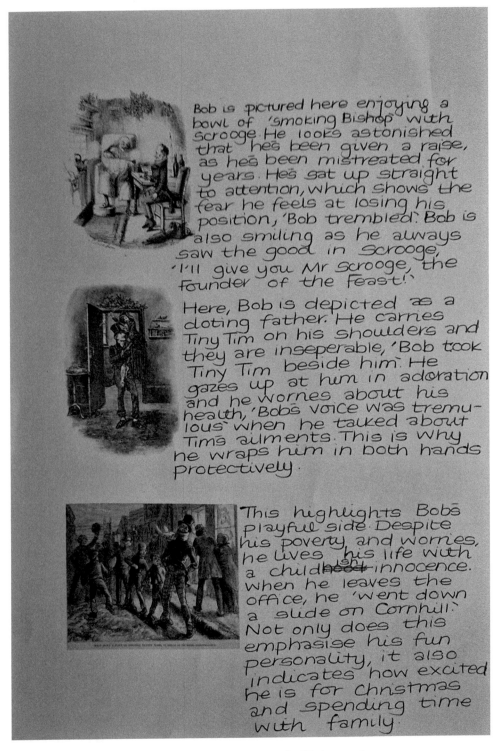

Bob is pictured here enjoying a bowl of 'smoking Bishop' with Scrooge. He looks astonished that he's been given a raise, as he's been mistreated for years. He's sat up straight to attention, which shows the fear he feels at losing his position, 'Bob trembled'. Bob is also smiling as he always saw the good in Scrooge, 'I'll give you Mr Scrooge, the founder of the Feast!'

Here, Bob is depicted as a doting father. He carries Tiny Tim on his shoulders and they are inseperable, 'Bob took Tiny Tim beside him'. He gazes up at him in adoration and he worries about his health, 'Bob's voice was tremulous' when he talked about Tim's ailments. This is why he wraps him in both hands protectively.

This highlights Bob's playful side. Despite his poverty and worries, he lives his life with a childish innocence. When he leaves the office, he 'went down a slide on Cornhill'. Not only does this emphasise his fun personality, it also indicates how excited he is for Christmas and spending time with family.

Figure 9.6 Student's deconstruction of the portrayal of Bob using images.

AO2: List four qualities of Mrs Cratchit and match them up with quotes from the text. Annotate the quotes, zooming in and completing single word/phrase analysis, exploring layers of meaning.

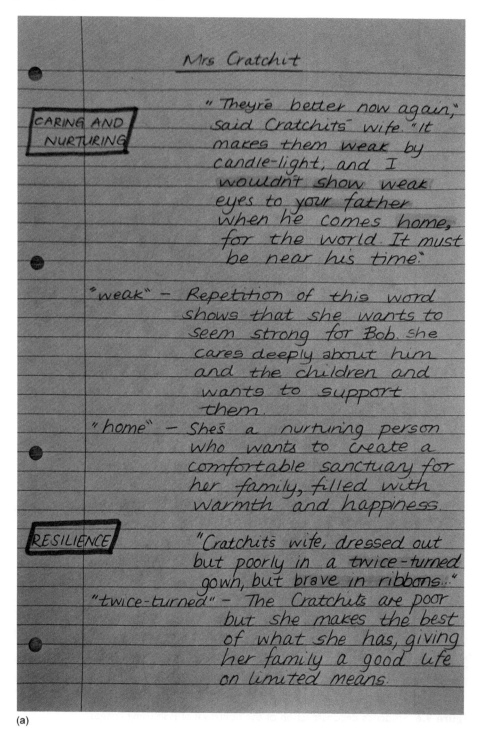

(a)

Figure 9.7 (a, b, c) Student's quote analysis of Mrs Cratchit. (Continued)

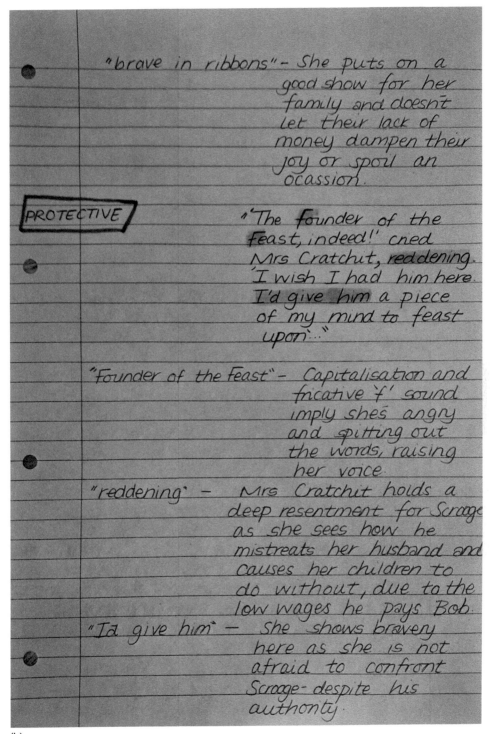

"brave in ribbons" - She puts on a good show for her family and doesn't let their lack of money dampen their joy or spoil an ocassion.

PROTECTIVE

"'The founder of the Feast, indeed!' cried Mrs Cratchit, reddening. 'I wish I had him here. I'd give him a piece of my mind to feast upon...'"

"Founder of the Feast" - Capitalisation and fricative 'f' sound imply she's angry and spitting out the words, raising her voice.

"reddening" - Mrs Cratchit holds a deep resentment for Scrooge as she sees how he mistreats her husband and causes her children to do without, due to the low wages he pays Bob.

"I'd give him" - She shows bravery here as she is not afraid to confront Scrooge - despite his authority.

(b)

(Continued)

Figure 9.7 (Continued) (a, b, c) Student's quote analysis of Mrs Cratchit.

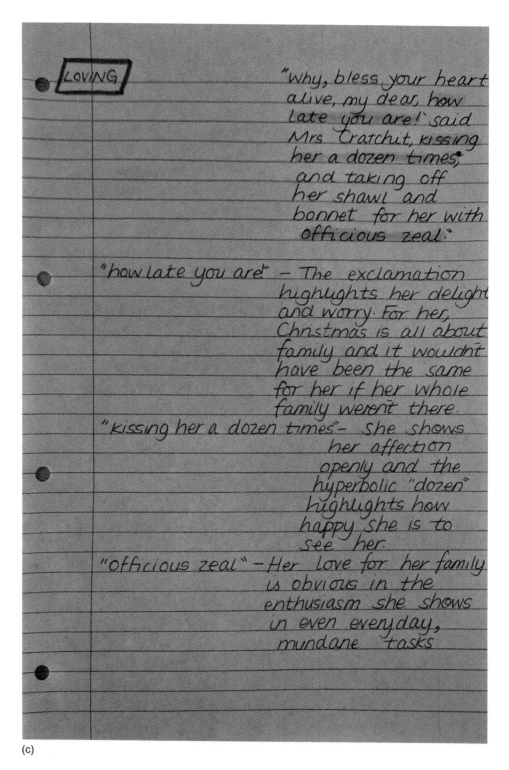

LOVING

"Why, bless your heart alive, my dear, how late you are!' said Mrs Cratchit, kissing her a dozen times; and taking off her shawl and bonnet for her with officious zeal."

"how late you are" – The exclamation highlights her delight and worry. For her, Christmas is all about family and it wouldn't have been the same for her if her whole family weren't there.

"kissing her a dozen times" – She shows her affection openly and the hyperbolic "dozen" highlights how happy she is to see her.

"officious zeal" – Her love for her family is obvious in the enthusiasm she shows in even everyday, mundane tasks.

(c)

Figure 9.7 (Continued) (a, b, c) Student's quote analysis of Mrs Cratchit.

AO3: Can you situate the Cratchit family within beliefs about the poor in the Victorian era, particularly when considering Thomas Malthus' comments about the poor having excessive amounts of children? How did Dickens' depiction of them seek to refute this?

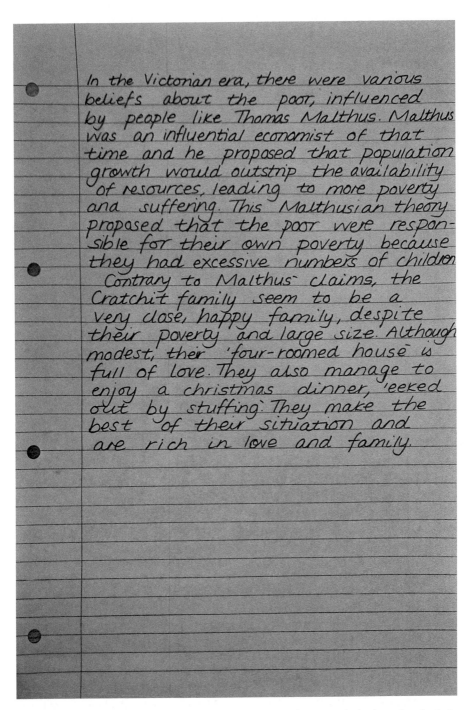

In the Victorian era, there were various beliefs about the poor, influenced by people like Thomas Malthus. Malthus was an influential economist of that time and he proposed that population growth would outstrip the availability of resources, leading to more poverty and suffering. This Malthusian theory proposed that the poor were responsible for their own poverty because they had excessive numbers of children.

Contrary to Malthus' claims, the Cratchit family seem to be a very close, happy family, despite their poverty and large size. Although modest, their 'four-roomed house' is full of love. They also manage to enjoy a christmas dinner, 'eeked out by stuffing'. They make the best of their situation and are rich in love and family.

Figure 9.8 Student's analysis of Victorian beliefs about the poor linked to the depiction of the Cratchit family.

Notes

1 Charles Dickens, *A Christmas Carol* (London: Wordsworth Classics, 2018), 55–56.

2 Ibid., 58.

3 Clara Debus, 'Negotiating Family and Community in Anglo-American Christmas Discourses from 1843 to 2020,' University of the Balearic Islands, (April 28, 2021), https://bora.uib.no/bora-xmlui/handle/11250/2759131, 75.

4 Charles Dickens, *A Christmas Carol*, 53.

5 Victor Witter Turner, 'Introduction,' In: *Celebration. Studies in Festivity and Ritual* (Washington D.C.: Smithsonian Institution Press, 1982), 16.

6 Michael Slater, *The Great Charles Dickens Scandal* (New Haven: Yale, 2012), 112.

7 Charles Dickens, *A Christmas Carol*, 60.

8 Audrey Jaffe, 'Spectacular Sympathy: Visuality and ideology in Dickens's A Christmas Carol,' *Modern Language Association* 109, no. 2 (March 1994): 254–265.

9 G. Major, 'Scrooge's Chambers,' *Dickensian* 29, no. 225 (December 1932): 11–15.

10 Mark Duell, 'Revealed: The 25 boroughs with the largest number of high earners (and only two are outside the south-east),' *The Daily Mail*, May 2, 2021, https://www.dailymail.co.uk/news/article-6821941/Britains-richest-boroughs-revealed.html.

11 Angus Wilson, *The World of Charles Dickens* (Harmondsworth: Penguin Books, 1972).

12 Simon Gunn, 'Urbanization,' In Chris Williams (Ed.), *A Companion to Nineteenth-Century Britain* (Malden: Blackwell, 2004): 238–252.

13 Walter Allen, *The English Novel: A short critical history* (Harmondsworth: Penguin Books, 1986), 163.

14 Humphry House, *The Dickens World* (London: Oxford University Press, 1965), 165.

15 G. Major, 'Scrooge's Chambers': 11–15.

16 Jane Ridley, *Victoria: Queen, Matriarch, Empress* (London: Penguin, 2015).

17 Judith Butler, *Undoing Gender* (New York & London: Routledge, 2004), 10.

18 Charles Dickens, *A Christmas Carol* (London: Wordsworth Classics, 2018), 59.

19 Ibid., 59.

20 Paul Davis, *The Lives and Times of Ebenezer Scrooge* (New Haven & London: Yale University Press, 1990), 232.

21 Charles Dickens, *A Christmas Carol*, 81.

22 Jon Mee, *The Cambridge Introduction to Charles Dickens* (Cambridge: Cambridge University Press, 2010), 76.

23 Marie-Luise Kohlke, Christian Gutleben, *Neo-Victorian Families: Gender, sexual and cultural politics* (Leiden: BRILL, 2011).

24 Charles Dickens, *A Christmas Carol*, 93.

25 Natalie McKnight, 'Dickens's Philosophy of Fathering,' *Dickens Quarterly* 18, no. 3 (September 2001): 129–138.

26 John Tosh, *A Man's Place: Masculinity and the middle-class home in Victorian England* (New Haven: Yale UP, 1998), 4.

27 Charles Dickens, *A Christmas Carol*, 93.

28 David Parker, *Christmas and Charles Dickens* (New York: AMS Press, 2005).

29 Paul Davis, *Charles Dickens A to Z: The essential reference to his life and work* (New York: Facts on File, 1998).

30 Charles Dickens, *A Christmas Carol*, 15.

31 Hera Cook, *The Long Sexual Revolution: English women, sex, and contraception 1800–1975* (Oxford: Oxford UP, 2004).

32 Goldie Morgentaler, 'Fertility as Sociological Metaphor; or the Ambiguities of Unchecked Reproduction,' *Dickens Quarterly* 37, no. 2 (January 2020): 176–185.

33 Charles Dickens, *A Christmas Carol*, 61.

34 Lynn Hollen Lees, *The Solidarities of Strangers: The English poor laws and the people, 1700–1948*. Cambridge: Cambridge University Press, 1998).

35 Michael Grogan, 'Generosity and the Ghosts of Poor Laws Passed,' *NARRATIVE* 12, no. 2 (May 2004): 151–166.

36 Les Standiford, *The Man Who Invented Christmas: How Charles Dickens's A Christmas Carol rescued his career and revived our holiday spirits* (London: Crown/Archetype, 2017), 10.

37 'Dickens to an American friend, January 2, 1844,' The New York Public Library, http://web-static.nypl.org/exhibitions/lifeofauthor/3detail7.html.

38 Martha Stoddard Holmes, *Fictions of Affliction: Physical disability in Victorian culture* (Michigan: University of Michigan Press, 2009), 18.

39 Ibid., 99.

40 Ibid., 100.

41 Ibid., 100.

42 Lucinda Hawksley, 'How Did A Christmas Carol Come to Be?' BBC, May 2, 2021, https://www.bbc.com/culture/article/20171215-how-did-a-christmas-carol-come-to-be.

43 Russell W. Chesney, 'Environmental Factors in Tiny Tim's Near-Fatal Illness,' *Paediatrics and Adolescent Medicine 166*, no. 3 (March 2012): 271–275. DOI: 10.1001/archpediatrics.2011.852.

44 Charles Dickens, *A Christmas Carol*, 54.

45 Ibid., 60.

46 Rene Jules Dubos, Jean Dubos, *The White Plague: Tuberculosis, man and society* (Chapel Hill. NC: Rutgers University Press, 1987).

47 Charles Dickens, 'Poverty. In All Year Round,' *Dickens Journal Online*, May 2, 2021, https://www.djo.org.uk/all-the-year-round/volume-xiii.html.

48 Russell W. Callahan Jr., 'Tiny Tim: The child with a crippling fatal illness,' *Dickensian* 89, no. 431 (March 2012): 214–217.

49 Pierre Bourdieu, *Forms of Capital: General Sociology, Volume 3: Lectures at the Collège de France 1983–84* (London: Polity, 2021).

50 Charles Dickens, *A Christmas Carol*, 93.

51 Ibid.

References

Walter Allen, *The English Novel: A short critical history* (Harmondsworth: Penguin Books, 1986).

Pierre Bourdieu, *Forms of Capital: General sociology, Volume 3: Lectures at the Collège de France 1983–84* (London: Polity).

Judith Butler, *Undoing Gender* (New York & London: Routledge, 2004).

Russell W. Callahan, Jr., 'Tiny Tim: The child with a crippling fatal illness,' *Dickensian* 89, no. 431 (March 2012): 214–217.

Russell W. Chesney, 'Environmental Factors in Tiny Tim's Near-Fatal Illness,' *Paediatrics and Adolescent Medicine* 166, no. 3 (March 2012): 271–275. DOI: 10.1001/archpediatrics.2011.852

Hera Cook, *The Long Sexual Revolution: English Women, Sex, and Contraception 1800–1975* (Oxford: Oxford UP, 2004).

Paul Davis, *Charles Dickens A to Z: The essential reference to his life and work* (New York: Facts on File, 1998).

Paul Davis, *The Lives and Times of Ebenezer Scrooge* (New Haven, CT: Yale University Press, 1990).

Clara Debus, 'Negotiating Family and Community in Anglo-American Christmas Discourses from 1843 to 2020,' *University of the Balearic Islands*, (April 28, 2021), https://bora.uib.no/bora-xmlui/handle/11250/2759131

Charles Dickens, 'Poverty. In All Year Round,' *Dickens Journal Online*, (May 2, 2021), https://www.djo.org.uk/all-the-year-round/volume-xiii.html

Charles Dickens, *A Christmas Carol* (London: Wordsworth Classics, 2018).

Rene Jules Dubos, Jean Dubos, *The White Plague: Tuberculosis, man and society* (Chapel Hill. NC: Rutgers University Press, 1987).

Mark Duell, 'Revealed: The 25 boroughs with the largest number of high earners (and only two are outside the south-east),' *The Daily Mail*, May 2, 2021, https://www.dailymail.co.uk/news/article-6821941/Britains-richest-boroughs-revealed.html

Michael Grogan, 'Generosity and the Ghosts of Poor Laws Passed,' *NARRATIVE* 12, no. 2 (May 2004): 151–166. DOI: 10.1353/nar.2004.0005

Simon Gunn, 'Urbanization,' In Chris Williams (Ed.), *A Companion to Nineteenth-Century Britain* (Malden: Blackwell, 2004): 238–252.

Lucinda Hawksley, 'How Did A Christmas Carol Come to Be?' BBC, (May 2, 2021), https://www.bbc.com/culture/article/20171215-how-did-a-christmas-carol-come-to-be

Martha Stoddard Holmes, *Fictions of Affliction: Physical disability in Victorian culture* (Michigan: University of Michigan Press, 2009), 18. DOI: 10.3998/mpub.11877

Humphry House, *The Dickens World* (London: Oxford University Press, 1965).

Audrey Jaffe, 'Spectacular Sympathy: Visuality and ideology in Dickens's A Christmas Carol,' *Modern Language Association* 109, no. 2 (March 1994): 254–265. https://doi.org/10.2307/463120

Marie-Luise Kohlke, Christian Gutleben, *Neo-Victorian Families: Gender, sexual and cultural politics* (Leiden: BRILL, 2011).

Lynn Hollen Lees, *The Solidarities of Strangers: The English Poor Laws and the people, 1700-1948* (Cambridge: Cambridge University Press, 1998).

G. Major, 'Scrooge's Chambers,' *Dickensian* 29, no. 225 (December 1932): 11–15.

Natalie McKnight, 'Dickens's Philosophy of Fathering,' *Dickens Quarterly* 18, no. 3 (September 2001): 129–138. https://www.jstor.org/stable/45291822

Jon Mee, *The Cambridge Introduction to Charles Dickens* (Cambridge: Cambridge University Press, 2010).

Goldie Morgentaler, 'Fertility as Sociological Metaphor, or the Ambiguities of Unchecked Reproduction,' *Dickens Quarterly* 37, no. 2 (January 2020): 176–185.

"Dickens to an American Friend, January 2, 1844," The New York Public Library, (May 3, 2021), http://web-static.nypl.org/exhibitions/lifeofauthor/3detail7.html

David Parker, *Christmas and Charles Dickens* (New York: AMS Press, 2005).

Jane Ridley, *Victoria: Queen, Matriarch, Empress* (London: Penguin, 2015).

Michael Slater, *The Great Charles Dickens Scandal* (New Haven: Yale, 2012).

Les Standiford, *The Man Who Invented Christmas: How Charles Dickens's A Christmas Carol rescued his career and revived our holiday spirits* (London: Crown/Archetype, 2017).

John Tosh, *A Man's Place: Masculinity and the middle-class home in Victorian England* (New Haven: Yale UP, 1998).

Victor Witter Turner, 'Introduction,' In *Celebration. Studies in Festivity and Ritual* (Washington DC: Smithsonian Institution Press, 1982).

Angus Wilson, *The World of Charles Dickens* (Harmondsworth: Penguin Books, 1972).

It's all in the name: How does Dickens' use of names help us understand his characters?

The naming of names. It is one of 'those devices of language and rhetoric that produce the characteristic ring of Dickens' style,'[1] and his wonderful name choices work on both literal and connotative levels. The names in Dickens' stories didn't just appear as by accident, it is a well-known fact that Dickens had experimental lists where he jotted down names he liked the sound of, and took great care in assigning these names to characters.

This list of names is something which biographer and friend, John Forster, also refers to, and he recounts an anecdote where Dickens struggled with the naming of his character Martin Chuzzlewit, from his eponymous novel. Before deciding on Chuzzlewit, he tried out Sweezleden, Sweezleback, Sweezlewag, Chuzzletoe, Chuzzleboy, Chubblewig and Chuzzlewig, before finally settling on Chuzzlewit.[2]

This fondness for peculiar names did not only reveal itself in his writing but was also evident in the nicknames he gave to his children. In a letter to Henry Austin, he added at the end,

> P. S.-The children's present names are as follows:
> Katey (from a lurking propensity to fieryness),
> Marney (as generally descriptive of her bearing),
> Mild Glo'ster. Charley (as a corruption of Master
> Toby), Master Floby. Walter (suggested by his high
> cheek bones), Young Skull. Each is pronounced with a
> peculiar howl which I shall have great pleasure in
> illustrating.[3]

Some of these nicknames, such as 'Chicken-Stalker' (one of the nicknames for his third son Francis) were even used in his stories, as this name was appropriated for one of Dickens' other Christmas stories from 1844, 'The Chimes.' As is evident

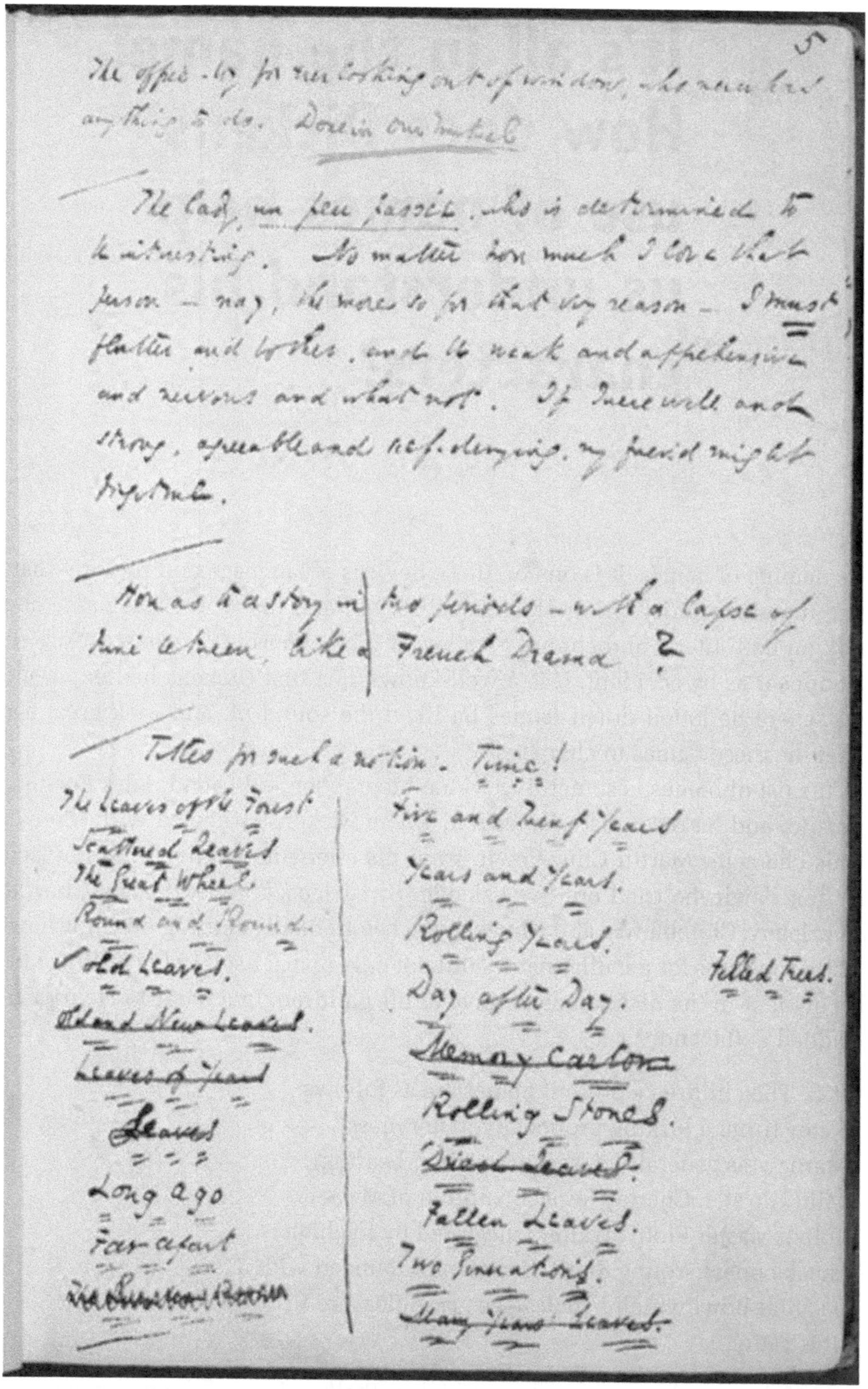

Figure 10.1 Dickens's *Book of Memoranda*.

© The New York Public Library, Berg Collection of English and American Literature.

from these nicknames and his literary character names, they often came from a corruption of words, or were indicative of some character trait the figures embodied – often negative as well as positive. With many of Dickens' choices, there seems to be affinity between the names and the characters, they are what Plato labelled 'cratylic'[4] – the name is a sign. Some meanings are obvious, they are puns, which Dickens may have been inspired to do through reading Elizabethan drama or Ben Jonson's descriptive names.[5] At his time of writing, this kind of nomenclature, where names gave away somebody's job or personality, was no longer in fashion, but Dickens made excellent use of it in his literary career.

The Victorians and names

However, that isn't to imply that he was the only person who had an interest in names. The Victorians seemed to have a fascination with the naming of names and exploring the history of them.[6] There were also many essays published in the periodical Dickens edited, *Household Words*, including explorations of the social implications of forms of address and more unusual name choices. Indeed, in 1857, Nathaniel Ingersoll Bowditch penned *Suffolk Surnames*, where he gathered and curated a list of curious and sometimes grotesque names. Bowditch lived in Boston but he did meet Dickens and gave him copies of his books which he later reviewed for *Household Words*, and he retained both editions of the book in his Gadshill library, and annotated them[7] so he may have been further inspired by this collection in the naming of his own characters.[8] But some of his names also may have come from institutional records,[9] or even from court proceedings, as in the Parliamentary inquiry into the conduct of the Duke of York, 1809, the names of Wardle, Lowten and Dowler were all found – which are all used in *The Pickwick Papers* in 1836.[10]

Some academics have claimed that names were so important to Dickens that he needed to determine the names of characters before he could tell their stories. Harry Stone asserts that he 'felt uncomfortable and inhibited, unable to proceed, until he settled on a name – the right name. He agonized especially over the names of his chief characters.'[11] Furthermore, six of Dickens' fifteen novels are actually named after the protagonists in the books, which indicates their importance. Dickens himself re-named himself at different points in his career, for his sketches, he rebranded himself as Boz, after one of his favourite characters in Goldsmith's *Vicar of Wakefield*, Moses (who became Boses, which became Boz).[12] But one of his lesser nicknames was The Sparkler of Albion, which appeared in *Collected Letters* in 1880. This nickname seemed to be of his own devising, but it did allow him to draw rays next to the customary flourish of his famous signature on letters![13] But what about Dickens' use of names in *A Christmas Carol*? Where may these names have come from and what might they signify about the characters who own them?

are told he became exceedingly prosperous and had male and female servants, large flocks, camels and donkeys.[26] A further monetary link comes with the name of an obscure golden coin called a 'Jacobus,' which was minted under the reign of King James I. As somebody whose 'spirit never walked beyond our counting house'[27] it might fit Jacob Marley's character, as he wasted his life counting out coins and being pre-occupied with wealth, rather than living his life.

The Cratchit family

As Kelsie B. Harder said, Dickens 'was a master at concocting names with tonal and allegorical qualities'[28] and Cratchit is a great example of this. The name is a pleasure to say and the sound of the name is 'evocatively positive' as it has a 'low, front, lax vowel' which is opposite to Scrooge's 'high, back, relatively tense vowel.'[29] When we are first introduced to Scrooge's clerk, Bob, he is working away at the counting house by the feeble light and warmth of one coal. Hearn proposes that 'cratch' suggests the 'scratching of the clerk's pen,'[30] which evokes a kind of sympathy in the audience for the cruel way he is treated.

Cratchit could also derive from the French 'criquet,' which means 'feeble person,' and may seem to link to Tiny Tim. Another link to Tim could be that Cratchit also derives from 'cratch' which sounds a bit like 'crutch' – an item the reader certainly associates with Tiny Tim, as we are told 'his active little crutch was heard upon the floor'[31] and it is almost symbolic of his determination to live as full a life as he can as a Christian stoic figure. Yet Cratchit also derives from 'cratch' meaning cradle or manger. With some critics pointing out that Tim is almost Christ-like in his perfection, this may be a subtle hint.

In Old English, Cratchet was a word used for the stomach, meaning to eat heartily or like a horse.[32] Considering that the family preside over one of the most well described meals in literature, the name is quite apt. However, it may also be tinged with a sense of irony, as the family may have struggled with hunger and the goose for the Christmas feast is very small – a visual reminder of Scrooge's meanness – but they make the best of it. Finally, Crotchet, meaning 'a peculiar notion held by an individual in opposition to popular opinion,'[33] which may link to Bob's refusal to condemn his boss. At the Christmas feast, as they gather round the fire to roast chestnuts, Bob Cratchit makes a toast to his employer and calls him 'the Founder of the Feast,' meaning the provider of the Cratchit family's Christmas dinner. What's surprising is that Scrooge treats Bob very poorly and pays him very little, which are some of the things Mrs Cratchit resents about Scrooge, whom she considers an 'odious, stingy, hard, unfeeling man.'[34]

Bob, probably short for Robert, was also Victorian slang for a shilling and it is a word which is still used today as slang for a pound coin. This reminds us of the pittance Bob makes as a clerk for Scrooge, and Dickens even tells us, 'Think of that! Bob had but fifteen "bob" a week himself.'[35] Although this may have been an average wage for clerks like Bob, it still would have made it extremely difficult to make ends meet and feed a wife and six children.

For Tiny Tim, his full name, Timothy is an English form of the Old Greek name Timotheos which means 'honouring God or honoured by God.'[36] We read in the novella that Tim honours God, as we are told that he 'hoped the people saw him in the church, because he was a cripple, and it might be pleasant to them to remember upon Christmas Day, who made lame beggars walk and blind men see.'[37] Dickens also indicates that despite his short life, Tiny Tim was indeed honoured by God as he tells us, 'Spirit of Tiny Tim, thy childish essence was from God.'[38] In the New Testament, Timothy was a companion of the Apostle Paul, who met him during his second missionary journey. He suffered from frequent ailments like his namesake and decided to follow Paul after he witnessed him healing a crippled person – perhaps predicting Tim's recovery at the end of the novella. As Harry Stone attests,

'Dickens's names are deceptive. They often seem
clear or even simple, but this is frequently a figment
of hindsight, a wisdom that comes only after we have
been made privy to the grand design of a novel.'[39]

Other characters

Although Dickens used some obvious puns and references in his names, some of the other name choices were more unobtrusive and are what Fowler terms 'self-effacing,'[40] as they don't stand out particularly and their associations are much more general, meaning that they are more determined by the reader. More minor characters like Belle, Fred and Little Fan may still have something to impart to us, however. Of course, Belle has French origins and means beautiful. It belongs to the language of love, something which Scrooge may once have tasted and now no longer has. Perhaps the memory of his former fiancé's beauty and the tenderness they once felt for one another is placed there as a juxtaposition between Scrooge's former life and the cold world he now inhabits; it reminds him that there is another way and that if he is to open his heart to beauty and love once again, he would come out of the shadows and again feel the warmth of human affection. It strikes a contrast between emotional love and the love of money.

Scrooge's nephew Fred's name derives from German roots and means peaceful ruler. We see in Fred a cheerful disposition, who despite his uncle's coldness and goading, manages to remain calm and positive:

I want nothing from you; I ask nothing of you; why cannot we be friends? ...I am sorry, with all my heart, to find you so resolute. We have never had any quarrel, to which I have been a party. But I have made the trial in homage to Christmas, and I'll keep my Christmas humour to the last. So, a Merry Christmas, uncle![41]

He attempts to keep the peace and implores his uncle to accept his invitation, breaking down the barriers between them in an attempt to get to know his uncle more, and invite him into his life.

Even Scrooge's little sister Fanny, affectionately referred to as 'Little Fan,' which is derived from the French 'Francis,' could give us clues. It translates as 'free one' and she certainly seems to be free of the melancholy malaise which suffocates Scrooge and her father. When she bursts into the school room, her joy is almost contagious:

> darting in, and putting her arms about his neck, and often kissing him, ad-dressed him as her 'Dear, dear brother. I have come to bring you home, dear brother!' said the child, clapping her tiny hands, and bending down to laugh. 'To bring you home, home, home!'[42]

The dynamic verbs 'darting' and 'clapping' demonstrate her exuberance. Her childlike repetition of 'dear' and 'home' are drenched with the excitement of see-ing her older brother, and it also emphasises to the reader that Scrooge is a product of his own experiences. His sister is at home, treated well by their father, while Scrooge is abandoned at school, so his father doesn't have to lay eyes on him, and he's treated cruelly by the school master. Charles Dickens' own sister was also called Fanny, and with only two years between them, he was particularly close to her. She studied at the Royal Academy of Music and met her husband there, Henry Burnett, who she married in 1837. The couple had two sons – one of which, Henry Junior, was disabled and sickly, and is said to have been the inspiration for Tiny Tim. Fanny later moved to Manchester, where Dickens visited her often, but she sadly died in 1848, at the young age of 38, after suffering from tuberculosis. Dickens was greatly affected by her death, remarking in a letter to his friend, John Forster, that displaying 'such an affecting exhibition of strength and tenderness in all that early decay, is quite indescribable.'[43] It seems only natural then that he should be inspired to name one of Scrooge's most beloved relatives after one of his own.

Summed up in six

- The names in Dickens' stories didn't just appear as by accident; it is a well-known fact that Dickens had experimental lists where he jotted down names he liked the sound of and took great care in assigning these names to characters.

- There is often an affinity between the names and the characters, they are what Plato labelled 'cratylic' – the name is a sign. Some meanings are obvious puns, some use nomenclature, where names gave away somebody's job or personality. Some are less obvious and have more of an unobtrusive significance.

- Ebenezer derives from the Bible and is a name given to a stone that commemorated an Israeli victory against invaders. God helped them defeat their enemies, and it is said that from then on, every time an Israelite saw the Ebenezer stone it would be a constant reminder that God had protected them – a visual reminder of that truth. Scrooge himself acts as a visual reminder of the truth that being selfish and cold will result in loneliness and purgatory. Many critics agree that Dickens based Scrooge on 'scrouging' which is an 18th-century word, probably evolved from the 16th century word 'scruze' which means to squeeze, and was perhaps a blend of screw and squeeze. 'Screw' was also Victorian slang for a miser.

- Jacob Marley - 'Marl' is a 14th century word meaning soil, which reminds the reader that Marley was dead. Jacob has its roots in the Bible, and it belonged to the son of Isaac and Rebecca, who was a shrewd businessman, just like Marley. There was also an obscure golden coin called a 'Jacobus,' which was minted under the reign of King James I. Marley wasted his life counting out coins and being pre-occupied with wealth, rather than living his life.

- There are many suggestions for where Cratchit may come from. Among them, Hearn proposes that 'cratch' suggests the 'scratching of the clerk's pen' which evokes a kind of sympathy in the audience for the cruel way he is treated. In Old English, 'Cratchet' was a word used for the stomach, meaning to eat heartily or like a horse.

- More minor characters could also be significant: Belle is French, the language of love and means 'beautiful.' She is a visual reminder of all Scrooge has forsaken due to greed. Fred comes from Germanic roots and means 'peaceful ruler,' a quality he definitely demonstrates in the face of Scrooge's coldness. Little Fan translates as 'free one' and could be inspired by Dickens' own sister Fanny, whom he was very close to and who died young – just like Scrooge's sister in the novella.

Ideas for teaching

AO1: Do you think the studying of names can add something to our analysis of characters? Choose one of the characters and find three quotations from the novella which seem to provide evidence that the character is behaving in a way their name suggests.

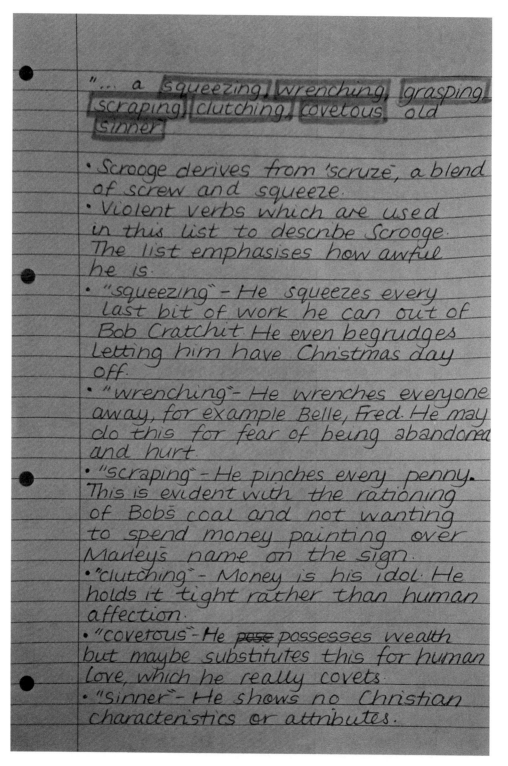

"... a squeezing, wrenching, grasping, scraping, clutching, covetous old sinner"

- Scrooge derives from 'scruze', a blend of screw and squeeze.
- Violent verbs which are used in this list to describe Scrooge. The list emphasises how awful he is.
- "squeezing" - He squeezes every last bit of work he can out of Bob Cratchit. He even begrudges letting him have Christmas day off.
- "wrenching" - He wrenches everyone away, for example Belle, Fred. He may do this for fear of being abandoned and hurt.
- "scraping" - He pinches every penny. This is evident with the rationing of Bob's coal and not wanting to spend money painting over Marley's name on the sign.
- "clutching" - Money is his idol. He holds it tight rather than human affection.
- "covetous" - He ~~pose~~ possesses wealth but maybe substitutes this for human love, which he really covets.
- "sinner" - He shows no Christian characteristics or attributes.

Figure 10.3 Quotes to demonstrate the characteristics of Scrooge based on etymology.

AO2: Explore the quotations from the previous task, zooming into words, labelling language techniques and exploring multiple layers of possible meaning for key words.

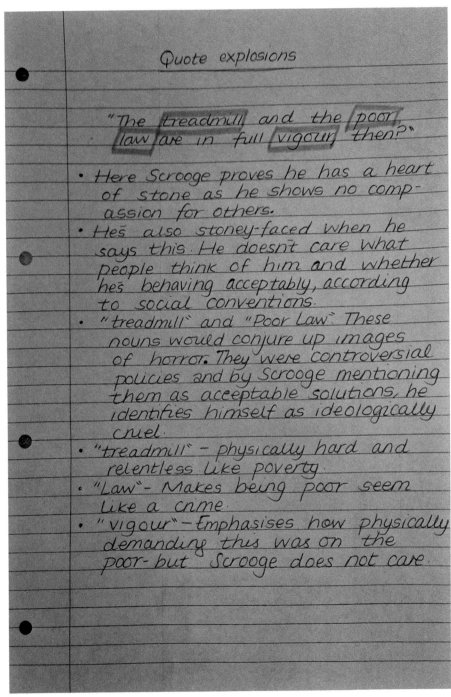

(a)

Figure 10.4 (a, b) Quote explosions. *(Continued)*

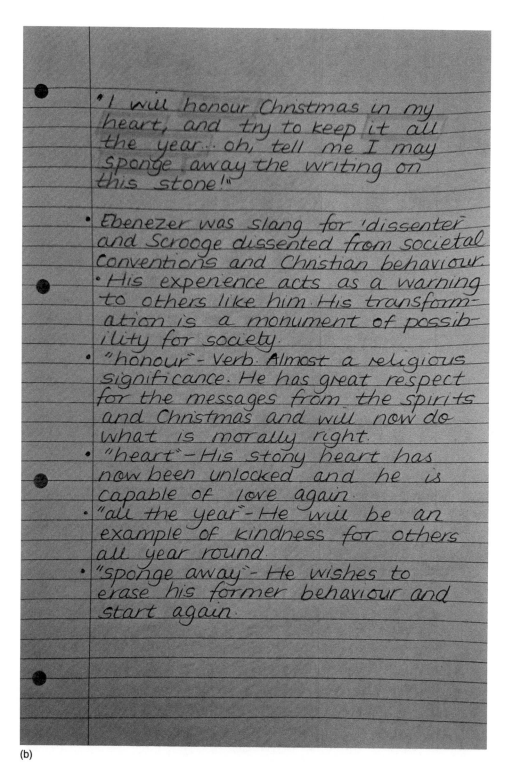

"I will honour Christmas in my heart, and try to keep it all the year. Oh, tell me I may sponge away the writing on this stone!"

- Ebenezer was slang for 'dissenter' and Scrooge dissented from societal conventions and Christian behaviour.
- His experience acts as a warning to others like him. His transformation is a monument of possibility for society.
- "honour" - Verb. Almost a religious significance. He has great respect for the messages from the spirits and Christmas and will now do what is morally right.
- "heart" - His stony heart has now been unlocked and he is capable of love again.
- "all the year" - He will be an example of kindness for others all year round.
- "sponge away" - He wishes to erase his former behaviour and start again.

(b)

Figure 10.4 (Continued) (a, b) Quote explosions.

Notes

1 Taylor Stoehr, (1966) *Dickens: The Dreamer's Stance.* (Ithaca, NY: Cornell University Press, 1966), 7.

2 John Forster, *The Life of Charles Dickens* (Boston: Estes & Lauriat, 1875), 464.

3 Charles Dickens, *Letters: Edited by Miss Hogarth and Mamie Dickens* (London: Macmillan and Co, 1880), 76.

4 Catherine Dalimier, *Platon, Cratyle* (Paris: Flammarion, 1998).

5 Elizabeth Home Gordon, 'The Naming of Characters in the Work of Charles Dickens,' *University of Nebraska Studies in Language, Literature, and Criticism* 5 (January 1917): 2-35.

6 Alastair Flower, *Literary Names: Personal Names in English Literature* (Oxford: Oxford University Press, 2012).

7 H. Stonehouse, *Catalogue of the Library of Charles Dickens from Gadshill* (London: Piccadilly Fountain Press, 1935).

8 Daniel Bever, 'The Higher Court of Heaven: Dr. Henry Ingersoll Bowditch and Violent Abolition,' *William and Mary*, May 6, 2022, https://scholarworks.wm.edu/honorstheses/369/.

9 Alastair Flower, *Literary Names.*

10 W. K. R. B., 'Dickens' Names,' *Notes and Queries* 11, no. 293 (1855), 443.

11 Marjorie Stone, 'Dickens, Bentham, and the Fictions of the Law: A Victorian controversy and its consequences,' *Victorian Studies* 29, no. 1 (October 1985), 141.

12 'Who Is Boz?' *Charles Dickens Info*, (May 21, 2022), https://www.charlesdickensinfo.com/novels/boz/.

13 Stephen B. Dobranski, 'Names in Dickens: The trouble with Dombey,' *Modern Philology* 114, no. 2 (November 2016): 388-410.

14 Charles Dickens, *A Christmas Carol* (London: Wordsworth Classics, 2018), 8.

15 Philip V. Allingham, 'The Naming of Names in Charles Dickens's A Christmas Carol,' *The Victorian Web*, May 21, 2022, https://victorianweb.org/authors/dickens/xmas/names.html.

16 Philip V. Allingham, 'Vocabulary Notes for Dickens" A Christmas Carol.' *The Victorian Web*, May 21, 2022, https://victorianweb.org/authors/dickens/xmas/pva116.html.

17 1 Samuel 7:12, *Bible Hub*, https://biblehub.com/1_samuel/7-12.htm.

18 Maurice Waite, Sara Hawker (Eds.), *Oxford Paperback Dictionary and Thesaurus* (Oxford: Oxford University Press, 2009), 832.

19 Bryan Kozlowski, 2016 *What the Dickens?!: Distinctly Dickensian words and how to use them* (Philadelphia: Running Press, 2016), 28.

20 'Scrouge,' *Collins Dictionary*, https://www.collinsdictionary.com/dictionary/english/scrouge.

21 Charles Dickens, *A Christmas Carol*, 8.

22 Bryan Kozlowski, *What the Dickens?!*, 31.

23 Charles Dickens, *A Christmas Carol*, 78.

24 'Marl,' *Collins Dictionary*, https://www.collinsdictionary.com/dictionary/english/marl.

25 Charles Dickens, *A Christmas Carol*, 7.

26 Genesis 30, *Bible Gateway*, https://www.biblegateway.com/passage/?search=Genesis+30&version=NIV.

27 Charles Dickens, *A Christmas Carol*, 23.

28 Kelsie B. Harder, 'Dickens and His Lists of Names,' *Names* 30, no. 4 (December 1982), 35.

29 Michael Adams, 'Cratchit: The etymology,' *Journal of Literary Onomastics* 1, no. 1 (2011), 33.

30 Charles Dickens, Michael Patrick Hearn, *The Annotated Christmas Carol* (New York: Clarkson
N. Potter, 1976), 119.

31 Charles Dickens, *A Christmas Carol*, 54.

32 Philip V. Allingham, 'The Naming of Names in Charles Dickens's A Christmas Carol,' *The Victorian Web*, (May 21, 2022), https://victorianweb.org/authors/dickens/xmas/names.html.

33 Philip V. Allingham, 'Vocabulary Notes for Dickens's A Christmas Carol.'

34 Charles Dickens, *A Christmas Carol*, 59.

35 Ibid., 53.

36 'Timothy,' *Baby Names*, https://babynames.net/names/timothy.

37 Charles Dickens, *A Christmas Carol*, 54.

38 Ibid., 83.

39 Harry Stone, 'What's in a Name: Fantasy and calculation in Dickens,' *Dickens Studies Annual* 14, (1985), 191.

40 Alastair Flower, *Literary Names*, 139.

41 Charles Dickens, *A Christmas Carol*, 11.

42 Ibid., 34.

43 'Death of Fanny (Dickens) Burnett,' *Charles Dickens Page*, https://www.charlesdickenspage.com/fannys-death.html.

References

Michael Adams, 'Cratchit: The etymology,' *Journal of Literary Onomastics* 1, no. 1 (2011): 31–52.

Philip V. Allingham, 'The Naming of Names in Charles Dickens's A Christmas Carol,' *The Victorian Web*, (May 21, 2022a), https://victorianweb.org/authors/dickens/xmas/names.html

Philip V. Allingham, 'Vocabulary Notes for Dickens's A Christmas Carol,' *The Victorian Web*, (May 21, 2022b), https://victorianweb.org/authors/dickens/xmas/pva116.html

'Timothy,' *Baby Names*, (May 21, 2022), https://babynames.net/names/timothy

Daniel Bever, 'The Higher Court of Heaven: Dr. Henry Ingersoll Bowditch and violent abolition,' *William and Mary*, (May 6, 2022), https://scholarworks.wm.edu/honorstheses/369/

'Genesis 30,' *Bible Gateway*, (May 21, 2022), https://www.biblegateway.com/passage/?search=Genesis+30&version=NIV

'1 Samuel 7:12,' *Bible Hub*, (May 21, 2022), https://biblehub.com/1_samuel/7-12.htm

Catherine Dalimier, *Platon, Cratyle* (Paris: Flammarion, 1998).

'Scrouge,' *Collins Dictionary*, (May 21, 2022), https://www.collinsdictionary.com/dictionary/english/scrouge

'Marl,' *Collins Dictionary*, (May 21, 2022), https://www.collinsdictionary.com/dictionary/english/marl

Charles Dickens, *A Christmas Carol* (London: Wordsworth Classics, 2018).

Charles Dickens, *Letters: Edited by Miss Hogarth and Mamie Dickens* (London: Macmillan and Co., 1880).

'Who Is Boz?' *Charles Dickens Info*, (May 21, 2022), https://www.charlesdickensinfo.com/novels/boz/

Charles Dickens, Michael Patrick Hearn, *The Annotated Christmas Carol* (New York: Clarkson N. Potter, 1976).

'Death of Fanny (Dickens) Burnett,' *Charles Dickens Page*, (May 28, 2022), https://www.charlesdickenspage.com/fannys-death.html

Stephen B. Dobranski, 'Names in Dickens: The trouble with Dombey,' *Modern Philology* 114, no. 2 (November 2016): 388–410.

Alastair Flower, *Literary Names: Personal names in English literature* (Oxford: Oxford University Press, 2012).

John Forster, *The Life of Charles Dickens* (Boston: Estes & Lauriat, 1875).

Elizabeth Home Gordon, 'The Naming of Characters in the Work of Charles Dickens,' *University of Nebraska Studies in Language, Literature, and Criticism* 5 (January 1917): 2–35.

Kelsie B. Harder, 'Dickens and His Lists of Names,' *Names* 30, no. 4 (December 1982):16–35. https://doi.org/10.1179/nam.1982.30.4.235

Bryan Kozlowski, 2016 *What the Dickens?!: Distinctly Dickensian words and how to use them*, (Philadelphia: Running Press, 2016).

Taylor Stoehr, (1966) *Dickens: The Dreamer's Stance.* Ithaca (New York: Cornell University Press, 1966).

Harry Stone, 'What's in a Name: Fantasy and calculation in Dickens,' *Dickens Studies Annual* 14 (1985a): 191–204.

Marjorie Stone, 'Dickens, Bentham, and the Fictions of the Law: A Victorian controversy and its consequences,' *Victorian Studies* 29, no. 1 (October 1985b): 125–154.

H. Stonehouse, *Catalogue of the Library of Charles Dickens from Gadshill* (London: Piccadilly Fountain Press, 1935).

Maurice Waite, Sara Hawker (Eds.), *Oxford Paperback Dictionary and Thesaurus* (Oxford: Oxford University Press, 2009).

W.K.R.B., 'Dickens' Names,' *Notes and Queries* 11, no. 293 (1855).

Food glorious food! Feast and famine in *A Christmas Carol*: Do Dickens' descriptions of food and starvation in the novella help contribute to the novel's meaning?

Like any literature, *A Christmas Carol* is defined by the time it was written. As we know, Dickens was influenced by the disparity of wealth he witnessed around him and the change in his family's fortunes he experienced as a child, when his father was sent to a debtor's prison and Charles was forced to work in the blacking factory. One of the most profound events of the early 1800s was the introduction of The Corn Laws in 1815. The Corn Laws were tariffs and restrictions which were placed on the trade of imported food – not just 'corn' but all cereal grains, such as oats, wheat and barley. The tariffs meant that the importation of cheap 'corn' was blocked, and steep import duties were imposed so that it was far too expensive to import it from abroad. This raised food prices and the cost of living for many normal working people. But for those who owned land, The Corn Laws enhanced their power and profits.

On September 18, 1838, a nation-wide organisation was launched, who were dedicated to free trade. They demanded a repeal of the Corn Laws, which they felt served the interests of the landed classes and aristocracy, who had dominated Parliament. The organisation was made up of the rising class of industrialists and merchants, who emerged from the Industrial Revolution and wanted cheap food for their workers to stave off upward pressure on wages. They were based

DOI: 10.4324/9781003453468-12

in Manchester, and campaigners such as John Bright and Richard Cobden distributed pamphlets, wrote newspaper articles and gave public speeches, supported financially by many of the Northern industrialists. Their campaigns for free trade (particularly in food) gained a hugely popular following, resulting in them even having MPs elected to parliament, where their influence eventually won over the opposition.

Yet it was another horrific event, the Great Hunger in Ireland, sometimes called the Irish Potato Famine, which persuaded even the most ardent supporter of The Corn Laws to reconsider. The famine, which killed around 1 million people and forced over a million more to flee the country, was a period of mass starvation which occurred from 1845 to 1852.[1] The famine was caused by a potato infected with late blight, showing typical rot symptoms,[2] which then infected potato crops throughout Europe. Of course, the impact of the blight was exacerbated even further by The Corn Laws, and a resolution was forced as there was an urgent need for food supplies. In 1846, the Prime Minister, Sir Robert Peel, achieved repeal against his own party, and the result was announced to the applause of Cobden and Bright.

Just ten years prior to this, the government launched The Poor Law of 1843. Poverty was a widespread issue, which needed to be tackled by the government, but they were reluctant to get involved. The new laws provided two types of 'help': the workhouse – which many poor Victorians greatly feared due to the hard labour, meagre meals and cruel treatment, or so called 'outdoor relief' which saw food and money being given to those in poverty in their homes. However, there was a great deal of social stigma around this, so people were reluctant to accept the help. This earned the government a lot of criticism from social commentators and scholars, such as Thomas Malthus and Dickens himself.

Malthusian Theory

Thomas Malthus FRS was an English cleric, scholar and economist, who observed in his 1798 book, *An Essay on the Principle of Population*, that an increase in a nation's food production improved the well-being of the population, but the improvement was temporary because it led to population growth, which did not help with the shortage of food. This link between abundance and population growth has become known as the 'Malthusian trap.' He criticised The Poor Laws for leading to inflation rather than improving the well-being of the poor[3] and also supported The Corn Laws, as he felt it encouraged domestic production and would guarantee British self-sufficiency in food.

Malthus' opinions would have been well known to Dickens, who fundamentally disagreed with them. Dickens argued that there was plenty to go round if the rich were more generous and shared their wealth. Through the characters in some of

Figure 11.1 Christmas pudding, 'The wonderful pudding!'

There was a religious significance to the making of the pudding, with the Church demanding that they be made on the 25th Sunday after Trinity and prepared with 13 ingredients to represent Christ and the 12 Apostles. Every member of the family had to have their turn at stirring, from east to west, in honour of the Wise Men and their journey, following the star.

Food and Freud

Dickens had great faith in the humanising power of the Christmas feast. Yet food also has a special significance in *A Christmas Carol*, as food is shown as a way for men like Scrooge to redeem their mistakes as the comfort and fulness food represents is symbolic of values like generosity and kindness. Which is why when Scrooge is a reformed man at the end of Stave 5, his first thought is to demonstrate his newfound benevolence by buying the prize turkey for his dedicated clerk and his family.[14] It can be argued that through a Freudian lens, 'Dickens's imagination remained rooted in the perceptions of childhood,' so he 'creates people in his novels who are marked by residues of the oral stage according to Freudian theories of character development.'[15]

According to Sigmund Freud, a child's personality develops through certain phases, known as 'psychosexual stages.' Children go through these stages, and this is what leads them to the formation of their adult personalities. Within these various childhood stages, there are pleasure-seeking energies: oral, anal, phallic, latent, and genital stage. The areas that are related to these psychosexual stages act as bases of pleasure. The oral stage focuses on oral satisfaction and occurs between birth and 18 months old. From his observations in his studies, Freud believed that an infant's mouth was the only organ of pleasure, so they seek to fulfil this need by drinking milk from their mother's breast or a bottle, thumb-sucking or insertion of objects into the mouth. If the need isn't gratified, oral fixation occurs, which can lead to overeating or excessive drinking. It is a sign then perhaps, that the corpulent capitalists Dickens criticises in the book have substituted abundance and excess – whether that be in food, drink or money, for the really important things in life, such as love, kindness and human connection.

However, there is also the power of connection that food represents. When the Cratchit family all work together to prepare for the Christmas feast, the table gets set and Mrs Cratchit begins to carve the turkey. Dickens describes the 'one murmur of delight' which arose all around the table and Tiny Tim, who was so excited he 'beat on the table with the handle of his knife, and feebly cried Hurrah!'[16] This demonstration of unbridled joy is evidence of the personal and collective pleasure of the fulfilling experience of the feast laid before them.[17]

The thread of food

Of course, the Cratchit feast is not the only mention of food in the story. During Stave 2, the Ghost of Christmas Past shows Scrooge a scene from his youth, when he was an apprentice to Mr Fezziwig and he encouraged them to eat, drink and be merry at their Christmas party. The narrative tells us that the fiddler 'plunged his hot face into a pot of porter' and that 'there was cake, and there was negus, and there was a great piece of cold roast, and there was a great piece of cold boiled, and there were mince-pies, and plenty of beer.'[18] This listing of delicious foods equates the pleasure of eating with joyful events and juxtaposes with Scrooge's meagre meal in

Stave 1, at the melancholy tavern, which he seems to take no pleasure in. These delicious foods are associated with a happier time in his life, and his later darker years are characterised by him outwardly showing no pleasure in the past time of eating.

Perhaps it is the Ghost of Christmas Present who is the spirit most associated with food. When the ghost made his appearance, he was seated on a great throne made up of heaps of:

> turkeys, geese, game, poultry, brawn, great joints of meat, sucking-pigs, long wreathes of sausages, mince-pies, plum-puddings, barrels of oysters, red-hot chestnuts, cherry-cheeked apples, juicy oranges, luscious pears, immense twelve-cakes, and seething bowls of punch, which made the chamber dim with their delicious steam.[19]

This mouth-watering asyndetic list represents the delicious foods the wealthiest can afford, which should be available to all, as there is plenty to go round. The ghost sits on it instead and decorates the room with it, as a nod to those greedy people who waste food by harbouring it all for themselves and use it as a status symbol. In the same Stave, when the ghost leads Scrooge through a market, Dickens describes the wonderful foods on display:

> There were great, round, pot-bellied baskets of chestnuts, … There were ruddy, brown-faced, broad-girthed Spanish onions, … There were pears and apples, … there were bunches of grapes, … there were piles of filberts, mossy and brown, … there were Norfolk biffins (red cooking apples), squab and swarthy.[20]

The pleasing aroma and spectacle of such delicious foods must have acted as a form of torture for London's poor who could not even dream of tasting them and were confronted with their image day after day. This is truly the season where poverty and indulgence clash[21] and even someone as seemingly blind to poor people's plight as Mr Scrooge could not have helped but be drawn to this unfair dichotomy of the haves and have nots.

Food and the gothic

Some critics have argued that the motif of food in *Carol* borders on the Gothic, in that the Gothic sometimes has a 'penchant for pleasure often simultaneous with pain.'[22] Dodworth claims that Victorians were fearful of food as they saw it as somehow 'other' but were also acutely aware of the need to grow and diversify. Cozzi reinforced this view by adding 'nothing is more familiar and domestic than food. Thus, the sheer mundanity of eating conceals deeply embedded power structures,'[23] suggesting that the lack of food, or fear of food being taken away, can be seen as a threat to domesticity or one's comfort zone, and the 'other' doesn't have to just be a fear of the unknown. Indeed, Scrooge himself is isolated and marginalised based on the gothic and food. He is 'othered' due to his inability to be involved in the convivial human process of sharing food, and his lack of interest in the commodity culture which had begun to permeate Victorian Britain. He also marginalises his self by refusing to have any diversity in this diet, his typical 'melancholy dinner in his usual melancholy tavern'[24] is juxtaposed with the later vivid descriptions of exotic abundant foods described in the market.

Even Scrooge's change of heart can be linked to allusions of food and beverage imagery, his frugal meal of 'gruel' is revisited when he has finished his lessons from the ghost, and this may inspire him straight after to ask the boy on the street to buy the big prize turkey hanging up at the poulterers, with the intention to send it to the Cratchits. The gruel is a symbol of Scrooge's former isolated and miserly self, as well as a sign of how economically solitary he has been when it comes to food and his immediate impulse to buy the biggest, most expensive item of food he can think of, is an attempt at compensating for it. The turkey is a symbol of his newfound pleasure in life, for human company and the economic and commercial consumption that was becoming associated with Christmas – which of course Scrooge had hitherto resisted. He can now allow himself to be seduced by the 'pears and apples, clustered high in blooming pyramids' and 'piles of filberts, mossy and brown.'[25] He has opened his heart to the joy that eating food with loved ones at Christmas can bring.

Food and the middle classes

For the middle classes in the 1800s, 'food touches everything and is the foundation of every economy, marking social differences, boundaries, bonds, and contradictions – an endlessly evolving enactment of gender, family and community relationships.'[26] Thomas M. Wilson builds on this idea by suggesting, 'both food and alcohol build and enhance peoples' senses of belonging and becoming, the twin bases to social identity.'[27] Therefore, at Christmas time, when families get together and form stronger bonds with their communities, food customs can strongly contribute to an imagined community,[28] which makes people feel more of a sense of fellowship and belonging to those around them. This food vocabulary can indicate the way in which particular groups identify themselves and become part of a shared culture.[29]

Food and power

Yet food was also associated with wealth and power, and the huge amount of food, which the Ghost of Christmas Present uses as a throne, 'turkeys, geese, game, poultry, brawn, great joints of meat, sucking-pigs, long wreaths of sausages, mince-pies, plum-puddings, barrels of oysters, red-hot chestnuts, cherry-cheeked apples, juicy oranges, luscious pears, immense twelfth-cakes, and seething bowls of punch,'[30] symbolises the gluttony that those who are wealthy at Christmas partake in, while those who have little may starve.

If food in *A Christmas Carol* is to be examined in Foucaultian terms of power discourses, we need to analyse food in the novella as something which circulates, rather than something that only functions in the form of a chain. This can certainly be demonstrated by the way that the food the Ghost of Christmas Present brings with him is used to form a throne, the seat of kings, who can exercise ultimate power over their subjects. This implies that those who possess it and need worry about it so little that they can sit upon it, hold dominion over those at the other side of the scale, with no thought for their sustenance or survival, in a grim act of gluttony and selfishness. Foucault also states that 'power is neither given, nor exchanged, nor recovered, but rather exercised and that it only exists in action.'[31] Whilst food does not exist only as an action, its symbolic power is complicated by the meanings we attach to our food, especially at Christmas. This includes the traditions of the turkey or goose and the plum pudding, which had come to symbolise Christmas itself – as much as the religious significance of the holiday.

As we see in the novella though, not everyone is given access to this wealth and abundance. The starving figures of Ignorance and Want, which peek out from the spirit's robe are 'wretched, abject, frightful, hideous, miserable,' they are:

> yellow, meagre, ragged, scowling, wolfish, but prostrate, too, in their humility. Where graceful youth should have filled their features out, and touched them with its freshest tints, a stale and shriveled hand, like that of age, had pinched, and twisted them, and pulled them into threads.[32]

Dry, shriveled and yellow skin are all signs of extreme starvation,[33] so to go back to Foucault, these children have had food as power put into action against them, where 'it incites, it induces, it seduces, it makes easier or more difficult; in the extreme it constrains or forbids absolutely.'[34]

Food as a symbol of commerce

It is useful to consider food as a power dynamic in the context of the Victorian era, as an Empire heavily concerned with commerce. The holiday feasts depicted in the novella became part of social consciousness and brought about changes in the eating habits of the nation. The scene of the Cratchit's Christmas dinner, with the goose whose 'tenderness and flavour, size and cheapness were themes of universal admiration,'[35] established domestic achievement, despite a lack of wealth and abundance as the true sign of a happy home. The Cratchits are delighted by their dinner, even though it is 'eked out by apple sauce,'[36] and food is used here as a symbol of family security.

Of course, a large portion of the British Empire may have recognised themselves in this portrayal as they reminisced on their own enjoyment of the holiday season, where they gathered with family to feast and enjoy the fruits of their labour. This dinner, which is witnessed in Scrooge's dreamlike state with the spirit, is replaced by the real dinner when Scrooge awakes from his strange slumber a changed man. The small yet succulent goose is replaced by the prize turkey and even eighteen years later, the influence of this on society could be seen when *Mrs Beeton's Book of*

Household Management claimed that 'a Christmas dinner, with the middle classes of this empire, would scarcely be a Christmas dinner without its turkey.'[37] The Cratchit's turkey then, not only changed the seasonal eating habits of the nation but also came to symbolise the rising middle-classes of the British Empire. With Scrooge's help, the Cratchits are going up in the world and their values of thrift, family happiness and personal betterment embodied not only the age but drove the British Empire.

Food and famine

Food, or lack of food, in *A Christmas Carol* also speaks to the national fear of famine. Moore states that 'starvation entered the print matter of Christmas first as part of a social argument and later as a concern for the abiding national identity that had become intertwined with Christmas itself.'[38]

Following a surge in the 1840s of seasonal books, stories and pamphlets which specifically taught about charity and benevolence, *Carol* carried a familiar message, which was similar to Jerrold's messages in *Punch* to an audience eager to placate its own feelings of guilt during a season in which indulgence and poverty clashed in both real life and print. It seems that Christmas literature in the 1840s often contained a rhetoric of social reform, 'specifically noblesse obliges, that urges the middle classes to reach out to the poor.'[39]

Dickens was not the only writer who chose this medium to impart a moral message, Henry and Augustus Mayhew also launched a scathing attack on the Corn Laws in the 1846 novel, *The Good Genius That Turned Everything into Gold or the Queen Bee and the Magic Dress: A Christmas Fairy Tale*.[40] These books have left memorable and visceral images attesting to the societal and political failures of the time – starvation among them. These images of hungry people seemed to haunt the imagination of the Victorians, and in J. Lhotsky's *On Cases of Death by Starvation and Extreme Distress among the Humbler Classes*,[41] the writer highlights the cruelty of Malthusian doctrine by exploring in great detail the medical descriptions of starvation and the physical suffering it brings. His accounts of the suffering of real life people are harrowing. He recounts newspaper reports about a mother who threw her starving month-old infant into a river when she could no longer nurse it, and a 'man who lay howling for six days in a manger of one of the lanes of London' until he was taken to a hospital and died.[42]

No doubt, these shocking accounts detail the extreme effects of poverty, but the signs of starvation would have been unavoidable for the middle-classes as it was all around them. Lhotsky estimates the number of beggars in London to be around 40,000, in 1844 when he wrote and published his book.[43] He described streets where there were '[d]rooping, emaciated half-naked men, lying on the steps of some church, or on the footpath, with the inscription in chalk, or on a bit of paper, 'I am starving.'[44] These moralistic tales highlighted how important food was to the Victorians, particularly at Christmas, when it was packaged as part of the commodification culture, but also illuminated the vast swathes of the population who were unable to feed themselves and their families – let alone partake in the feasting associated with the seasons.

Yet, Michelle Persell feels these books sometimes miss the mark. She states, 'the ethos of charity is dependent upon the unequal distribution of wealth, an economic state none of [Dickens's] Christmas books seriously seek to undo.'[45] In essence, rather than these stories helping to rework or quash class hierarchies and prevent future generations from suffering the same fate, they instead paint a nostalgic view where the middle and upper classes awaken their paternalistic fervour and aid the destitute for just one day a year. The scathing rhetoric in *Punch* also adopts this viewpoint, with articles about the workhouse reminding readers that 'Christian England' only feeds its poor one day out of the year.[46] In 1849, it almost seemed like *Punch* was inspired by the markets in the Ghost of Christmas Present's visitation, as they ran a poem called 'The Shops at Christmas' where the poet wrote about shops bursting with 'Crystal sugar, candied citron, clotted currants...' then contrasted with an account of a hungry family desperately trying to ignore the largesse displayed in the shop windows, as they know they could never taste its pleasures.[47]

Like many real life Londoners living in poverty, they were outsiders to the joyful tableaux of seasonal feasting around them and instead lived an existence on the margins of society. Again, we can revisit the images of Ignorance and Want here, as the juxtaposition of them against the Ghost of Christmas Present and his association with plenty, was a stark reminder to the reader of their moral obligations to help society's most vulnerable and desperate. But Moore believes their appearance is even more symbolic, as she posits, 'Want's public birthing process symbolizes Dickens's consistent Christmas argument that the starving are concealed just beneath the social patina of English middle-class institutions.'[48] They are easy to ignore throughout the year, until the Christmas season and its associated benevolence comes around, and we can bind our conscience for another year by opening our hearts for just this special time.

Food and identity

Not only is food associated with economics in *A Christmas Carol*, but it is also used a symbol of both class and ethnic identity. The Cratchits are a demonstrable example of this, when they signify that they are a loving family unit by staying at home together on Christmas morning to prepare the food together. Not only will this fulfil their physical need for sustenance, but it will also accomplish a spiritual need for closeness, love and a sense of belonging.[49] The feast they prepare is robust in its Englishness, comprising of the typical English food prepared at Christmas time. It is not unusual to people to use foods to 'demarcate their own...group,'[50] so it seems natural to associate the warm and flavourful food with the warmth and generosity of the Cratchit family and Scrooge's bowl of gruel with his pitiful, sallow personality.

Christmas tipples

What Christmas dinner is complete without a delicious beverage to serve alongside it? There are several beverages mentioned in the novella, but perhaps the most well remembered one comes from this extract in Stave Five:

> 'A merry Christmas, Bob!' said Scrooge, with an earnestness that could not be mistaken, as he clapped him on the back. 'A merrier Christmas, Bob, my good fellow, than I have given you, for many a year! I'll raise your salary, and endeavour to assist your struggling family, and we will discuss your affairs this very afternoon, over a Christmas bowl of smoking bishop, Bob!'[51]

According to The Victorian Web, bishop was a popular seasonal drink in taverns of the 1700 and 1800s and was defined in Johnson's *Dictionary* as 'a cant word for a mixture of wine, oranges, and sugar.'[52] Allegedly, the drink was a favourite of Charles Dickens' father, John Dickens,[53] and it received its name because of its purple colouring. In his middle and later life, Ackroyd claims that Dickens was not a great consumer of food and drink himself, but that instead he chose 'to participate in other people's enjoyment of what was laid before them rather than to have any pleasure in the good things himself.'[54] This enjoyment of the sentiment, rather than the thing is now beginning to be appreciated by Scrooge himself, who recognises that food is not just something which gives us fuel but it also gives us the fire and warmth of human companionship.

However, it seems that his numerous references to alcohol in his works led some members of the public to believe that he promoted drunkenness. In typical Dickensian pizazz and humour, he replied to a letter of complaint in 1847 intimating this with:

> I have no doubt whatever that the warm stuff in the jug at Bob Cratchit's Christmas dinner, had a very pleasant effect on the simple party. I am certain that if I had been at Mr. Fezziwig's ball, I should have taken a little negus – and possibly not a little beer – and been none the worse for it, in heart or head. I am very sure that the working people of this country have not too many household enjoyments, and I could not, in my fancy or in actual deed, deprive them of this one when it is so innocently shared.[55]

Like food, a pleasant beverage at Christmas time brings people together and seems a fitting reward for the hard work they've completed throughout the rest of the year. Scrooge finally realises this and begins to show his appreciation for his clerk through the commodities of food and drink. As we know from the closing words of the novella, Scrooge:

> did it all, and infinitely more; and to Tiny Tim, who did not die, he was a second father. He became as good a friend, as good a master, and as good a man, as the good old city knew, or any other good old city, town, or borough, in the good old world.[56]

Through his transformation, he was able to change his love shown through commodities, such as food and drink, to real love and care.

Summed up in six

- The Corn Laws, the Potato Famine and the Poor Laws all contributed to life being made incredibly difficult for those who were most vulnerable in society in the 1800s.

- Thomas Malthus FRS was an English cleric, scholar and economist, who believed an increase in a nation's food production improved the well-being of the population, but the improvement was temporary because it led to population growth, which did not help with the shortage of food. He criticised The Poor Laws for leading to inflation rather than improving the well-being of the poor and also supported The Corn Laws, as he felt it encouraged domestic production and would guarantee British self-sufficiency in food. Dickens fundamentally disagreed with him and argued that there was plenty to go round if the rich were more generous and shared their wealth.

- According to food historian, Pen Vogler, Dickens' wrote a lot about food as 'he knew what it was like to be hungry.' She claims that Dickens used food to create character and comedy but also to highlight social issues.

- Characters such as the Cratchits, who share food are portrayed as inherently good and pure and profess their emotions about food openly. Food and emotions are entwined in the novella.

- Many believe that the Christmas feast enjoyed by the Cratchits has set the template for the way we celebrate Christmas dinner today. It also emphasises the power of human connection that is so important – especially at Christmas time.

- Some critics have argued that the motif of food in Carol borders on the Gothic, in that the Gothic sometimes has a 'penchant for pleasure often simultaneous with pain. Scrooge himself is isolated and marginalised based on the gothic and food. He is 'othered' due to his inability to be involved in the convivial human process of sharing food and his lack of interest in the commodity culture which had begun to permeate Victorian Britain. Even his change of heart can be linked to allusions of food and beverage imagery, the gruel is a symbol of Scrooge's former isolated and miserly self, as well as a sign of how economically solitary he has been when it comes to food. The turkey is a symbol of his newfound pleasure in life, for human company and the economic and commercial consumption that was becoming associated with Christmas – which of course Scrooge had hitherto resisted.

Ideas for teaching

AO1 and AO2: Can you find any quotations in the text which show food and drink being used to exert power and show status?

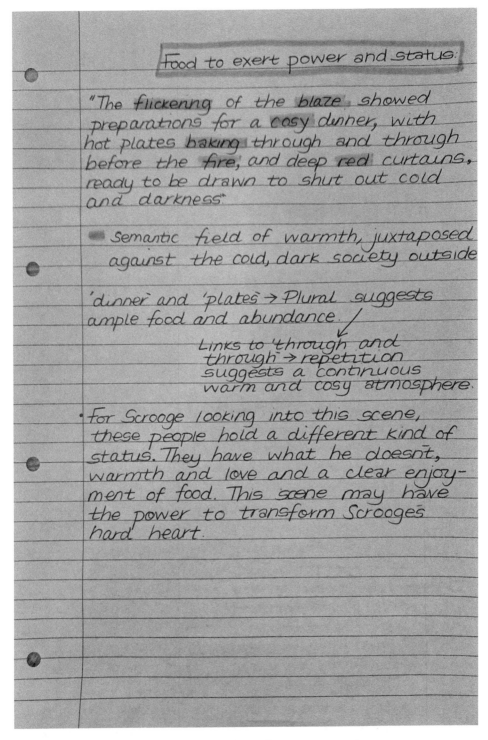

Food to exert power and status:

"The flickering of the blaze showed
preparations for a cosy dinner, with
hot plates baking through and through
before the fire, and deep red curtains,
ready to be drawn to shut out cold
and darkness."

■ Semantic field of warmth, juxtaposed
against the cold, dark society outside

'dinner' and 'plates' → Plural suggests
ample food and abundance. ✓

Links to 'through and
through' → repetition
suggests a continuous
warm and cosy atmosphere.

• For Scrooge looking into this scene,
these people hold a different kind of
status. They have what he doesn't,
warmth and love and a clear enjoyment of food. This scene may have
the power to transform Scrooge's
hard heart.

Figure 11.2 Quotes showing food and drink conferring power and status.

AO3: Explain how Dicken's background and childhood may have influenced his writing about food and starvation.

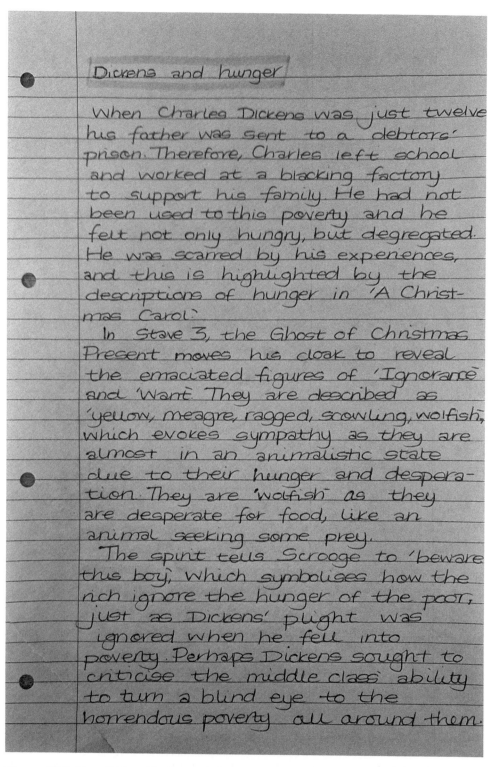

Dickens and hunger

When Charles Dickens was just twelve his father was sent to a 'debtors' prison. Therefore, Charles left school and worked at a blacking factory to support his family. He had not been used to this poverty and he felt not only hungry, but degregated. He was scarred by his experiences, and this is highlighted by the descriptions of hunger in 'A Christmas Carol.'

In Stave 3, the Ghost of Christmas Present moves his cloak to reveal the emaciated figures of 'Ignorance' and 'Want.' They are described as 'yellow, meagre, ragged, scowling, wolfish,' which evokes sympathy as they are almost in an animalistic state due to their hunger and desperation. They are 'wolfish' as they are desperate for food, like an animal seeking some prey.

The spirit tells Scrooge to 'beware this boy,' which symbolises how the rich ignore the hunger of the poor, just as Dickens' plight was ignored when he fell into poverty. Perhaps Dickens sought to criticise the middle class' ability to turn a blind eye to the horrendous poverty all around them.

Figure 11.3 How Dickens' background links to ideas about food and starvation.

Notes

1 David Ross, *Ireland: History of a Nation* (New Lanark: Geddes & Grosset, 2002).
2 Cormac Ó Gráda, *Ireland's Great Famine: Interdisciplinary perspectives* (Dublin: Dublin Press, 2006).
3 Thomas Malthus, *An Essay on the Principle of Population* (Oxfordshire, England: Oxford World's Classics, 2010).
4 Charles Dickens, *A Christmas Carol* (London: Wordsworth Classics, 2018), 14.
5 Pen Vogler, *Dinner with Dickens: Recipes inspired by the life and work of Charles Dickens* (London: CICO Books, 2017), 18.
6 Ibid.
7 Peter Ackroyd, *Dickens* (London: Vintage, 2002).
8 Ibid., 19.
9 Charles Dickens, *A Christmas Carol*, 56.
10 Mamie Dickens, 'Christmas Traditions – Christmas with Charles Dickens,' *Victoriana*, June 3, 2022, http://www.victoriana.com/christmas/dickenschristmas.htm.
11 Simon Callow, 'Charles Dickens and the Victorian Christmas Feast,' *The British Library*, June 3, 2022, https://www.bl.uk/romantics-and-victorians/articles/a-victorian-christmas-feast.
12 Simon Callow, 'Charles Dickens and the Victorian Christmas Feast.'
13 Ibid.
14 Francesca Orestano, Michael Vickers, *Not Just Porridge: English literati at table* (Oxford: Archaeopress, 2017).
15 Ian Watt, 'Oral Dickens,' *Dickens Studies Annual* 3 (1974), 174.
16 Charles Dickens, *A Christmas Carol*, 56.
17 Francesca Orestano, Michael Vickers, *Not Just Porridge*.
18 Charles Dickens, *A Christmas Carol*, 38.
19 Ibid., 46–47.
20 Ibid., 50.
21 Tara Moore, 'Starvation in Victorian Christmas Fiction,' *Victorian Literature and Culture* 36, no. 2 (2008): 489–505.
22 C. Dodworth, 'Fears of Consumption and Being Consumed: The gothicization of food in Victorian literature.' In: Piatti-Farnell, L. and Brien, D. L. (Eds.). *The Routledge Companion to Literature and Food* (1st ed.). (London: Routledge, 2018), 329.
23 Annette Cozzi, *The Discourses of Food in 19th Century British Fiction* (New York: Palgrave Macmillan, 2015), 4.
24 Charles Dickens, *A Christmas Carol*, 16.
25 Ibid., 50.
26 Ibid., 1.
27 T. M. Wilson, *Food, Drink and Identity in Europe: 22 (European Studies).* (Amsterdam: Rodopi, 2006), 6.
28 Benedict Anderson, *Imagined Communities: Reflections on the origin and spread of nationalism* (London: Verso Books, 2006).
29 Theresa M. Kostelc, 'Lessons in Acquisition: How domestic instruction for women shapes the middle-class,' *Pro Quest*, June 8, 2022, https://www.proquest.com/docview/520410562?pq-origsite=gscholar&fromopenview=true.
30 Charles Dickens, *A Christmas Carol*, 50.
31 Michael Foucault, *History of Sexuality Volume I* (New York: Random House, 1978), 93.
32 Charles Dickens, *A Christmas Carol*, 68.

33 Renata Strumia, 'Skin Signs in Anorexia Nervosa,' *Dermatoendocrinol* 1, no. 5 (September-October 2009): 268–270.

34 Michael Foucault, *History of Sexuality*, 220.

35 Charles Dickens, *A Christmas Carol*, 56.

36 Ibid.

37 Isabella Mary Beeton, 'Mrs Beeton's Book of Household Management,' *Project Gutenberg*, June 22, 2022, https://www.gutenberg.org/cache/epub/10136/pg10136.html.

38 Tara Moore, 'Starvation in Victorian Christmas Fiction,' *Victorian Literature and Culture 36*, no. 2 (2008), 489.

39 Ibid.

40 Henry Mayhew, Augustus Mayhew, *The Good Genius That Turned Everything into Gold or the Queen Bee and the Magic Dress: A Christmas Fairy Tale* (London: David Bogue, 1847).

41 John Lhotsky, (1844) *On Cases of Death by Starvation and Extreme Distress among the Humbler Classes, Considered as One of the Main Symptoms of the Present Disorganization of Society* (London: John Olivier, 1844).

42 Ibid., 23.

43 Ibid.

44 Ibid., 19.

45 Michelle Persell, 'Dickensian Disciple: Anglo- Jewish Identity in the Christmas Tales of Benjamin Farjeon,' *Philological Quarterly* 73 (Autumn 1994), 453.

46 George R. Sims, 'Christmas Day in the Workhouse,' *Punch* 45 (1863): 257.

47 Punch, 'The Shops at Christmas,' *Punch* 17 (1849), 25.

48 Tara Moore, 'Starvation in Victorian Christmas Fiction,' 496.

49 Don Richard Cox, Elliot L. Gilbert, 'Scrooge's Conversion,' *PMLA* 90, no. 5 (October 1975): 922–924.

50 Peter Scholliers, 'Meals, Food Narratives, and Sentiments of Belonging in Past and Present,' In: Peter Scholliers (Ed.) *Food, Drink, and Identity: Cooking, Eating, and Drinking in Europe Since the Middle Ages* (New York: Berg, 2001), 8.

51 Charles Dickens, *A Christmas Carol*, 93.

52 Samuel Johnson, *A Dictionary of the English Language* (London: Consortium, 1755), 82.

53 Philip V. Allingham, 'Charles Dickens and Two Kinds of Punch,' *The Victorian Web*, June 28, 2022, https://victorianweb.org/authors/dickens/pva/pva40.html.

54 Peter Ackroyd, *Dickens*, 248.

55 Charles Dickens, Walter Dexter (Ed.), *The Letters of Charles Dickens: The Nonesuch Dickens* (London: The Nonesuch Press, 1938), 20–21.

56 Charles Dickens, *A Christmas Carol*, 93.

References

Peter Ackroyd, *Dickens* (London: Harper Collins, 1990).

Peter Ackroyd, *Dickens* (London: Vintage, 2002).

Philip V. Allingham, 'Charles Dickens and Two Kinds of Punch,' *The Victorian Web*, (June 28, 2022), https://victorianweb.org/authors/dickens/pva/pva40.html

Benedict Anderson, *Imagined Communities: Reflections on the origin and spread of nationalism* (London: Verso, 2006).

Isabella Mary Beeton, 'Mrs Beeton's Book of Household Management.,' *Project Gutenberg*, (June 22, 2022), https://www.gutenberg.org/cache/epub/10136/pg10136.html

Simon Callow, 'Charles Dickens and the Victorian Christmas Feast,' *The British Library*, (June 3, 2022), https://www.bl.uk/romantics-and-victorians/articles/a-victorian-christmas-feast

Carole Counihan, *Food and Culture: A reader* (London: Routledge, 2012).

Don Richard Cox, Elliot L. Gilbert, 'Scrooge's Conversion,' *PMLA* 90, no. 5 (October 1975): 922–924. https://doi.org/10.2307/461477

Annette Cozzi, *The Discourses of Food in 19th Century British Fiction* (New York: Palgrave Macmillan, 2015).

Charles Dickens, *A Christmas Carol* (London: Wordsworth Classics, 2018).

Charles Dickens, Walter Dexter (Ed.), *The Letters of Charles Dickens: The Nonesuch Dickens* (London: The Nonesuch Press, 1938).

Mamie Dickens, 'Christmas Traditions – Christmas with Charles Dickens,' *Victoriana*, (June 3, 2022), http://www.victoriana.com/christmas/dickenschristmas.htm

Michael Foucault, *History of Sexuality Volume I* (New York: Random House, 1978).

Samuel Johnson, *A Dictionary of the English Language* (London: Consortium, 1755).

Theresa M. Kostelc, 'Lessons in Acquisition: How domestic instruction for women shapes the middle-class,' *Pro Quest*, (June 8, 2022), https://www.proquest.com/docview/52041 0562?pq-origsite=gscholar&fromopenview=true

John Lhotsky, (1844) *On Cases of Death by Starvation and Extreme Distress among the Humbler Classes, Considered as One of the Main Symptoms of the Present Disorganization of Society* (London: John Olivier, 1844).

Thomas Malthus, *An Essay on the Principle of Population* (Oxfordshire, England: Oxford World's Classics, 2010).

Henry Mayhew, Augustus Mayhew, *The Good Genius That Turned Everything into Gold or the Queen Bee and the Magic Dress: A Christmas fairy tale* (London: David Bogue, 1847).

Tara Moore, 'Starvation in Victorian Christmas Fiction,' *Victorian Literature and Culture* 36, no. 2 (2008): 489–505. https://www.jstor.org/stable/40347201

Cormac Ó Gráda, *Ireland's Great Famine: Interdisciplinary Perspectives* (Dublin: Dublin Press, 2006).

Francesca Orestano, Michael Vickers, *Not Just Porridge: English literati at table* (Oxford: Archaeopress, 2017).

Michelle Persell, 'Dickensian Disciple: Anglo- Jewish identity in the Christmas tales of Benjamin Farjeon,' *Philological Quarterly* 73 (Autumn 1994): 451–468. https://www.jstor.org/stable/40347201

Punch, 'The Shops at Christmas' *Punch* 17 (1849), 25.

David Ross, *Ireland: History of a Nation* (New Lanark: Geddes & Grosset, 2002).

Peter Scholliers, 'Meals, Food Narratives, and Sentiments of Belonging in Past and Present,' In Peter Scholliers (Ed.) *Food, Drink, and Identity: Cooking, eating, and drinking in Europe Since the Middle Ages* (New York: Berg, 2001).

George R. Sims, 'Christmas Day in the Workhouse,' *Punch* 45 (1863): 257.

Renata Strumia, 'Skin Signs in Anorexia Nervosa,' *Dermatoendocrinol* 1, no. 5 (September-October 2009): 268–270. DOI: 10.4161/derm.1.5.10193

Pen Vogler, *Dinner with Dickens: Recipes inspired by the life and work of Charles Dickens* (London: CICO Books, 2017).

Ian Watt, 'Oral Dickens,' *Dickens Studies Annual* 3 (1974), 165–181. https://www.jstor.org/stable/44372321

12 Suffer the little children: The depictions of children in *A Christmas Carol*: How does Dickens portray children in *A Christmas Carol*?

Dickens may have been somewhat of a social reformer, but he was also incredibly astute about the best way of getting his hard-hitting missives across to the masses. Therefore, he wrapped up his opinions on the shortcomings in society, and the divide between rich and poor in the shiny wrapping of an entertaining Christmas story. The ribbon on top of it meant that readers were then invited to construct their own understandings about what society was lacking. That Dickens disapproved of the cruel treatment of children in the 1800s is widely known. In fact, his campaigning and coverage of the plight of the poor Victorian child has led one critic to pronounce him as 'one of the most effective advocates for children' and that he 'probably did more than any other author to raise public awareness of the plight of children, laying the groundwork for a variety of social reforms.'[1] Consultant paediatrician Patricia Brennan reinforces this by referring to *Oliver Twist* as a 'textbook of child abuse,'[2] where through his astonishing perceptiveness, Dickens is able to hold a magnifying glass over the plight of children and bring them into the wider public consciousness.

Through Bob Cratchit's son, Tiny Tim, a small disabled boy, Dickens prompts his readers, and indeed his protagonist Scrooge, into feeling empathy and compassion towards not just children but also the entire underprivileged population. In addition to this, he confronts the upper classes with their lack of charity, and the insufficiency of the government's welfare system. Through Scrooge's questions to the two portly gentlemen, who are collecting for charity, 'Are there no prisons?...And the Union workhouses?' and 'The Treadmill and the Poor Law are in full vigour, then?'[3] Dickens makes his disdain for such solutions clear here, through the disgust and disdain that the reader already feels for Scrooge. Of course, it wasn't only poor

DOI: 10.4324/9781003453468-13

men and women who lived in workhouses; entire families, as well as orphaned children did too – by 1839, almost half of the workhouse's population were children. In the *Poor Law Handbook of the Poor Law Officer's Journal*, it stated:

> The care and training of children are matters which should receive the anxious attention of Guardians. Pauperism in the blood, and there is no more effectual means of checking its hereditary nature by doing all in our power to bring up our pauper children in such a manner as to make them God-fearing, useful and healthy members of society.[4]

How the Guardians in the workhouse made the child inmates more 'useful' and 'God-fearing' is well documented. As soon as they entered the workhouse, families were separated and deprived of a family life and the presence of their parents, where they sometimes only saw each other at mealtimes or in the chapel, where they were unable to speak.[5] For a largely Christian society, it was hardly subscribing to Jesus' teachings in the New Testament to 'Suffer little children, and forbid them not, to come unto me: for of such is the kingdom of heaven.'[6]

Education

But for some poor children in the workhouse, there were some education opportunities. Under the 1934 Act, it was a requirement for children to be educated for at least three hours a day, during which time a schoolmaster or mistress would teach reading, writing, arithmetic and the principles of Christianity, to make them fit for service, usefulness, industry and virtue. However, records show that some workhouse Guardians saw this as a waste of time and money and that there was little point in these types of children being taught to read.[7] It was this attitude of certain parts of society being unworthy of education that Dickens sought to change, as he:

> proposed schooling and religious education for these poor children, because those who live in filth will not see any hope and they will no longer have faith and believe in God. But giving them access to education and religion will give them the prospect of surviving and eventually overcoming their hardships.[8]

He took a particular interest in education, especially in the way pauper children were catered for, as he recognised that it had the potential to transform their lives. In the poverty stricken and crime ridden streets of London, the dregs of the population had 'minds and bodies destitute of proper nutriment'[9] and a 'good education could be the bulwark against ignorance, cyclical poverty and crime.'[10]

Dickens' own experiences

Although there are no specific mentions of children in the workhouse or explicit descriptions of child cruelty in *A Christmas Carol*, unlike some of Dickens' other novels, the messages about children may be more subtle, but they are almost certainly there. The exploitative nature of child labour isn't explored, although we know that some of Bob's children are set to work to contribute to the family's economic survival. Martha works long hours at a stretch and Peter will also soon be put to work.

Dickens himself had to work as a child. He was abruptly plunged into poverty in 1822 when the growing Dickens family moved back to London to the less salubrious area of Camden Town. His father, John, had an unfortunate propensity for living beyond his means, which resulted in him being thrown into debtor's prison in 1824 at the infamous Marshalsea prison in Southwark. The rest of the family, including Dickens' mother, joined him at Marshalsea, but the 12-year-old Charles was sent to work in Warren's blacking warehouse, where he spent 10 hours a day pasting labels onto pots of shoe polish for 6 shillings a week, which went towards his family's debts and his own modest lodgings. The Dickens family were able to settle their debts after John's grandmother Elizabeth gave an inheritance to them, and Charles was finally able to go back to school at the Wellington House Academy in North London.

However, the plight of the poor and the inhumane working conditions that he had experienced at such a young age never left Dickens, so the portrayal of children in his works – including in *A Christmas Carol*, was very much inspired by his own experiences and the things he had seen. The focus of the philanthropy, which played a large part in his adult life, was to have made a lasting impression.

Ignorance and Want

Most of the children we meet in *A Christmas Carol* play bit parts or are there in the background, but there are three children in particular who stand out: Tiny Tim, and Ignorance and Want – the two filthy children who hide under the cloak of the Ghost of Christmas Present. To start with, Ignorance and Want, whom Scrooge is warned to be wary of, their bedraggled and destitute appearance shocks Scrooge and he asks the spirit if they belong to him. The spirit replies, 'They are Man's [...] This boy is Ignorance. This girl is Want.'[11] Scrooge shrinks away when he is told that he needs to be wary of the boy because he perhaps realises that these characters are allegorical and symbolise mankind's ignorance and even more importantly, his own ignorance about the plight of poor children. He implores the spirit, 'Have they no refuge or resource?'[12] but instead of giving him some comfort, the spirit repeats Scrooge's earlier sentiments, 'Are there no workhouses?'[13] When Scrooge is confronted with his former words, accompanied by the reality of the poverty that helpless children face, he has his eyes opened to what is really happening to innocent people, and the seeds for repentance are sowed. The two children, Ignorance and Want, represent British society's worst traits: the demand for having more and more that most people feel is Want, while Ignorance mirrors the unawareness, but also carelessness, in regard to the poor population and the impact of such abandonment within society.

The symbolic associations of the boy Ignorance tells us much about the behaviour of Scrooge. Throughout the novella, he displays many different types of ignorance, including of the world, of society, of religious society and of love and relationships. Indeed, when Jacob Marley visits Scrooge he tells him he needs to be less ignorant of the world and that 'the spirit within him should walk abroad among his fellow-men, and travel far and wide' to see how other men are living, and, 'if that spirit goes not forth in life, it is condemned to do so after death.'[14] The warning here is clear, if Scrooge does not open his eyes to the plight of the poor and show some compassion, he will pay for it in his afterlife and be forced into a kind of purgatory, where he walks the earth forever, faced with the suffering of mankind. He is also ignorant of the desperation that poor people feel, as is demonstrated by the theft of his curtains and other personal possessions by his staff. With the threat of starvation, anyone is capable of theft. But in addition, Scrooge also seems completely ignorant of religious society; his disrespectful dismissal of Christmas as a Christian holiday, which he sees as 'humbug'[15] and perhaps the naming of the male child also has religious significance.

The largely Christian society of the 1800s might have heard missives in church on a Sunday, which talked about truth. Truth as a revelation of things that man can never discover from any other source than the Scriptures and therefore an assumption, that those who wilfully neglect the Scriptures or question or reject them, are ignorant. Scrooge seems to be entirely agnostic, as the definition of an agnostic is somebody who lives by the 'doctrine that humans cannot know of the existence of anything beyond the phenomena of their experience.'[16] He doesn't seem to really know or care about the existence of poor people or the widespread poverty which was evident all around him. There are also many references to the ignorance of man in the Old and New Testaments, but one in particular resonates with the character of Scrooge and those gentlemen like him, which seemed to dominate Victorian society, 'They are darkened in their understanding, alienated from the life of God because of the ignorance that is in them, due to their hardness of heart.'[17] This is Scrooge in a nutshell really, so perhaps Ignorance is male as he represents the ignorance of men like Scrooge and indeed mankind.

Ignorance's female counterpart, Want, with her 'Yellow, meagre, ragged, scowling, wolfish'[18] appearance again has religious significance. She may be symbolic of the Old Testament's enduring icon of Eve, whose sin of wanting the apple from the forbidden tree, cast Adam and all mankind with him, out of paradise. She also symbolises the characteristics of Scrooge, who prioritises 'want' over human relationships and encounters. After all, right near the beginning of the novella, we learn that his grip on his purse strings was so tight that he couldn't spare more than a single coal to warm his own office. Of course, 'want' is not only a negative feeling, the longing for more equality or the need to change can be a more positive mode of wanting. Indeed, we see this in Scrooge himself, when he wants another chance and implores the spirit, '"Spirit!" he cried, tight clutching at its robe, "hear me! I am not the man I was. I will not be the man I must have been but for this intercourse. Why show me this, if I am past all hope?'"[19]

After his lessons from the spirits, he now wants a second chance at life, so perhaps Dickens' message here is that we need to want the right things and eschew the greed of commodities, in order for things in society to really change. But why did Dickens choose to impart this hugely important message through children? Well, perhaps he recognised that most people will have more sympathy for children rather than adults, and it is the children in the novella who are able to break through Scrooge's icy exterior and warm his heart. But these metaphors in turn stretch to adulthood, as we are told that we need to 'beware this boy, for on his brow I see that written which is Doom, unless the writing be erased.'[20] So, these children will be destined to a future of struggle and poverty, their future is literally written on their foreheads, due to the unfortunate conditions they were born into. Just as Scrooge is the person he is because of his childhood and relationship with his father, these children will find it difficult to leave behind the poverty they have grown up in.

Tiny Tim

The other significant child, Tiny Tim, has a profound effect on Scrooge. Like many children of the time, Tim had a disability, and Kryger spoke about how common it was to encounter children who bore 'the countenances of old men, deformities with irons upon their limbs, boys of stunted growth, and others whose long meagre legs would hardly bear their stooping bodies.'[21] Dickens's novels confronted the reader with the reality of not only the poor, but also of ill people, particularly children. Kryger also explains that Dickens was usually very explicit in describing medical conditions that his characters suffered from and that perhaps helps to build sympathy and empathy in the reader.

Although Tiny Tim was probably suffering from the common condition of tuberculosis,[22] it was still associated with a high mortality rate and also sadly elicited suspicion from some sections of society, who were prejudicial against the 'lame.'[23] Yet despite this, Tiny Tim is a happy child and is also incredibly astute for his young age. He perceives that he is not entirely accepted by society, and Bob tells his wife that Tim said, 'he hoped that people saw him in the church, because he was a cripple, and it might be pleasant to them to remember upon Christmas Day, who made lame beggars walk and blind men see.'[24] Tim's pure heart wins Scrooge's and he asks the spirit if the child will survive the next year and the spirit replies that he most likely will not.

So, when Scrooge revisits the Cratchit family with the Ghost of Christmas Yet to Come and Tim is not there, the responsibility for his potential death is almost too much to bear. Here Dickens levels the daring accusation that the wealthy are responsible for deaths within the lower classes through their failure to help them and improve their living conditions. Interestingly, Dickens did practice what he preached in his literary work, in his real life and he supported the establishment of a children's hospital in London in 1858 and gave readings of *A Christmas Carol* to help raise funds, while giving a speech to appeal to the upper class sponsors to support the hospital in any way.[25] His support of the hospital perhaps came from the fact that his night walks through London illuminated the plight of sick, poor children and saw first-hand how they were affected by poverty and disease.[26] By highlighting the conditions caused by poverty, and 'wringing people's hearts, it got something done in the end.'[27] Carter concludes that the character of Tiny Tim enables Dickens to explicitly show the connection and relationship between poverty and disease and through this, he manages to prompt the nation into consciously acknowledging the issues that society had so far been happy to ignore.[28]

Carol is not just a story about Scrooge needing to change, but is a warning that every single member of society needs to redeem themselves; like Scrooge, they need to be reawakened 'I'm quite a baby. Never mind. I don't care. I'd rather be a baby.'[29] Scrooge develops a new, child-like innocence towards Christmas and life, becoming a generous and benevolent person, and again, the child is used as a symbol of innocence here, of all that is good in the world. We are encouraged to be more like him and open our hearts to those who are less fortunate, with the generosity and enthusiasm that children naturally possess.

Children and hunger

As has been explored in other chapters of this book, Dickens wrote often of food, and Hardy noted he 'loves feasts and scorns fasts…eating and drinking are valued by him as proofs of sociability and gusto, but more important still, as ceremonies of love.'[30] So, if feeding someone is to be seen as an act of love, then starvation is seen as act of abuse. The lack of nourishment for Dickens' fictional children plays a significant role in their childhood – especially Pip in *Great Expectations*, Oliver Twist and David Copperfield.

In *Carol* we see the Cratchits eking out their dinner to make it go around their considerably sized family, and the description of Ignorance and Want, 'Where graceful youth should have filled their features out, and touched them with its freshest tints, a stale and shrivelled hand, like that of age, had pinched, and twisted them, and pulled them into threads.'[31] This can be read as a description of starvation, as they have no plumpness, instead their sallow skin is hollowed out and shrivelled, making them old before their time. Burgan claims that this is an example of Dickens' view that 'the worst cases of child starvation were likely when the institutional dogmas – inspired by either religious doctrine or social penury – invaded the private home.'[32]

Dickens rejected the use of food for moral instruction and social control,[33] and this is made clear by the shock felt by Scrooge when he laid eyes upon the starved and meagre flesh of Ignorance and Want. The children are without a mother and instead, huddle under the phantom's cloak for warmth. Kaplan claims that in many of Dickens' novels, the woman is 'the nurturer-protector but...also has the potential to be the vehicle of deprivation.'[34] Just like Dickens' relationship with his own mother, which was complicated, the failure of the mother here to nurture and protect could be symbolic of society's neglect of the lower-class child. In many portrayals of mothers in his works, he seemed to delight in making mothers suffer – which critics have seen as a desire to wreak revenge on his own mother, whose love for him failed to meet his needs.[35]

He had similar opinions of his wife Catherine, and in the famous letter he wrote to explain his separation from her, he hinted that she lacked a maternal instinct, hinting that she employed a wet nurse and foisted her children on somebody else.[36] In *Carol* he wants society to suffer, which is why his grotesque descriptions of the children aim to shock an apathetic middle-class into action.

The imperfect child

There has been much written on the binaries between the Romantic and the deprived, socially unredeemable child in Victorian literature. Dickens seems to be most drawn towards creating a construct of the imperfect child, and examples can be seen in *The Old Curiosity Shop, Oliver Twist, Bleak House* and of course, in *A Christmas Carol*. Dickens 'uses the child protagonist throughout his work both to indicate the influences society and culture have on children and to show how this, in turn, affects society and culture.'[37] The children in the novella and the struggles they face play upon the readers' conscience and emotions; the sympathy they evoke illuminates the difficulties they face in the harsh social and cultural conditions of the Victorian era. The children in question are imperfect because they have been tarnished by their social and cultural conditions, but some of them seem ever hopeful, such as Tiny Tim, who radiates love and positivity, despite his condition.

These characters act as a projection of Dickens' own struggles but also highlight the rise in social and cultural consciousness regarding the plight of the poor, which was improving due to 'the rise in literacy, journalism, literature, and many other mediums.'[38] Victorian culture was not perfect, and like the imperfect child, who was often ignored by society, the Victorians often ignored the problems of their own period. But as the era progressed, so too did the image of the child – away from the value of the physical contributions they could make in the dark satanic mills of the industrial revolution, to the emotional ones. Childhood rather became something that should be cherished and preserved.

In her essay, 'Dickens for Children,' Margaret Hodges explained that an overarching memory of her childhood was an annual reading of *A Christmas Carol* and how this permeated into her own routine as a mother, many years later. She felt that it had universal appeal as Dickens 'makes us see what he had seen as a child and remembered as a man.'[39] While our memories of childhood may dissipate as we grow older, it is the nostalgia of treasured characters like Tiny Tim that make us remember certain elements of our own histories with fondness, and to feel a sense of guilt that some children may have not been as lucky.

Ethical considerations

As we have discussed, Dickens did not shy away from such depictions of unhappy and mistreated children in his work, and readers were continually exposed to harrowing scenes of suffering; children in pain seemed to evoke pity and provoke the most response from the reader. Such depictions perhaps existed in order to reproach the world and its inhabitants who sanctioned it. Langbauer claimed that:

> their thunderous denunciations damn the morals around them without necessarily claiming moral high ground, without obscuring their own involvement, complicity, guilt. These works empathize with the impossible contradictions people must negotiate in their relations to one another, and yet they don't let us off the hook because of that either.[40]

Consequently, Dickens' depictions of children in *Carol* are surrounded by ethical considerations. They encourage readers to take part in an exploration of their own moral dilemmas and to examine and critique our own choices. Indeed, the very fact that Tim is described as 'Tiny' makes it seem like he is need of our care, but we hear that he is stared at in church for seeming abnormal and imperfect. This contrast between the way we should behave and the way we actually do is a constant source of ethical dilemma, and this reflects the way Scrooge feels when he is faced with Ignorance and Want. He thinks that they must be children, and yet, he's not sure, as they seem more like monsters perhaps, or demons, pinched and wizened old men. They are the antipathy of everything he thinks childlike: 'where graceful youth should have filled their features out, and touched them with its freshest tints,'[41] he sees degradation.

Their metaphorical status makes them seem even more unworldly and un-childlike. Unlike when Scrooge sees his former child self, alone in his school at Christmas time, he does not feel an immediate sense of connection and empathy. This is because the child he sobs for, his former self, he still recognises as being within him. His ignorance of children, and inability even to see them, except as some shadow of himself, may be the path to man's doom. It seems that Dickens had been reading 'parliamentary bluebooks about the horrors of child labour before he began *A Christmas Carol*.'[42]

Dickens' own childhood

While there is no direct representation of child labour in the novella, this could be a deliberate choice, as when discussing his own time as a child labourer, Dickens often referred to the invisible plight of the child. It is clear from his friend Forster's biography of him that he was haunted by how powerless he felt during this most vulnerable of times. He described a memory where he was sat behind a plate glass window as a living advertisement for shoe polish and had attracted quite a crowd when his father entered the shop, and he wondered how he could bare everybody staring at his son while he worked. Both his father and the other adults around him seemed completely oblivious to his suffering, 'that I suffered in secret, and that I suffered exquisitely, no one ever knew but I. How much I suffered, it is… utterly beyond my power to tell. No man's imagination can overstep the reality.'[43] This feeling that his suffering and agony should have been visible to the people who cared about him never left Dickens, and children in his books became almost a poignant symbol of how we can allow our own self-absorptions to blind us and they may even lead us to mistreat others as well. In *Carol* Scrooge forgot his own suffering as a child, '"strange to have forgotten it for so many years!" observed the Ghost.'[44]

Representing children's suffering forces us to regard it, rather than to screen ourselves from such disturbing images. Langbauer suggests that this is also perhaps why the Ghost of Christmas Past is forced to extinguish his light and 'dim the clarity of the pictures of the past—including lonely miserable children—he wishes to show us.'[45] It is just too distressing. But if Scrooge and society do not confront the truth about children's suffering, then the whole message behind the novella becomes self-defeating. We need to see it in all its grotesque depravity – as does Scrooge himself and no matter how hard he 'pressed it down with all his force, he could not hide the light.'[46] The figures of children are so effective as a rhetorical device that the shock of their depictions shakes the reader into action, and forces us to take responsibility for the construction of the way we want society to be.

Victorian culture and children

The release of *A Christmas Carol* coincided with a wider reform of the Victorian's ideas of self and state.[47] The patriarchal model of the monarch having the authority of a father over the family was eroding, and ideas about the welfare of the individual family being linked inextricably with the state were becoming more popular. This meant a more public consideration of the guardianship of England's children, where the domain of the previously private home was now more subject to other authorities, such as the legal system, social welfare, medical establishments or education. It seems that childhood and the child had become public categories, and according to Katharina Boehm,[48] children were routinely said to be the victims of an uncaring society, which was obsessed with progress.

This sparked a public discourse that stressed the need to protect children, which focused on doing things for the 'best interests' of the child, such as philanthropist Jonas Hanaway's efforts to highlight the dangerous practices of chimney sweeping and attempts to regulate apprenticeships.[49] This came from a movement in the last 1700s which began to view childhood in more Constructivist terms. J. H. Plumb suggested that 'the child is no longer viewed as the miniature adult, but rather as an essentially different and discrete biological and social category.'[50] This resulted in what Aries labelled as a movement towards children being more associated with traits such as innocence and naturalness.[51]

Although this reconfiguration of childhood may have come from Romantic culture, writing about Victorian children is different, as it focuses more on their physical wellbeing, often casting the child as a victim. This is certainly the version of the child we see in *A Christmas Carol* and many of Dickens' other works. In fact, in Berry's *The Child, the State, and the Victorian Novel*,[52] she claims that these stories of victimised children were circulated as part of a wider longing for social reform. These dramatised depictions of childhood cruelty often played into the ideas of the old fashioned child[53] who had more of the ways of knowing or behaving which would be associated with adults. This quality was defined by Adye as an introspectiveness and reflectiveness beyond their years which combines with a natural sweetness.[54] This can certainly be seen as the case for Tiny Tim, whom Bob tells us 'gets thoughtful, sitting by his self so much' and he 'hoped the people saw him in the church, because he was a cripple, and it might be pleasant to them to remember upon Christmas Day, who made lame beggars walk, and blind men see.'[55] This ability to look beyond his own suffering belies his young age and evokes our pity, respect and admiration.

Gavin adds that Dickens also 'contributed to both realist portrayals of childhood – which critiqued social and cultural systems that fail to understand and accommodate children – and fantasy "depictions of the angelic child as too good for this fallen world."'[56] Again, this is a category that certainly Tiny Tim could have been seen as belonging to. His pure behaviour and personality make him seem almost angelic. If Tiny Tim is in this category, then the children Ignorance and Want are more like the products of hell, or a fallen world. They can be linked to Blake's ideas of experience, opposing the innocence of Tiny Tim. Childhood as a lived experience, complete with homelessness, poverty and cruelty for these children has aged and decayed them. Tiny Tim may be poor, but he lives within the caring bosom of his family, whose love protects him from the savagery of society.

Dickens as the inventor of a new kind of childhood

Some critics have even argued that Dickens reconfigured childhood through Christmas texts published alongside the industrialisation and global capitalism of the time. Saltmarsh[57] states that children in *Carol* are vulnerable, as their access to both financial and symbolic capital is limited by the vagaries of an adult world. Indeed, there is this clear motif in all the visions Scrooge is shown by the apparitions. First in the figure of Scrooge himself, the lonely and abandoned schoolboy who becomes a young apprentice. Then in the emaciated forms of Ignorance and Want, who cower under the spirit's robes. Notably also in the crippled form of Tiny Tim, the son of Scrooge's clerk. Each of these children live in conditions which have been cruelly imposed on them by the adult world: loneliness, starvation and poverty. They are vulnerable and powerless to intervene in either the political or economic circumstances in which they find themselves, as both victims and inheritors of a broken social system. Through the novella, Dickens implies that the only hope these children have, is that the privileged males who decide their fate will make more moral choices. Scrooge is representative of these privileged males, who must simultaneously confront and alter their attitudes.

As this chapter is about children, it seems apt to end it with a last exploration of Ignorance and Want. Brandon Chitwood claims that they are figures of horror, not pathos, who are meant to chill the blood, not warm the heart.[58] There are claims that the children were based on Dickens' visit to a 'ragged school' in Field Lane,[59] which inspired a speech a few weeks later that Dickens made in Manchester where he stated that 'ignorance itself was the most prolific parent of misery and crime.'[60] In essence, it seems Dickens believed that ignorance was at the heart of many social evils, as he is more concerned about the lack of education for children than about the work that they do.[61] His novella then, attempts to appeal to the recent reconfiguration of thoughts about childhood and the longing for state intervention, to open up the eyes of the privileged to the suffering of children – something which he does with the evocative portrayal of children throughout the text.

Summed up in six

- Dickens did a great deal to raise awareness about the plight of children and laid the groundwork for a variety of different social reforms.

- He took a particular interest in how pauper children were educated and believed that education had the power to change poor children's lives.

- His own childhood and the shame and embarrassment he felt when polishing shoes with an audience fed into his concerns.

- Ignorance and Want are important child characters as they represent society's sins and warn of the danger of what may happen if mankind does not change their ways. These children will find it almost impossible to escape the poverty they have experienced.

- The character of Tiny Tim is also significant as it allows Dickens to demonstrate the parallels between poverty and disease. He can be seen as an angelic child, who is too good for this world, or an old-fashioned child, whose wisdom belies his years.

- This depiction of children came at a time when society was beginning to see children differently, not as little adults but as distinct entities who were more innocent and natural. Society began to see more involvement from the state, so the depictions of children in the novella feed into a wider call for more social reforms.

Ideas for teaching

AO1: Explore how Dickens' depiction of children in *A Christmas Carol* emphasises his intention to shock the Victorian audience into action.

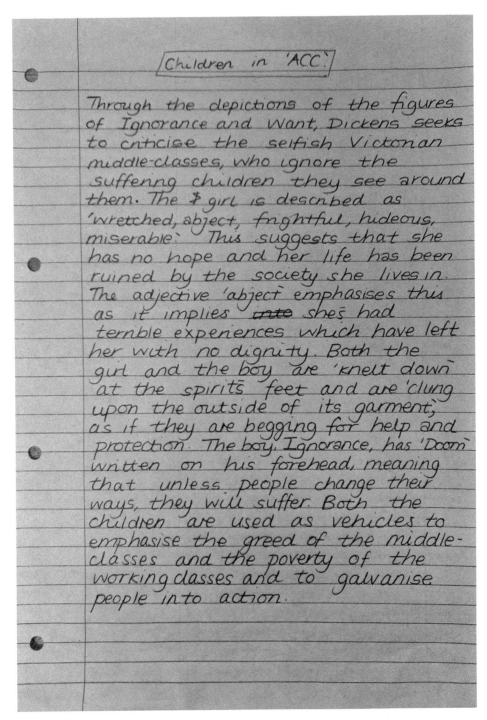

Children in 'ACC'

Through the depictions of the figures of Ignorance and Want, Dickens seeks to criticise the selfish Victorian middle-classes, who ignore the suffering children they see around them. The girl is described as 'wretched, abject, frightful, hideous, miserable.' This suggests that she has no hope and her life has been ruined by the society she lives in. The adjective 'abject' emphasises this as it implies she's had terrible experiences which have left her with no dignity. Both the girl and the boy are 'knelt down' at the spirits' feet and are 'clung upon the outside of its garment,' as if they are begging for help and protection. The boy, Ignorance, has 'Doom' written on his forehead, meaning that unless people change their ways, they will suffer. Both the children are used as vehicles to emphasise the greed of the middle-classes and the poverty of the working classes and to galvanise people into action.

Figure 12.1 Analytical paragraph on authorial intention and children's depictions.

AO3: Research how society viewed children in the 1800s. As a novella which was written in the middle of the century, how do the portrayals of children in *Carol* fit with society's changing perceptions?

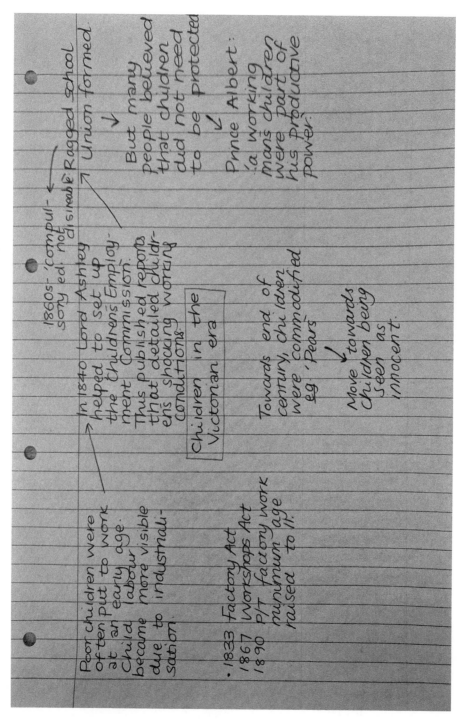

Figure 12.2 Research on Victorian children.

Notes

1 Richard B. Gunderman, 'Advocating for Children: Charles Dickens,' *Pediatric Radiology* 50 (January 2020), 467.

2 Patrick Butler, 'A Novel Insight into Child Abuse,' *The Guardian*, March 2023, https://www.theguardian.com/society/2001/nov/30/childrensservices.

3 Charles Dickens, *A Christmas Carol* (London: Wordsworth Classics, 2018), 13.

4 D. W. Roberts, 'How Cruel Was the Victorian Poor Law?' *The Historical Journal* 6, no. 1(March 1963), 98.

5 James Schoonmaker, 'Children in the Workhouse,' *Manchester Historian*, March 8, 2023, https://manchesterhistorian.com/2015/children-in-the-workhouse/.

6 Matthew 19:14, *Bible Gateway*, https://www.biblegateway.com/passage/?search=Matthew%2019%3A14&version=KJV.

7 'Education in the Workhouse,' *Workhouses*, https://www.workhouses.org.uk/education/workhouse.shtml.

8 Charles Dickens, *Speeches: Literary and Social* (London: The Floating Press, 2015), 255.

9 Charles Dickens, 'London Pauper Children,' *Household Words*, vol. 1, 551, https://www.djo.org.uk/household-words/volume-i/page-551.html.

10 Patricia Pulham, Brad Beaven, *Dickens and the Victorian City* (London: Tricorn Books, 2012), 18.

11 Charles Dickens, *A Christmas Carol*, 69.

12 Ibid., 69.

13 Ibid., 69.

14 Ibid., 22.

15 Ibid., 10.

16 'Agnosticism,' *Britannica*, https://www.britannica.com/topic/agnosticism.

17 'Ephesians 4:18,' *Bible Gateway*, https://www.biblegateway.com/passage/?search=Ephesians%204%3A18&version=NIV.

18 Charles Dickens, *A Christmas Carol*, 68.

19 Ibid., 85.

20 Ibid., 69.

21 Meir Kryger, 'Charles Dickens: Impact on medicine and society,' *Journal of Clinical Sleep Medicine* 8, no. 3 (June 2012), 336.

22 A. J. Carter, 'A Christmas Carol: Charles Dickens and the birth of orthopaedics,' *Journal of the Royal Society of Medicine* 86, no. 1, (January 1993): 45-48.

23 Ibid.

24 Charles Dickens, *A Christmas Carol*, 54.

25 John Forster, *The Life of Charles Dickens* (Cambridge: Cambridge University Press, 2011).

26 Charles Dickens, *Speeches: Literary and Social*.

27 L. C. B. Seaman, *Victorian England: Aspects of English and imperial history 1837-1901* (London: Routledge, 2002), 12.

28 A. J. Carter, 'A Christmas Carol: Charles Dickens and the birth of orthopaedics,' 45-46.

29 Charles Dickens, *A Christmas Carol*, 88.

30 Barbara Nathan Hardy, *The Moral Art of Charles Dickens* (London: Athlone, 1970), 139.

31 Charles Dickens, *A Christmas Carol*, 68.

32 Mary Burgan, 'Bringing Up by Hand: Dickens and the Feeding of Children,' *Mosaic* 24, no. 3(August 1991), 73.

33 Ibid.

34 Fred Kaplan, *Dickens: A Biography* (New York: Morrow, 1988), 19.

35 Natalie McKnight, 'Making Mother Suffer and Other Fun in Dickens,' *Dickens Quarterly* 11, no. 4(1994): 177-186.

36 M. Slater, *Dickens and Women* (Stanford: Stanford University Press, 1983).

37 Amberyl Malkovich, *Charles Dickens and the Victorian Child: Romanticizing and socializing the imperfect child* (London: Routledge, 2012).

38 Ibid., 135.

39 Margaret Hodges, 'Dickens for Children,' *The Horn Book Magazine* 58 (1982), 626.

40 Laurie Langbauer, 'Ethics and Theory: Suffering children in Dickens, Dostoevsky, and Le Guin,' *ELH 75* (Spring 2008), 89.

41 Charles Dickens, *A Christmas Carol*, 68.

42 Laurie Langbauer, 'Ethics and Theory, 91.

43 John Forster, *The Life of Charles Dickens* (Cambridge: Cambridge University Press, 2011), 29.

44 Charles Dickens, *A Christmas Carol*, 33.

45 Laurie Langbauer, 'Ethics and Theory, 95.

46 Charles Dickens, *A Christmas Carol*, 44.

47 Laura C. Berry, *The Child, the State, and the Victorian Novel* (Charlottesville: University Press of Virginia, 1999).

48 K. Boehm, *Charles Dickens and the Sciences of Childhood: Popular medicine, child health and Victorian culture* (London: Palgrave, 2013).

49 Laura Peters, *Dickens and Childhood* (London: Routledge, 2012).

50 J. H. Plumb, 'The New World of Children in Eighteenth-century England,' *Past & Present* 67, no. 1 (May 1975), 68.

51 Philippe Aries, *Centuries of Childhood* (London: Pimlico, 1996).

52 Laura C. Berry, *The Child, the State, and the Victorian Novel.*

53 Paul Goetsch, 'Old-Fashioned Children: From Dickens to Hardy and James,' *Anglia-zeitschrift Fur Englische Philologie* 123, no. 1 (January 2005): 45-69.

54 Frederick Adye, 'Old-Fashioned Children,' *Macmillan's Magazine* 68 (1893): 286–292.

55 Charles Dickens, *A Christmas Carol*, 54.

56 Adrienne E. Gavin, *The Child in British Literature: Literary constructions of childhood, medieval to contemporary* (Palgrave Macmillan, Basingstoke, 2012), 9.

57 Sue Saltmarsh, 'Spirits, Miracles and Clauses: Economy, patriarchy and childhood in popular Christmas texts,' *Papers: Explorations into Children's Literature* 17, no. 1 (May 2007): 5-18.

58 Brandon Chitwood, 'Eternal Returns: A Christmas Carol's ghosts of repetition,' *Victorian Literature and Culture* 43, no. 4 (July 2015): 675–687.

59 Peter Ackroyd, *Dickens: Public and private passion* (London: BBC Books, 2002).

60 Ibid., 93.

61 Hugh Cunningham, 'Dickens as a Reformer,' In: David Paroissien (Ed.), *A Companion to Charles Dickens* (London: Wiley, 2011): 159–173.

References

Peter Ackroyd, *Dickens: Public and private passion* (London: BBC Books, 2002).

Frederick Adye, 'Old-Fashioned Children,' *Macmillan's Magazine* 68 (1893): 286–292.

Philippe Aries, *Centuries of Childhood* (London: Pimlico, 1996).

Laura C. Berry, *The Child, the State, and the Victorian Novel* (Charlottesville: University Press of Virginia, 1999).

'Ephesians 4:18,' *Bible Gateway*, (March 8, 2023), https://www.biblegateway.com/passage/?search=Ephesians%204%3A18&version=NIV

'Matthew 19:14,' *Bible Gateway*, (March 8, 2023), https://www.biblegateway.com/passage/?search=Matthew%2019%3A14&version=KJV

K. Boehm, *Charles Dickens and the sciences of childhood: popular medicine, child health and Victorian culture* (London: Palgrave, 2013).

Mary Burgan, 'Bringing Up by Hand: Dickens and the feeding of children,' *Mosaic* 24, no. 3 (August 1991): 69–88. https://www.jstor.org/stable/24780466

Patrick Butler, 'A novel insight into child abuse,' *The Guardian*, (March 8, 2023), https://www.theguardian.com/society/2001/nov/30/childrensservices

A. J. Carter, 'A Christmas Carol: Charles Dickens and the Birth of Orthopaedics,' *Journal of the Royal Society of Medicine 86*, no. 1, (January 1993): 45–48.

Brandon Chitwood, 'Eternal Returns: A Christmas Carol's ghosts of repetition,' *Victorian Literature and Culture* 43, no. 4 (July 2015): 675–687. DOI:10.1017/S1060150315000200

Hugh Cunningham, 'Dickens as a Reformer,' In David Paroissien (Ed.), *A Companion to Charles Dickens* (London: Wiley, 2011): 159–173.

Charles Dickens, *A Christmas Carol* (London: Wordsworth Classics, 2018).

Charles Dickens, 'London Pauper Children' in *Household Words*, vol. 1, p. 551, https://www.djo.org.uk/household-words/volume-i/page-551.html

Charles Dickens, *Speeches: Literary and Social* (London: The Floating Press, 2015), 255.

John Forster, *The Life of Charles Dickens* (Cambridge: Cambridge University Press, 2011).

Adrienne E. Gavin, *The Child in British Literature: Literary constructions of childhood, medieval to contemporary* (Palgrave Macmillan, Basingstoke, 2012).

Paul Goetsch, 'Old-Fashioned Children: From Dickens to Hardy and James,' *Anglia-zeitschrift Fur Englische Philologie* 123, no. 1 (January 2005): 45–69. DOI:10.1515/ANGL.2005.45

Richard B. Gunderman, 'Advocating for Children: Charles Dickens,' *Pediatric Radiology* 50 (January 2020): 467–469. doi: 10.1007/s00247-019-04608-w

Barbara Nathan Hardy, *The Moral Art of Charles Dickens* (London: Athlone, 1970).

Margaret Hodges, 'Dickens for Children,' *The Horn Book Magazine* 58 (1982): 626–635.

Fred Kaplan, *Dickens: A Biography* (New York: Morrow, 1988).

Meir Kryger, 'Charles Dickens: Impact on Medicine and Society,' *Journal of Clinical Sleep Medicine* 8, no. 3 (June 2012): 333–338. DOI: 10.5664/jcsm.1930

Laurie Langbauer, 'Ethics and Theory: Suffering children in Dickens, Dostoevsky, and Le Guin,' *ELH* 75 (Spring 2008): 89–108. DOI: 10.1353/elh.2008.0005

Amberyl Malkovich, *Charles Dickens and the Victorian Child: Romanticizing and socializing the imperfect child* (London: Routledge, 2012).

Natalie McKnight, 'Making Mother Suffer and Other Fun in Dickens,' *Dickens Quarterly* 11, no. 4 (1994): 177–186.

Laura Peters, *Dickens and Childhood* (London: Routledge, 2012).

J. H. Plumb, 'The New World of Children in Eighteenth-century England,' *Past & Present* 67, no. 1(May 1975): 64–95. https://doi.org/10.1093/past/67.1.64

Patricia Pulham, Brad Beaven, *Dickens and the Victorian City* (London: Tricorn Books, 2012).

D. W. Roberts, 'How Cruel Was the Victorian Poor Law?' *The Historical Journal* 6, no. 1 (March 1963): 97–107. DOI:10.1017/S0018246X00000935

Sue Saltmarsh, 'Spirits, Miracles and Clauses: Economy, patriarchy and childhood in popular Christmas Texts,' *Papers: Explorations into Children's Literature* 17, no. 1 (May 2007): 5–18. https://doi.org/10.21153/pecl2007vol17no1art1201

James Schoonmaker, 'Children in the Workhouse,' *Manchester Historian*, (March 8, 2023), https://manchesterhistorian.com/2015/children-in-the-workhouse/

'Education in the Workhouse,' Workhouses, (March 8, 2023), https://www.workhouses.org.uk/education/workhouse.shtml

It's the most wonderful time of the year! How does Dickens depict Christmas?

How many of us check the weather report in the week running up to Christmas and long for the perfect, picture postcard white Christmas of myth and legend? For those of us who grew up in the UK like me, white snowy Christmases have been few and far between in the 20th century. The actual definition of a 'white Christmas' is that just one snowflake has to be recorded on the roof of the local Met Office Weather Centre.[1] While I have been alive, only 1995 has brought immense snowdrifts and even then, much of the south remained unaffected. Yet, like many people, I grew up with cards displayed in my living room throughout the whole festive season, bedecked with idyllic snowy scenes. Perhaps this came from tradition, as 1906, 1917, 1923, 1938 and 1970 all had great snow falls,[2] which are all years lying within living memory of the adults during my childhood. Or perhaps, as some academics believe, we associate Christmas so much with snow due to Dickens' popular novels set during this period, where a snowy London is often evocatively described within its pages. This may come from the description of Dingley Dell in *The Pickwick Papers*:

> 'How it snows!' said one of the men, in a low tone. 'Snows, does it?' said Wardle. 'Rough, cold night, Sir,' replied the man; 'and there's a wind got up, that drifts it across the fields, in a thick white cloud.'[3]

This recollection of a snowy Christmas Eve may have been based upon the cold, snowy late Decembers of both 1829 and 1830 and as *The Pickwick Papers* was released in 1836, it is a popular cultural reference which most readers would have been able to imagine and relate to. Indeed, 1836 itself was a particularly snowy Christmas, which Ian Currie, from *Weather Eye Magazine* (2017) describes as causing 'mountainous drifts... on the South Downs in Sussex and an avalanche swept onto the town of Lewes and demolished a whole street called Boulder Row burying alive a number of its residents.'[4]

DOI: 10.4324/9781003453468-14

So perhaps this influenced Dickens' descriptions of the snow covered festive period in London we see in *A Christmas Carol* or it could have even been his own childhood Christmases, as Dickens 'grew up during the coldest decade England has seen since the 1690s.'[5] In 1814, even the River Thames froze, where frost fairs were held with people camping out on the river in tents and even more unbelievably to a modern reader, an elephant was led across the river next to Blackfriars Bridge.[6] Like many writers, Dickens was inspired by his own childhood experiences and memories,[7] so perhaps these vivid experiences made their way into his descriptions of Christmas in *A Christmas Carol* and in turn, have worked their way into our psyches when we think about Christmas, even today.

However, it isn't just our nostalgia about a white Christmas which Dickens has made popular. Some critics, like Peter Ackroyd, claim that Dickens can be said to have almost singlehandedly created the modern idea of Christmas we celebrate today. Stephen Jarvis, the author of *Death and Mr Pickwick*, denies that this is the case, claiming instead that Dickens made Christmas fashionable again, as during the early part of the Victorian era, most newspapers didn't even mention Christmas.[8] Yet even as an adult, Christmas was always an important time for Dickens. His oldest daughter, Mary 'Mamie' Dickens, wrote extensively about her childhood experiences of Christmas with her father,[9] and we can see many of her own experiences echoed in her father's depictions in the novella. One particular influence is clear – the importance of family and celebrating the festive spirit with merriment and dancing. Mamie writes:

> When 'the boys' came home for the holidays there were constant sieges of practice for the Christmas and New Year's parties…He was very fond of a country dance which he learned at the house of some dear friends at Rockingham Castle, which began with quite a stately minuet to the tune of 'God Save the Queen,' and then dashed suddenly into 'Down the Middle and up Again.'

It is easy to see the parallels here between his own love of dancing and the joys it brings, particularly at Christmas, and the dancing described at Fezziwig's Christmas party. Mamie also writes about having a house full of guests throughout their time at Gad Hill, where games passed their evenings in jollity – much like the games Scrooge witnesses at his nephew Fred's house accompanied by the spirit. But perhaps the clearest link between Mamie's memories and the descriptions in the novella belong to the feast – in particular the Christmas pudding. She recalls:

> The Christmas plum pudding had its own special dish of colored 'repoussé' china, ornamented with holly. The pudding was placed on this with a sprig of real holly in the center, lighted, and in this state placed in front of my father, its arrival being always the signal for applause.[10]

So, if Dickens and his family celebrated Christmases in this way, was this common in Victorian England? Probably not. The festive period prior to the 1830s was seen as a holy day, but as there was a strong Calvinist and Puritan theology, it had much more of a focus on what Scripture allowed for Christian worship. The Christmas that we now celebrate with Christmas trees, wreathes and holly decorations, was only an invention of the late 1800s and certainly had some help from Dickens in being made popular. Although there is not a Christmas tree in *A Christmas Carol*, just after its publication, trees as a festive decorative item inside houses were being popularised due to Queen Victoria's husband, Albert, bringing the tradition with him from his native Germany.[11] Yet in some of his other seasonal works, there are magical descriptions of lavishly decorated trees, such as in one of his first Christmas stories, which appeared in *Household Words* in 1850: 'The tree was planted in the middle of a great round table, and towered high above their heads. It was brilliantly lit by a multitude of little tapers; and everywhere sparkled and glittered with bright objects.'[12]However, these superficial details, such as decoration, food and the weather are not the only way that the writing of Dickens has influenced the way we regard and celebrate Christmas today. Charles Dickens believed wholeheartedly in the humanising power of Christmas.[13] Throughout all of his works, there is a thread of criticising the rich, not just for their wealth but mostly for their indifference towards the suffering of others. This charitable spirit still surrounds Christmas today, as we see more than half of the population surveyed saying they are more likely to give to charity at Christmas.[14] Suddenly, Christmas was seen to be becoming a highly moral holiday, despite its pagan origins. What *A Christmas Carol* highlights is the ritualistic inclusion of an individual into a community, which ties people together as a glue. Edward Casey, writes that people are nostalgic for 'lost worlds,'[15] and perhaps this could also account for their longing to gather with family at Christmas, even today. Can we put this down to Dickens' writings? Probably not, but it is fair to say that his message of benevolence and generosity to fellow man has definitely become part of the cultural zeitgeist at Christmas.

To enhance this message, of course, Dickens often focuses on the abundance at Christmas, not just in *A Christmas Carol* but in other books, such as *David Copperfield* and with the missing pork pie in *Great Expectations*. This image of a family around the dinner table, enjoying the abundance of a Christmas feast was even replicated in Henry Cole's first commissioned illustration for a Christmas card in 1843.[16]

Clearly, the Victorians transformed the idea of Christmas, so that it was very much centred around family, and with his depictions of the merriment at Fred's and the peek into the Cratchit's household in *A Christmas Carol*, coupled with Mamie's descriptions of Dickens' own family festivities, it is evident Charles Dickens himself also agreed.

To conclude, Dickens may not have invented the Christmas we celebrate today but his name had become so synonymous with Christmas that on hearing of his death in 1870, a little girl who sold fruit and vegetables in London asked, 'Mr. Dickens dead? Then will Father Christmas die too?'[17] A Christmas Carol, with its portrayal of idyllic festive cheer, has helped to popularise and spread the traditions of the festival. Its illuminating of the importance of family, charity and goodwill help to encapsulate the spirit of the Victorian Christmas, and are still very much a part of the Christmas we celebrate today.

Summed up in six

- Dickens' portrayal of a white Christmas in London may have influenced our idealised vision of Christmas – despite a white Christmas being very rare in England in the 20th century. This may have been influenced by Dickens' own experiences of very cold Christmases in 1814 and only a decade before A Christmas Carol was written in 1830.

- Before the publication of A Christmas Carol, the celebration of Christmas had gone somewhat out of fashion for the Victorians. Yet Dickens had always celebrated it, indeed there are vivid accounts from his daughter Mamie who describes the exciting festivities, many of which mirror the fictional accounts in the novella.

- Even the food we eat at Christmas may have been influenced by A Christmas Carol. The description of the Christmas pudding at the Cratchits mirrors Mamie Dickens' own recollections of the reception to the pudding at her own Christmas dinners with her father. The Christmas pudding, with its sprig of holly and the ceremonial setting it on fire, is still a tradition in many households even today.

- Perhaps the biggest influence a modern Christmas gets from A Christmas Carol is the focus on people having a more charitable spirit and more of a sense of community during the festive period.

- It would be wrong to claim that Dickens singlehandedly invented the Christmas we celebrate today. However, his association with the festive period definitely highlights how he helped to popularise the Christmas holiday.

Ideas for teaching

AO1: Compile a list of quotations which portray Christmas as a time of community and charity and analyse them.

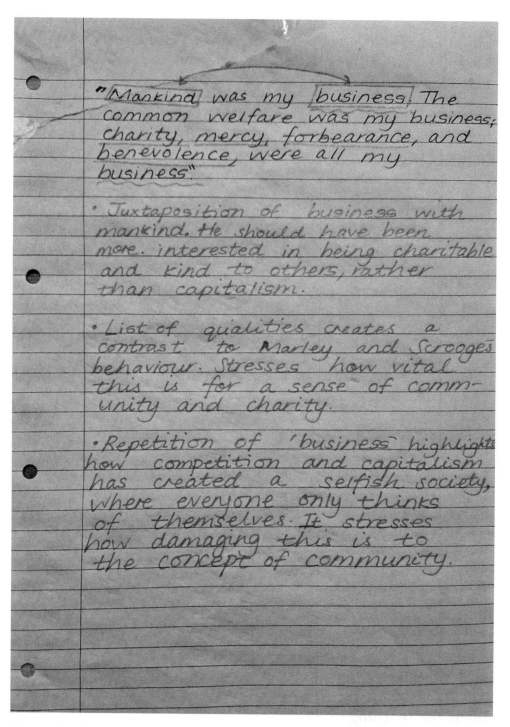

"Mankind was my business. The common welfare was my business; charity, mercy, forbearance, and benevolence, were all my business"

• Juxtaposition of business with mankind. He should have been more. interested in being charitable and kind to others, rather than capitalism.

• List of qualities creates a contrast to Marley and Scrooges behaviour. Stresses how vital this is for a sense of community and charity.

• Repetition of 'business' highlights how competition and capitalism has created a selfish society, where everyone only thinks of themselves. It stresses how damaging this is to the concept of community.

Figure 13.1 Analysed quotations focused on community and charity.

AO2: Re-study and annotate the Cratchit Christmas feast scene. What techniques, words and phrases and sentence forms does Dickens employ to portray the importance of community and family?

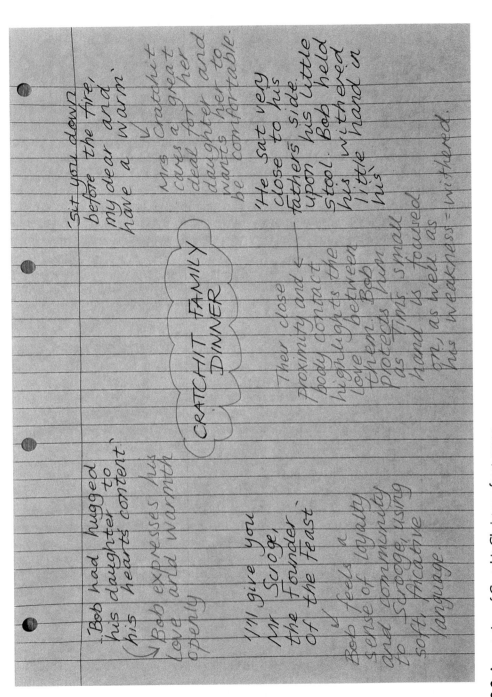

Figure 13.2 Annotation of Cratchit Christmas feast scene.

Notes

1 Ian Currie, 'A White Christmas Is Only for Dreamers,' *Met Check*, https://www.metcheck. co.uk/blogs/news/a-white-christmas-is-only-for-dreamers#:~:text=They%20were%20 1906%2C%201917%2C%201923,lines%20and%20cutting%20off%20communities.
2 Ibid.
3 Charles Dickens, 'The Pickwick Papers,' *Project Gutenberg*, https://www.gutenberg.org/ cache/epub/580/pg580-images.html.
4 Ian Currie, 'A White Christmas Is Only for Dreamers.'
5 Brian Fagan, *The Little Ice Age* (New York: Perseus Books, 2002), 134.
6 Diego Arguedas Ortiz, 'How Dickens Made Christmas White,' *BBC Future*, https://www. bbc.com/future/article/20181217-how-dickens-made-white-christmas-a-myth.
7 Melissa Dickson, 'Dickens's Nightmare: Dreams, memory and trauma,' *Interface Focus* 10, no. 3 (April 2020): 1–8.
8 What Was Christmas Really Like for Charles Dickens? *Penguin Books*, https://www. penguin.co.uk/articles/2016/11/what-was-christmas-like-for-charles-dickens.
9 Mamie Dickens, 'Christmas Traditions – Christmas with Charles Dickens,' *Victoriana Magazine*, June 6, 2023, http://www.victoriana.com/christmas/dickenschristmas.htm.
10 Ibid.
11 'How "A Christmas Carol" Became a Holiday Classic,' *University of Denver*, https://news. ucdenver.edu/how-a-christmas-carol-became-a-holiday-classic/#:~:text=%E2%80%9 CInterestingly%2C%20there's%20not%20a%20Christmas,him%20from%20his%20 native%20Germany.
12 Ibid.
13 Simon Callow, 'Charles Dickens and the Victorian Christmas Feast,' *The British Library*, June 6, 2023, https://www.bl.uk/romantics-and-victorians/articles/a-victorian-christmas-feast.
14 Melanie May, 'Half of People More Inclined to Give at Christmas, Despite Many Feeling Worse Off,' *UK Fundraising*, June 6, 2023, https://fundraising.co.uk/2022/12/07/half-of-people-more-inclined-to-give-at-christmas-despite-many-feeling-worse-off/#:~:text= Features-,Half%20of%20people%20more%20inclined%20to%20give%20at,despite% 20many%20feeling%20worse%20off&text=Half%20(48%25)%20of%20people,to%20 new%20research%20from%20Enthuse.
15 Edward S. Casey, 'The World of nostalgia,' *Man and World* 20, no. 4 (October 1987): 361–384.
16 'History of Christmas,' *BBC*, June 6, 2023, https://www.bbc.co.uk/victorianchristmas/ history.shtml#:~:text=While%20Charles%20Dickens%20did%20not%20invent%20 the%20Victorian,a%20part%20of%20the%20Christmas%20we%20celebrate%20today.
17 'Dickens and Christmas,' *Victorian Vocabulary*, https://victorianvocabulary.weebly.com/ dickens-and-christmas.html.

References

'History of Christmas,' *BBC*, (June 6, 2023), https://www.bbc.co.uk/victorianchristmas/ history.shtml#:~:text=While%20Charles%20Dickens%20did%20not%20invent%20 the%20Victorian,a%20part%20of%20the%20Christmas%20we%20celebrate%20today.
Simon Callow, 'Charles Dickens and the Victorian Christmas Feast,' *The British Library*, (June 6, 2023), https://www.bl.uk/romantics-and-victorians/articles/a-victorian-christmas-feast

Edward S. Casey, 'The World of Nostalgia,' *Man and World* 20, no. 4 (October 1987): 361–384.

Ian Currie, 'A White Christmas Is Only for Dreamers,' *Met Check*, (June 4, 2023), https://www.metcheck.co.uk/blogs/news/a-white-christmas-is-only-for-dreamers#:~:text=They%20were%201906%2C%201917%2C%201923,lines%20and%20cutting%20off%20communities.

Charles Dickens, 'The Pickwick Papers,' *Project Gutenberg*, (June 4, 2023a), https://www.gutenberg.org/cache/epub/580/pg580-images.html

Mamie Dickens, 'Christmas Traditions – Christmas with Charles Dickens,' *Victoriana Magazine*, (June 6, 2023b), http://www.victoriana.com/christmas/dickenschristmas.htm

Melissa Dickson, 'Dickens's Nightmare: Dreams, Memory and Trauma,' *Interface Focus* 10, no. 3 (April 2020): 1–8. https://doi.org/10.1098/rsfs.2019.0076

Brian Fagan, *The Little Ice Age* (New York: Perseus Books, 2002), 134.

Stephen Jarvis, 'What Was Christmas Really Like for Charles Dickens?' *Penguin Books*, (June 5, 2023), https://www.penguin.co.uk/articles/2016/11/what-was-christmas-like-for-charles-dickens

Melanie May, 'Half of People More Inclined to Give at Christmas, Despite Many Feeling Worse Off.' *UK Fundraising*, (June 6, 2023), https://fundraising.co.uk/2022/12/07/half-of-people-more-inclined-to-give-at-christmas-despite-many-feeling-worse-off/#:~:text=Features-,Half%20of%20people%20more%20inclined%20to%20give%20at,despite%20many%20feeling%20worse%20off&text=Half%20(48%25)%20of%20people,to%20new%20research%20from%20Enthuse

Diego Arguedas Ortiz, 'How Dickens Made Christmas White,' *BBC Future*, (June, 2023), https://www.bbc.com/future/article/20181217-how-dickens-made-white-christmas-a-myth

'Dickens and Christmas,' *Victorian Vocabulary*, (June 6, 2023), https://victorianvocabulary.weebly.com/dickens-and-christmas.html

Oliver Ward, 'How A Christmas Carol Became a Holiday Classic,' *C U Denver*, (May 5, 2023), https://news.ucdenver.edu/how-a-christmas-carol-became-a-holiday-classic/#:~:text=%E2%80%9CInterestingly%2C%20there's%20not%20a%20Christmas,him%20from%20his%20native%20Germany.

Resources

Graphic Haunting: Illustration and Excluded Masculinity in Charles Dickens's Nicholas Nickleby (1838-9) and A Christmas Carol (1843) - Christine Chettle

Analysing Scrooge and Marley

01. Scrooge's bright colour contrasts with the stark whiteness of his nightgown, linking him to Marley's ghostly paleness.

02. This paleness stands up against the shadowed corner where he stands, emphasising his location in death and suggesting a poverty amidst all his wealth.

03. The connection with Marley underlines the warning that Marley gives. His greedy actions have loaded him in death with a punitive chain - Scrooge faces the same fate.

Image from Dickens' A Christmas Carol' - Copyright free and in the public domain.

AO3: DICKENS' CHILDHOOD AND CHILDREN IN ACC

01 When his father John Dickens experienced financial difficulties and was sent to Marshalsea prison, he took his entire family with him, with the exception of Charles. Charles was employed in Warren's blacking factory, putting labels onto bottles, he had just turned 12 year old. 'Just as the shock of going to work at Warren's factory had been worse than the actual hardship, so the loneliness of his new situation was harder to bear than penury. He had been cast into premature manhood and hankered for the childhood he had so traumatically lost' (Mackenzie & Mackenzie).

02 Once John Dickens's financial situation improved, it was no longer necessary for Charles to continue in the blacking factory. However, Mrs Dickens, his mother, felt that he should continue in this employment for the additional few shillings a week. Charles felt irrevocably betrayed by his mother's desire to return him to manual labour (Ackroyd 2002:11; Mackenzie & Mackenzie 1979:16). His father supported him, and instead of returning to work he returned to school. The episode in the blacking factory resulted in two things. Firstly, it interrupted and corrupted Dickens's own childhood and, secondly, it provided Dickens with a sense that childhood was a valuable period in life.

03 Another notable element of Dickens's childhood was his exposure to his father's library, which included books such as Tom Jones, Robinson Crusoe and other classics. Crusoe is also part of Scrooge's childhood reading. This intersection of lived experience and the experience of the characters is not coincidental. It was these books, Dickens later said, which 'kept alive my fancy, and my hope of something beyond that place and time', creating a private world into which he increasingly withdrew as he sat reading on his bed, taking imaginary voyages and dreaming of exotic adventures (Mackenzie & Mackenzie 1979:10). Slater makes a similar point about the value of Dickens's father's library and adds that the books were a source of inspiration for his own writing: 'Defoe's Robinson Crusoe, Goldsmith's The Vicar of Wakefield and The Arabian Nights and Tales of the Genii seem especially to have seized his imagination judging by the way that specific allusions and general references to them, along with Shakespearean ones, pervade all his writings, both public and private.... From the time of writing A Christmas Carol onwards, Dickens celebrated the wonder and delight of all his childhood reading many times.' (Slater 2009:11)

04 The images of characters from childhood reading are an assertion of the imagination of childhood, and the loneliness experienced by the child Scrooge is an echo of Dickens's own loneliness as a child. The young Scrooge escaped to an imaginary world, and the ghosts escort Scrooge through other imaginings or dreams.

05 Hardy (2008) makes reference to Dickens's experience as a child, including the difficult times of the blacking factory. However, despite this hardship, for Hardy the exploration of the streets of the great city would be a source of inspiration for the creative works to follow: 'The solitude and humiliation he felt when he was 11 or 12 - of course many children of his time and class started work at that age - began his fearful, compassionate, amused, and excited discovery of London's mean streets...the terrible children Ignorance and Want in Scrooge's Christmas dream. In London's humanity Dickens found his own, and the discovery was painful and creative. (Hardy 2008:2)

'Redemption and the imagination of childhood: Dickens's representation of children in A Christmas Carol' by D.E Robinson

CHILDREN IN 'A CHRISTMAS CAROL'

Robinson, D.E. (2016) 'Redemption and the imagination of childhood: Dickens's representation of children in A Christmas Carol', Literator, Vol. 37, Iss. 1, pp. 1-8.

Context - Childhood in the Victorian era:
'By the standards of a later generation, European childhood, up to the 1860s, was like human life itself, nasty, brutish and short. Not only was infant mortality high, childhood itself, if we define childhood in modern terms as a time of play, of learning, of innocent idleness and amusement, was virtually non-existent for the majority. Millions of children in the nineteenth century had the experience of working in a grown-up world when aged ten. Thousands of middle-class boys like (John Stuart) Mill would have been expected to conform in manner and even in dress to the mores of middle-aged parents.' (Wilson 2007:131-132)

Another critic, Monica Flegel, provides several insights into the world of 19th century childhood in England. She states that attitudes to childhood were undergoing change during the Victorian period. In addition, the notion of children likely to experience neglect or emotional or physical abuse was not limited to the working class. Furthermore, the shift of attitude towards children had a basis in notions of morality or amorality, and how these elements were present or absent in the state of the child. Flegel comments on literary representations of childhood as follows:

'Although the 'children of the poor' were often represented as endangered in nineteenth-century texts, they were by no means the only ones. In Victorian literature, in particular, the children of the middle and upper classes were also often represented as victims in need of rescue and protection.... Residual conceptions of childhood as a time of innate moral depravity, bolstered by the growth of Victorian Evangelicalism, meant that fear and discipline were the norm in many Victorian households.. Throughout the nineteenth century, then, this conception of childhood as a time of innate sinfulness had to contend with the emergent 'idea of childhood as property a time of happiness'. (Flegel 2009:14)

TINY TIM

Despite his disability, he is described as 'active'. Tiny Tim's active nature is an indication of his resolution and fortitude. He is clearly an example of making the best of things in the face of adversity. After his death (in the vision of the Ghost of Christmas yet to come) the Cratchit family talks about Tiny Tim, and Mrs Cratchit remarks that Bob could walk swiftly with Tiny Tim on his shoulder, suggesting that the child was no burden at all. In this same vision, it is stated that the spot where Tiny Tim is buried is green, a colour connoting life. It differs from the dull environment in which he lived. Bob promised to walk there every Sunday, suggesting a continued parental commitment. This response to Tiny Tim's death is different from the vision that Scrooge has of his own death and grave. Scrooge's grave is neglected, and he is not loved by others. In Dickens's presentation of Tiny Tim, the physical infirmity is a central element of the child's description. It must be noted that, as a child, Dickens himself had spasms that lasted from the time in the blacking factory onwards - in short, he was disabled (Ackroyd 2002:10). Ackroyd points out that this infirmity prevented Dickens from participating in games and other activities with children.

It seems that Dickens created childhood figures that, although lacking in physical perfection, achieved a higher moral order, and, as such, could be regarded as the guides or touchstones of a society seeking moral direction. However, the moral significance is merely alluded to, rather than explicitly stated, and it is in this vagueness that some of the value of the children lies. It would seem that, in being a person with a disability, Tiny Tim acts as a measure for others about how much worse their own lives could be.

IGNORANCE AND WANT

"From the foldings of its robe, it brought forth two children: wretched, abject, frightful, hideous, miserable. They knelt down at its feet, and clung upon the outside of its garment.' (Dickens 1843:100)

The children are incongruous figures because the Ghost of Christmas Present is a resplendent figure clothed in green - the symbol of life. Their abject state is a notable contrast with the sense of plenty that is associated with this ghost. The first element of the description of these children is of a hand that is claw like - it is a description that removes humanity from the children. The hand, we may assume, is indicative of a human hand that lacks flesh, as a result of poverty and the associated lack of food. The lack of food results in a physically wasted condition. The terms 'pinched' and 'twisted' are similar to the terms mentioned in the initial description of Scrooge - 'squeezing', 'wrenching' and 'grasping' - suggesting, perhaps, that they are the consequences of similar trying circumstances. The fact that they are a boy and a girl suggests an ironic comment on ideal families. These children are not the product of happy homes. There is no sense of a joyful future about them, no sense of human potential. Instead, there is a sense of neglect and degradation. These children contrast strongly with the images of children playing in the fields, shown to Scrooge by the Ghost of Christmas Past in the previous Stave. Ignorance is regarded by the ghost as a very unfortunate condition - particularly ignorance of the human condition. Brandon Chitwood (2015) makes the following comment: 'Unlike Dickens's gallery of poor orphans, these children are figures of horror, not pathos. They are meant to chill the blood, not warm the heart. The ghost's monstrous children suggest no program for change. Their rhetorical function is less logical than visceral.' (Chitwood 2015:680)

SCROOGE AS THE 'SOLITARY CHILD'

'The school is not quite deserted', said the Ghost. 'A solitary child, deserted by his friends, is left there still'. Scrooge said he knew it. And he sobbed. (Dickens 1843:47)

Scrooge's childhood home is a place lacking in warmth, both emotional and physical. The child Scrooge is sitting by a feeble fire, reading. The room is described as bare and melancholy, and the only furniture is desks and chairs. The image is one lacking in joy, but then Scrooge sees images deriving from the boy's book appear outside the window. The images, conjured up by the boy's imagination, pass in procession outside the window. The older Scrooge then lists the people and things that he sees, and he becomes animated and joyful. The first image and/or vision is 'dear old honest Ali Baba!' (Dickens 1843:48) This is swiftly followed by other visions from The Arabian Nights and images of Robinson Crusoe. The Arabian Nights figures are significant in that for a British child, like Scrooge (or Dickens himself), these are figures of the imagination. They are exotic, removed from the dull and dreary world in which Scrooge finds himself. They are of the world of adventure, which holds much potential. They are a shift from the material to the possible, or, even more interestingly, the world of the impossible, in that they exist in the imagination. Scrooge took refuge in the world of the imagination, because the material world in which he lived offered so little. He coped with the limitations of his world by venturing into fantasy worlds.

01 | He loved Christmas

John Forster, Dickens's first biographer, reflected that his friend had 'identified himself' with Christmas, and noted that 'its privilege to light up with some sort of comfort the squalidest of places, he had made his own'. ▌ From the earliest days of his writing career, Dickens had lighted upon Christmas as a season of good cheer and fellow feeling. Dickens similarly venerates Christmas as a 'brief season of happiness and enjoyment ... How many old recollections, and how many dormant sympathies, does Christmas time awaken'. Dickens came to be so strongly associated with Christmas that on the occasion of his death a story circulated that on hearing the dreadful news a young barrow girl in Covent Garden market exclaimed, 'Th en will Father Christmas die too?' ▌

02 | He didn't invent Xmas!

Dickens did not actually invent Christmas, though Robert Seymour , the initial illustrator for The Pickwick Papers , had brought out The Book of Christmas and this has many of the ingredients of the classic Dickensian Christmas. Prince Albert had popularised the German tradition of the Christmas tree, although it had first been introduced in England a few years earlier. Christmas cards were not introduced until 1846, and Christmas crackers emerged in the 1850s. ▌ At the mid century Christmas was still a one-day holiday: children were given presents, but it was not the extended season of festivity that we now know.

03 | Authorial intent

A Christmas Carol , The Chimes and The Haunted Man , in particular, all seem to be designed to educate the social conscience of Dickens's popular readership: the deprivation and social disruption that lurk within these tales could only be assuaged by the awakening of Dickens's readership into benevolent action.

DICKENS & Christmas

Based on the work of Sally Ledger in 'Dickens in Context' (2012)

04 | Context

Dickens's urging, in his Christmas books, of the regenerating power of human fellowship and fireside domesticity had a very particular resonance in the 1840s, when he was writing. For this decade was known as the 'Hungry Forties', a time when Britain's landscape was scarred by poverty and social unrest. It is clear that what Dickens is offering is an alleviation, in the realm of imaginative literature, of poverty and deprivation, and a fictional resolution of the very real class antagonisms which erupted in continental Europe in the revolutions of 1848.

05 | Domesticity

One of the main fictional devices Dickens deploys in his Christmas books to establish a sense of unity, comfort and harmony is a focus on domesticity as a panacea. Cosy, contented, cheerful and sheltering homes are presented as a social and emotional cure-all. It is the Cratchits' Christmas lunch that forms the focus for Dickens's realisation of the domestic ideal: after the meal 'the cloth was cleared, the hearth swept, and the fire made up ... Then all the Cratchit family drew around the hearth' (stave ▌). The hearth itself is an index of domestic happiness: whilst the Cratchits are united and comforted as they come together around their cosy domestic fireside, Scrooge's 'very small' fire burns meanly low as he huddles over it in an attempt to defy the frost.

06 | Legacy

Dickens's original conception of Christmas still alive and well. It is this warm-hearted, forgiving, benevolent and revel-making ideal of Christmas that has become associated with Dickens, and that has continued to infl ence yuletide celebrations in England ever since.

POLITICAL AND ECONOMIC ROOTS OF ACC

1

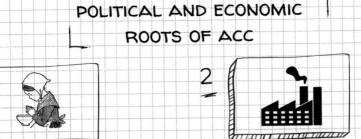

In 1843 Dickens gave a speech in Manchester at a benefit to raise money for an organisation that aimed to bring education and culture to the working masses. Dickens was deeply affected after he addressed the working class, he took a long walk after his speech and while thinking of the plight of exploited child workers he conceived the idea for A Christmas Carol.

2

In 1843, Dickens read the second report from the Parliamentary Commission on the Employment of Women and Children, and he was horrified by its findings. The report described the appalling conditions in which sometimes very young children were working, including dangerous jobs down mines and in factories. He saw them as the innocent victims of the Industrial Revolution.

3

In the novella, Scrooge characterises the poor as "idle". The prevalence of this viewpoint in Victorian society was one of the factors that led to the Poor Law Amendment Act of 1834, which established workhouses as a legal obligation for parishes. Workhouses reduced the cost of caring for the poor by providing (less than) the bare minimum in terms of living standards in exchange for long hours of often dangerous work.

4

The negative attitude towards the poor at this time is captured in the writings of economist Thomas Malthus. Malthus believed that the poor were responsible for their own poverty. In his writings, he presents the poor as stupid, feckless, and workshy. He also criticises poor families for having too many children, suggesting that there isn't enough food to go around, and blaming them for creating the conditions for famine.

'A golden idol'

Both Marley and Scrooge worshipped a golden idol (money). In the Old Testament, Jacob dreamt that this obsession with wealth is problematic and the ghost of Jacob Marley points this out to Scrooge.

Religious imagery and ACC

"He wanted his novels to be 'parables,' stories that would emphasize the teachings of Christ" Timko, 2013

Redemption and Salvation

The Spirits are narrative devices, which are used as tools to help Scrooge redeem himself and achieve salvation. They are sometimes likened to the Holy Trinity.

Bob & Tim

The image of Bob Cratchit with Tim on his shoulder can be seen as symbolic: for the people of the 1840s, he was associated with the image of the Madonna and Child. The child is seen as a symbol of hope and salvation, just like Tim.

Tim as the star

Tim shines bright in the Cratchit household as a source of warmth and positivity. Like the star that led the wise men to Jesus' birthplace, he also guides Scrooge to his rebirth and second chance at life.

Death & Resurrection

The themes of death and resurrection coexist in the story as "Dickens often linked Christmas and Easter" (Davies). At Christmas people remember the dead and celebrate the birth of Christ, this event foreshadows the redemption of the dead and their resurrection. The transformation of Scrooge turns the earthly city of London in the finale into a heavenly city, into the Kingdom of God on earth.

Tiny Tim

Little Tim is connected in the reader's imagination with the image of the Christ child. He plays the role of a child of Christ, born to carry the cross of his disability and metaphorically sacrificed so that Scrooge can be born again.

SCROOGE AND MONEY

Erickson, L (1997) 'The primitive Keynesianism of Dickens's A 'Christmas Carol', in Studies in the literary imagination, Vol.30 (1), p.51-66

THE ECONOMY IN THE 1840S

A period in the early 1840s when Britain experienced an economic depression, causing much misery among the poor. In 1839 there was a serious slump in trade, leading to a steep increase in unemployment, accompanied by a bad harvest. The bad harvests were repeated in the two following years and the sufferings of the people, in a rapidly increasing population, were made worse by the fact that the Corn Laws seemed to keep the price of bread artificially high. In 1845 potato blight appeared in England and Scotland, spreading to Ireland later in the year and ruining a large part of the crop. The potato blight returned in 1846, bringing the Irish Famine. Dickens' finances also suffered as readers could not afford to buy his books.

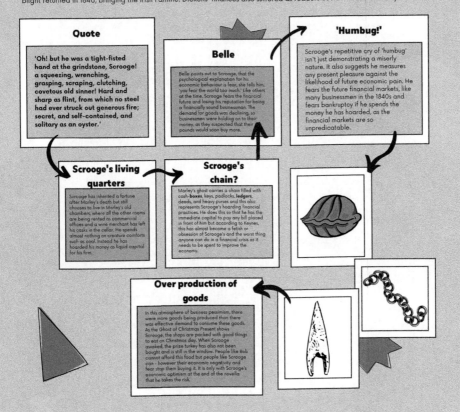

Quote

'Oh! but he was a tight-fisted hand at the grindstone, Scrooge! a squeezing, wrenching, grasping, scraping, clutching, covetous old sinner! Hard and sharp as flint, from which no steel had ever struck out generous fire; secret, and self-contained, and solitary as an oyster.'

Belle

Belle points out to Scrooge, that the psychological explanation for his economic behaviour is fear, she tells him, 'you fear the world too much.' Like others at the time, Scrooge fears the financial future and losing his reputation for being a financially sound businessman. The demand for goods was declining, so businessmen were holding on to their money, as they suspected that their pounds would soon buy more.

'Humbug!'

Scrooge's repetitive cry of 'humbug' isn't just demonstrating a miserly nature. It also suggests he measures any present pleasure against the likelihood of future economic pain. He fears the future financial markets, like many businessmen in the 1840s and fears bankruptcy if he spends the money he has hoarded, as the financial markets are so unpredicatable.

Scrooge's living quarters

Scrooge has inherited a fortune after Marley's death but still chooses to live in Marley's old chambers, where all the other rooms are being rented as commercial offices and a wine merchant has left his casks in the cellar. He spends almost nothing on creature comforts such as coal. Instead he has hoarded his money as liquid capital for his firm.

Scrooge's chain?

Marley's ghost carries a chain filled with cash-**boxes**, keys, padlocks, **ledgers**, deeds, and heavy purses and this also represents Scrooge's hoarding financial practices. He does this so that he has the immediate capital to pay any bill placed in front of him but according to Keynes, this has almost become a fetish or obsession of Scrooge's and the worst thing anyone can do in a financial crisis as it needs to be spent to improve the economy.

Over production of goods

In this atmosphere of business pessimism, there were more goods being produced than there was effective demand to consume these goods. As the Ghost of Christmas Present shows Scrooge, the shops are packed with good things to eat on Christmas day. When Scrooge awaked, the prize turkey has also not been bought and is still in the window. People like Bob cannot afford this food but people like Scrooge can - however their economic negativity and fear stop them buying it. It is only with Scrooge's economic optimism at the end of the novella that he takes the risk.

GRAPHIC HAUNTING: ILLUSTRATION AND EXCLUDED MASCULINITY IN CHARLES DICKENS'S NICHOLAS NICKLEBY (1838-9) AND A CHRISTMAS CAROL (1843)

Christine Chettle

'THE NATURE OF THE GHOST STORY IS LIMINAL, AS THE LIVING AND THE DEAD MEET. SUCH MEETINGS ARE ALMOST ALWAYS PROBLEMATIC: THE DEAD RETURN TO THE WORLD OF THE LIVING, BUT CANNOT BECOME MEMBERS OF THE LIVING AGAIN. JACQUES DERRIDA INTERPRETS GHOSTS AS A METAPHOR OF DEVIANCE FROM A PARTICULAR COMMUNITY. HE CONSTRUCTS GHOSTS AS 'THE BODY OF SOMEONE AS SOMEONE OTHER' IN SEARCH OF SOCIAL INTEGRATION, REPRESENTED BY 'A SPIRIT [...] THE PROMISE OR CALCULATION OF AN EXPIATION' (7, 135). CAROL COMPLICATES DERRIDA'S ASSOCIATIONS OF OTHERNESS AS SCROOGE, HIMSELF AN OUTCAST IN NEED OF EXPIATION, INITIALLY CONSTRUCTS THE CHRISTMAS SPIRITS AS 'OTHER' AND MUST IDENTIFY WITH CONTEMPORARY REPRESENTATIONS OF OTHERNESS (THE RAGGED OUTCASTS WANT AND IGNORANCE, FOR EXAMPLE) BEFORE HE DECIDES TO INCORPORATE ALL THREE SPIRITS IN HIMSELF.

Discuss this extract from an academic paper. What does it add to our understanding of the character of Scrooge and the theme of community?

Oh! but he was a tight-fisted hand at the grindstone, Scrooge! a squeezing, wrenching, grasping, scraping, clutching, covetous old sinner! Hard and sharp as flint, from which no steel had ever struck out generous fire; secret, and self-contained, and solitary as an oyster.[1]

'SOLITARY'

Scrooge is isolated from his fellow creatures as an oyster's body is by its enclosing shell. He edges his way 'along the crowded paths of life', 'warning all human sympathy to keep its distance.' By identifying reclusiveness and misanthropy with miserliness, Scrooge's habitual shunning of other people is a denial of the human commerce upon which a healthy society depends.

'SECRET'

There is something hidden inside of Scrooge. The comparison with an oyster implies it is something good, equivalent to the oyster's tasty flesh or cradled pearl.

At first this seems confusing as we are told by Dickens that there was 'more cold within him.' But the good is buried deep and we get clues about its exsistence with his craving for love at Christmas as a child and his gleeful celebrations as an apprentice at Fezziwigs.

A FLEETING GLIMPSE OF THE SECRET WITHIN

Within the first Stave, Scrooge cracks his shell for an instant:

> "But why?" cried Scrooge's nephew. "Why?"
> "Why did you get married?" said Scrooge.
> "Because I fell in love."

The question about marriage is inappropriate to the conversational context and it betrays his passionate involvement with marriage which still presses down on him. His repetition of Fred's answer marks Scrooge's remastery of what is within and the 'Good afternoon!' is the shell snapping shut again. Just like the potatoes bubbling in the saucepan at the Cratchits, Scrooge's goodness is beginning to bubble up and try to get out.

'SELF-CONTAINED'

Like an oyster, Scrooge has a crusty shell, which contains an organism quite shut off from the world around him, prevented from finding its way to the outside. Restriction defines Scrooge: his physique, his physiognomy and the stiff gait, as well as the small path he treads through London, on the margins of society.

Scrooge's restraint is in marked contrast to Bob Cratchit's elaborate celebrations on leaving the office, the frenzied activities of Belle's many children and Topper's tactile behaviour while playing 'Blind Man's Buff.'

BREAKING OPEN OF THE SHELL

At the end of the novella, Scrooge's shell breaks open and his behaviour is also no longer restricted; he flails his arms while he dresses and dances as he shaves. When out on the street, he shakes hands rather than sticking to the edges of the pavements. In short, Scrooge passes beyond his shell.

TO SUMMARISE:

Scrooge is lodged within his world and his story as a grain of sand against the fleshy part of an oyster. Like the grain of sand, he undergoes a transformation, through the visits of the three spirits, then finally emerges as the story's pearl.

Adapted from Buchwald, C. (1990) 'Stalking the Figurative Oyster: The Excursive Ideal in A Christmas Carol,' *Studies in Short Fiction*, 27, pp. 1–14 by @HughesHaili

Scrooge through a kierkegaardian lens

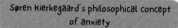

Inspired by Shale Preston

Søren kierkegaard's philosophical concept of anxiety

Søren Kierkegaard was a Danish theologian who developed The Concept of Anxiety (1844). Anxiety is "freedom's actuality as the possibility of possibility." This means when the man looks over the edge, he experiences an aversion to the possibility of falling, but at the same time, the man feels a terrifying impulse to throw himself intentionally off the edge. That experience is anxiety or dread because of our complete freedom to choose to either throw oneself off or to stay put.

Scrooge as the demonic or neurotic individual

The demonic person has **anxiety about the Good** which means he is both repelled by, and attracted to, the Good. This anxiety gives rise to **actions that seek to undermine the Good in order to free from the anxiety it causes.** There are 3 types of behaviour that come from: shutupness, the contentless and the sudden.

Shutupness

The demonic person's initial and fundamental strategy for defying the Good is **to shut himself up with himself to avoid meaningful communication.** Kierkegaard notes that this is the basic **form** of activity the demonic takes—**a form of withdrawal from other people.** We see this exemplified with Scrooge in Dickens' quote, 'As solitary as an oyster' and in his reluctance to go to Fred's for Christmas day.

the contentless

Interaction with the world are inauthentic and seek to empty the world of good content and the vitality it offers. Anxious people want to open up but then choose to defy and even destroy those sources of the Good that call them out of their hiding places. This is clear when Scrooge pushes away those close to him. It is a form of self-preservation, so he never has to again experience loss.

the sudden

According to Kierkegaard, a self is integrated when its choices and actions establish a thread of continuity from the past into the future. Through the ghosts, we see that Scrooge's past has resulted in his future - the events of his life impact on the way he behaves. The sudden interrupts this chain, so Marley and the other ghosts serve as this interruption and force Scrooge to face his past and realise that his true identity lies in committing to this realisation of who he really is.

Preston, S. (2012) 'Existential Scrooge: A Kierkegaardian Reading of A Christmas Carol', in **Literature Compass**, vol. 9, pp. 743-751

THE MOTIF OF FIRE IN 'CAROL'

'A cheerful company assembled round a glowing fire'

Fire symbolises the Christmas spirit, representing generosity and philanthropy.

'...lighted a great fire in the brazier, round which a party of ragged men and boys were gathered'

'Sit ye down before the fire my dear and have a warm'

Cold and the lack of fire demonstrates the hard feelings and lack of warmth Scrooge experiences and gives others.

Fire brings people together and opens their heart to the warmth that family and community can bring.

'Scrooge had a very small fire, but the clerk's fire was so very much smaller that it looked like one coal'

'A lonely boy was reading before a feeble fire'

Tiny Tim

'Tiny Tim, is disabled: he walks with a crutch and is also supported by an iron frame. A child with polio, wearing leg braces and supported on crutches, was, according to Halfon, Houtrow, Larson, and Newacheck, 'the iconic image of disability' until the 1960s (14).

SCANNED IMAGE AND TEXT BY PHILIP V. ALLINGHAM AT HTTPS://VICTORIANWEB.ORG/ART/ILLUSTRATION/DREAMCHILDREN/6.HTML

Such a portrayal of Tiny Tim was meant to induce sympathy amongst readers, who were likely to recognise the ailment, which was fairly common amongst Victorian children, and feel solidarity with the character. The character of Tiny Tim has a synecdochal function and is a representative of a stigmatised social group, the disabled. Dickens hoped that fictional suffering could help his contemporaries 'ameliorate the actual suffering they encountered around them' (Harrison 262).'

Vidovi, E. (2013) 'A Christmas Carol: Disability Conceptualised through Empathy and the Philosophy of 'Technologically Useful Bodies,' International Research in Children's Literature, 6(2), p.176-191.

What does this tell us about authorial intent?

Index

Page numbers in *italic* indicate a figure and page numbers in **bold** indicate a table on the corresponding page

interaction between students and teachers 2
internal struggle 89
Irish Potato Famine 143
Iser, Wolfgang 27

Jakobson, Roman 21
Jameson, Fredric 16, 26
Jarvis, Stephen 177
Jauss, Hans Robert 27
Jhirad, Susan 71
Job and Scrooge (fictional characters) 78–80
Jung, Carl 19

Kantian ethics 91; fundamental value 87;
    Scrooge's character through 87–88;
    student's Hexagon analysis template on
    92; views on human beings 88
Kant, Immanuel 15, 17, 87–88, 91–*92*
Keating, John 1
Kermode, Frank 77
kindness 35–36, 102, 130, 147
knowledge 1–6, 11–12, 20, 22–24, 26, 32,
    44, 58, 88, 91, 117; in English 4–5; priori
    and postiori factors 88; transcendental
    form of 88; of truths 12

Lacan, Jacques 21
laissez-faire system 97
language 2, 14, 16, 18–19, 21–26, 28–29,
    31, 34, 36, 47, 53, 58; body 22, 61; and
    discourse 16, 18; figurative 10; in novel
    16; philosophy of 16; tentative 3
large families, Dickens portrayals of
    115–116
Larson, Janet L. 80
learning 3, 31, 46, 51, 56
Le Cid (play) 13
Lévi-Strauss, Claude 20–21
linguistics 22
linguistic sign system 17
Litdrive 4
literary criticism 10–11, 14, 17–18, 20, 28–29,
    31, 44, 53–54, 56–58; academic sources
    45–46; Anxiety of Influence style of 18;
    AQA Literature spec 46–47; catalyst for
    46; effective curriculum 56; encouraging

conversation 44–45; evaluative questions
    52; gender stereotypes 47–51; importance
    of 44, 58; making precise and systematic
    20; on philosophical foundation 14;
    psychological impact of 46; on *Romeo
    and Juliet* 44; students' engagement
    44–45; teaching challenges 53–56; using
    Cornell notes 51–52; vocabulary teaching
    46
literary schools of thought 9, *9*, **35–38**;
    archetypal theory 19; classical theory 10–
    11; cultural studies 28–30; deconstruction
    24–25; feminist literary theory 31–33;
    formalism 16–17; Marxism 15–16;
    medieval theory 11–12; neoclassical
    theory 12–14; new criticism 19–20; new
    historicism 27–28; post-colonialism
    30–31; post-modernism 25–26; post-
    structuralism 23–24; psychoanalysis
    17–18; queer theory 34; Reader Response
    criticism 26–27; renaissance 12–14;
    romantic theory 14–15; semiotics 21–23;
    structuralism 20–21
literature: as autonomous aesthetic
    phenomenon 17; autonomous nature of
    16; interpretation 2
logocentrism 18
Lyotard, Jean-François 26

Macbeth (Shakespeare) 3, 45–48, 47–51, 54
Malthusian theory 143–144
Malthusian trap 143
Malthus, Thomas 97, 143–144
Marley, Jacob (fictional character) 59–60,
    59–61, 72, 79, 87, 101, 131, 135; biblical
    connections 61; ghost 61, 86–87, 98,
    100, 103; ideas for teaching 61–69;
    importance of 59–69; inspired fear
    in Scrooge 59–60; as key character in
    novella 60; name choice of 131–132;
    personal connection to Scrooge 60; as
    Scrooge's first guide 72
Marley scene, student's annotations of 61,
    62–64
Marxism 15–16, 35
Marxist critics 15